Crochet for Caring & Sharing™

I expect to pass through this world but once;
any good thing therefore that I can do,
or any kindness that I can show
to any fellow creature, let me do it now;
let me not defer or neglect it,
for I shall not pass this way again.

—Stephen Grellet

Edited by Carol Alexander

HOUSE of WHITE BIRCHES
PUBLISHERS
SINCE 1947

Crochet for Caring & Sharing

Editor: Carol Alexander
Associate Editor: Cathy Reef
Design Associate: Vicki Blizzard
Technical Editor: Agnes Russell
Copy Editors: Michelle Beck, Nicki Lehman, Mary Martin

Photography: Tammy Cromer-Campbell, Tammy Christian, Christena Green, Kelly Heydinger
Photography Assistant: Joshua J. Cromer

Production Coordinator: Brenda Gallmeyer
Graphic Arts Supervisor: Ronda Bechinski
Graphic Artist/Book Design: Edith Teegarden
Production Assistant: Marj Morgan
Traffic Coordinator: Sandra Beres
Technical Artist: Chad Summers

Chief Executive Officer: John Robinson
Publishing Director: David J. McKee
Book Marketing Manager: Craig Scott
Editorial Director: Vivian Rothe
Publishing Services Manager: Brenda R. Wendling

Printed in China
First Printing: 2004
Library of Congress Number: 2002113549
ISBN: 1-59217-014-5

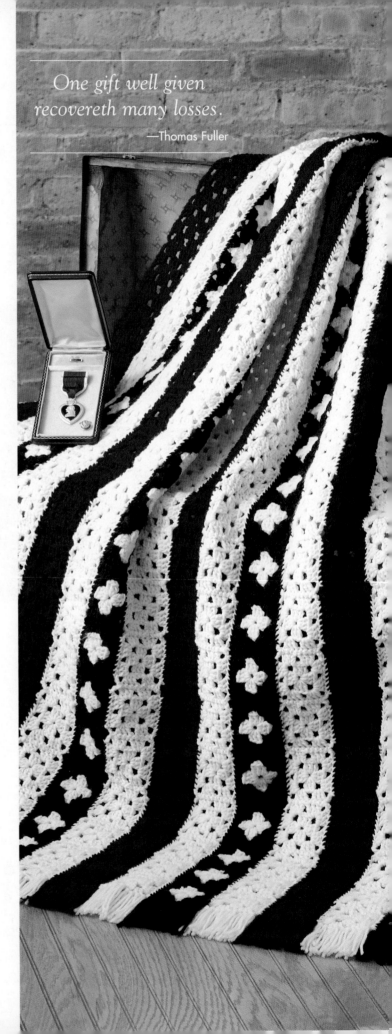

One gift well given recovereth many losses.

—Thomas Fuller

Made by Hand ...
Given From the Heart

We all know the simple joy of giving just the right gifts to special people in our lives, especially if they are handmade with love. In most of our communities, we have neighbors in need whose lives can be enhanced with wonderful, handcrafted gifts to lighten their spirits and ease their daily existence. Even though we may never directly realize how much our kindness improves someone's life, we can be sure that by giving generously of our crochet time and talents to help others, we brighten many lives in many ways.

Crocheters are well-known to be some of the most caring and compassionate folks around; in their tireless efforts to help people and animals in need, they spend endless hours making countless items for charitable causes all over the world.

With careful thought, we have created this very special book of crochet patterns that will make fabulous gifts for family and friends and also add a touch of beauty and comfort to the lives of others less fortunate.

At the back, you will find information about several well-deserving and respected charities that would welcome projects from this book. I also encourage you to seek out and help local charities and service organizations in your area. Nursing homes, crisis centers, animal shelters, hospices and veterans hospitals are just a few of the many recipients that would appreciate crocheted donations. The needs are great everywhere.

As you thoughtfully select just the right pattern in this book to make as a special gift for someone you care about, why not make a duplicate, or select another project, to share with someone in need? The rewards are many, and it is in sharing our time and talents for others that we create our greatest gifts.

Warm regards,

Carol Alexander

Contents

1 Wonderful Warmers

2 All-Around Afghans

3 Cuddly Comforts

4 Handy Helpers

Wonderful Warmers

Mittens and scarves, sweaters and socks, and soft, cozy caps are the everyday staples of warm winter wear. In this chapter you'll find a delightful array of patterns in a variety of designs and sizes to fit everyone in the family and please even the most discerning tastes in style!

There is new strength, comfort, and inspiration in fresh apparel.

—Ella Wheeler Wilcox

Pretty in Plum Scarf & Ski Band

Designs by Kazimiera Budak

Ski the slopes with fashionable flair with this pretty accessory set that's made doubly-thick to keep neck and ears extra warm in the cold winter wind!

Skill Level: Beginner

Size

Scarf: 5¼ x 53 inches

Ski band: 3½ x 20 inches

Materials

• Caron Simply Soft worsted weight yarn: 11 oz violet #9738, 8 yds orchid #9717

• Size H/8 crochet hook or size needed to obtain gauge

• Tapestry needle

• Compass

• Cardboard

Gauge

11 sts = 3 inches; 5 rnds = 3 inches

Check gauge to save time.

Pattern Notes

Weave in loose ends as work progresses.

Do not join rnds unless otherwise stated. Use a scrap of CC yarn to mark rnds.

Scarf

Rnd 1: With violet, ch 40, join to form a ring, ch 2 (counts as first dc), dc in each rem ch around, do not join. (40 dc)

Rnd 2: Dc in top of beg ch-2 of previous rnd, working in back lps only, dc in each st around.

Rnd 3: Working in back lps only, dc in each st around, do not join.

Rnds 4–84: Rep Rnd 3. At the end of Rnd 84, working in back lp only, sc in next st, fasten off.

Trim

Rnd 1: Attach orchid with sc between any 2 dc of Rnd 84, *ch

10, sk next 4 dc **, sc in sp between dc sts after 4th sk dc, rep from * around, ending last rep at **, sl st to join in beg sc, fasten off.

Rep Rnd 1 of trim on opposite end of scarf between dc sts of rnd.

Fringe

For each fringe, cut 3 strands of yarn each 6 inches long. Fold 3 strands in half, insert hook in ch-10 lp, draw strands through at fold to form a lp on hook, draw cut ends through lp on hook, pull gently to secure. Rep fringe in each ch-10 lp. Trim ends even.

Ski Band

Rnd 1: With violet, ch 28, join to form a ring, ch 2 (counts as first dc), dc in each ch around, do not join. (28 dc)

Rnd 2: Rep Rnd 2 of scarf.

Rnds 3–30: Rep Rnd 3 of scarf. At the end of Rnd 30, working in

Continued on page 30

North Country Caps

Designs by Michele Wilcox

Grownups and kids alike will appreciate the handsome styling and snuggly warmth of this quick-to-stitch cap. One easy pattern makes a perfect fit for both adults and children.

Skill Level: Beginner

Size

Adult's: Brim 22 inches unstretched

Child's: 21 inches unstretched

Materials
- Worsted weight yarn: Child's: 5 oz MC, small amount CC
- Chunky weight yarn: Adults: 6 oz MC, 2 oz CC
- Sizes H/8 and J/10 crochet hooks or sizes needed to obtain gauge
- Yarn needle
- 5-inch square cardboard

edge of brim rows, work 1 sc in each row, for child's cap turn, for adults fasten off CC, attach MC, turn. (75 sc)

Row 2: Ch 1, sc in each sc across, turn.

Rows 3 & 4: Rep Row 2.

Row 5: Ch 1, sc across, dec 3 sc evenly sp across, turn. (72 sc)

Rows 6 & 7: Rep Row 2.

Row 8: Ch 1, sc across, dec 6 sc evenly sp across, turn. (66 sc)

Rows 9–13: Rep Row 2.

Row 14: Rep Row 8. (60 sc)

Rows 15–17: Rep Row 2.

Row 18: Rep Row 8. (54 sc)

Rows 19–22: Rep Row 2.

Row 23: Rep Row 8. (48 sc)

Rows 24–26: Rep Row 2.

Row 27: Rep Row 8. (42 sc)

Rows 28–30: Rep Row 2.

Row 31: Rep Row 8. (36 sc)

Rows 32–36: Rep Row 2.

Continued on page 30

Gauge

Working brim with larger hook, 7 sc = 2 inches; 3 sc rows = 1 inch

Working brim with smaller hook, 9 sc = 2 inches; 4 sc rows = 1 inch

Check gauge to save time.

Pattern Notes

Weave in loose ends as work progresses.

Use larger hook for adult size cap and smaller hook for child size cap.

Brim

Row 1: With MC for child's and CC for adults, ch 13, sc in 2nd ch from hook, sc in each rem ch across, turn. (12 sc)

Row 2: Working in back lps only, ch 1, sc in each st across, turn.

Rows 3–75: Rep Row 2. At the end of Row 75, turn.

Cap

Row 1: Ch 1, working across side

Weekender Pullover

Design by Margret Willson

When it's time to leave work behind for some fun or relaxation, this easy-going pullover is a winning choice! A smart, yet simple, design worked in soft, cozy sport yarn creates this comfortable, tee-style sweater that any guy on your gift list will appreciate!

Skill Level: Intermediate

Size

Finished chest measurements:
40 (44, 48, 52, 56) inches

Materials
• Lion Brand Wool-Ease sport worsted weight yarn (5 oz per skein): 3 skeins each wheat #402 and blue mist #115
• Size I/9 crochet hook or size needed to obtain gauge
• Tapestry needle
• Size H/8 crochet hook

Gauge

16 sts = 4 inches; 14 pattern rows = 4 inches

Check gauge to save time.

Pattern Notes

Weave in loose ends as work progresses.

Join rnds with a sl st unless otherwise stated.

Carry color not in use loosely along edge.

Ch-3 counts as first dc throughout.

Pattern Stitches

3-dc dec: [Yo hook, insert hook in next st, yo, draw up a lp, yo, draw through 2 lps on hook] 3 times, yo, draw through all 4 lps.

3-sc dec: [Insert hook in next st, yo, draw up a lp] 3 times, yo, draw through all 4 lps on hook.

Body Pattern

Note: *Body pattern is a multiple of 2 sts plus 1 st; a rep of 4 rows.*

Foundation row (RS): With wheat, dc in 4th ch from hook, dc in each rem ch across, turn.

Row 1: Ch 4 (counts as first dc, ch 1 throughout), sk next st, dc in next st, [ch 1, sk next st, dc in next st] rep across, changing to blue mist with last yo, turn.

Row 2: Ch 1, sc in first st, [working behind ch-1 sp, dc in sk st 2 rows below, sc in next st] rep across, ending with sc in 3rd ch of ch-4, turn.

Row 3: Ch 3, dc in next st, [ch 1, sk next st, dc in next st] rep across, ending with dc in last st, changing to wheat with last yo, turn.

Row 4: Ch 1, sc in each of next 2 sts, [working behind ch-1 sp, dc in sk st 2 rows below, sc in next st] rep across, ending with sc in last st, turn.

Rep Rows 1–4 for pattern.

Back

With smaller hook, ch 83 (91, 99, 107, 115) and work foundation row, change to larger hook, work in pattern st on 81 (89, 97, 105, 113) sts until piece measures approximately 24½ (25, 25½, 26½, 27) inches from beg, ending with a RS row.

First shoulder shaping

Continuing in pattern, work across 23 (27, 29, 33, 37) sts, turn.

Work in pattern across next row, fasten off.

Second shoulder shaping

With WS facing, sk center 35 (35, 39, 39, 39) sts for neckline opening, attach yarn in next st and work in pattern across rem sts, turn.

Work in pattern across next row, fasten off.

Front

Work as for back until piece measures approximately 22 (22½, 23, 24, 24½) inches from beg, ending with a RS row.

First shoulder shaping

Work across 26 (30, 34, 36, 40) sts, turn, dec 1 st at neck edge every sc row 3 times. (23, 27, 29, 33, 37 sts) Work even until piece measures same as back from beg, ending on a RS row, fasten off.

Second shoulder shaping

With WS facing, sk center 29 (29, 29, 33, 33) sts for neckline opening, attach yarn in next st and complete row on rem sts. Work as first shoulder reversing shaping, fasten off.

Sleeve
Make 2

With smaller hook and wheat, ch 43 (43, 45, 47, 49) and work foundation row on 41 (41, 43, 45, 47) sts. Change to larger hook and work in pattern st inc on RS rows, 1 st each side every 2 rows 4 (8, 10, 14, 16) times, then every 4 rows 15 (13, 12, 10, 9) times. (79, 83, 87, 95, 99 sts)

How Old Sweaters Became New

By Rose Pirrone

Recycling had a very different meaning during the Depression years. It meant not discarding anything that could be reused, including clothing with parts that could be used to make new garments. Adult shirts, pants and jackets were taken apart, cut and sewn into articles of clothing for children.

Today's synthetic fibers weren't available back in those days. Most crochet and knitting yarns were made from wool. Women ripped out old sweaters so that the yarn could be reused to make new sweaters, vests, scarves, hats or mittens for the children.

The first step was to remove any buttons, and then carefully cut open the seams. Each section was ripped out and the yarn wound into balls. Any yarn that was worn thin, torn or badly stained was cut away and discarded.

The unraveled yarn was crimped and had to be straightened before crocheting or knitting with it. This was done by wrapping the yarn around another person's outstretched hands into a hank, or using two straight-back chairs placed back-to-back, two or three inches apart. The hank was securely tied off at each end, then thoroughly saturated in cold water and hung out on a clothesline to dry.

When the yarn had drip-dried, the strands had miraculously straightened out. The hank was then rewound into balls, ready to use. Once the new garment or accessory was made, no one was any the wiser that it had been made from an old one. It's one way that, even in those days, what's popularly known today as "recycling" was practiced and promoted.

Work in pattern until sleeve measures approximately 19½ inches from beg, ending with Row 2 of pattern st, fasten off.

Assembly
Sew shoulder seams. Measure 10 (10½, 11, 11½, 12) inches from shoulder seam and mark for sleeve placement. Sew sleeve in place, then sew sleeve and side seams.

Neckline Band
Rnd 1: With smaller hook, attach wheat with sc in right shoulder seam, working 2 sc around end of each row and 1 sc in each st of center front and back, sc evenly around, join in beg sc.

Rnd 2: Ch 3, dc in each sc around, working 3-dc dec at each inside corner, join in 3rd ch of beg ch-3.

Rnd 3: Ch 1, sc in each dc around, working a 3-sc dec at each inside corner, join in beg sc.

Rnd 4: Rep Rnd 2, fasten off. ✂

If honor be your clothing, the suit will last a lifetime.

—William Arnot

Neutral Tones Pullover

Design by Melissa Leapman

Neutral shades of sport weight yarn and a striking pattern created with long treble crochet stitches create a soft and sophisticated look in this fashionable pullover.

Skill Level: Intermediate

Sizes
Finished bust measurement:
35½ (39, 43, 46, 50) inches

Materials
- Lion Brand Wool-Ease sport weight yarn: 3 (3, 4, 4, 5) skeins mushroom #403 (A), 3 (3, 3, 4, 4) skeins fisherman #099 (B)
- Size G/6 crochet hook or size needed to obtain gauge
- Size F/5 crochet hook
- Yarn markers
- Yarn needle

Gauge
In block pattern with larger hook, 18 sts = 4 inches; 16 rows = 4 inches
Check gauge to save time.

Pattern Notes
Weave in loose ends as work progresses.

Ch-2 counts as first hdc of each row unless otherwise stated.

Pattern Stitch
Long tr: Tr is worked from top to bottom into st 3 rows directly below working through front lp only.

Block Pattern
Note: Block pattern is worked in a multiple of 4 sts.

Foundation Row 1 (RS): Hdc in 3rd ch from hook, hdc in each rem ch across, turn.

Foundation Row 2: Ch 2, sk first st, hdc in each st across, ending with hdc in top of beg ch-2, change color, turn.

Row 1 (RS): Ch 2, sk first st, working in back lps only, hdc in each st across, ending with hdc in top of beg ch-2, turn.

Row 2 & all WS rows: Ch 2, sk first st, hdc in each st across, ending with hdc in top of beg ch-2, change color, turn.

Row 3: Ch 2, sk first st, [working in back lps only, hdc in next 2 sts, long tr in each of next 2 sts] rep across to last 3 sts, working in back lps only, hdc in next 2 sts, hdc in top of beg ch-2, turn.

Row 5: Ch 2, sk first st, hdc in each st across, ending with hdc in top of beg ch-2, turn.

Row 7: Rep Row 1.

Row 9: Ch 2, sk first st, *long tr in each of next 2 sts **, hdc in back lp only of next 2 sts, rep from * across, ending last rep at **, hdc in top of beg ch-2, turn.

Row 11: Rep Row 5.

Row 12: Rep Row 2, change color, turn.

Back
With larger hook and A, ch 81 (89, 97, 105, 113), work block pattern even on 80 (88, 96, 104, 112) sts until piece measures approximately 27 inches from beg, ending after a Row 5 or 11 pattern row.

Shoulder shaping
Work in pattern across first 24 (28, 32, 36, 40) sts, fasten off. For neckline opening, sk center 32 sts, attach yarn with sl st in next st, ch 2, work in pattern across to end of row, fasten off.

Front
Work the same as for back until front measures approximately 25 inches from beg, ending after a Row 4 or 10 pattern row.

Neck shaping
Work across next 32 (36, 40, 44, 48) sts, ch 2, turn. Continue in established pattern, dec 1 st at neck edge every row 8 times, 24, (28, 32, 36, 40) sts rem. Continue even until piece measures same as back, fasten off.

Sk next 16 sts for neck opening, attach yarn in next st with a sl st, ch 2, complete as first side.

Sleeve
Make 2

With larger hook and A, ch 41 (45, 45, 45, 49), work in block pattern on 40 (44, 44, 44, 48) sts for 2 rows. Continue in established pattern, inc 1 st each side every other row 1 (3, 8, 10, 11) times, then every 4th row 17 (16, 13, 11, 10) times. (76, 82, 86, 86, 90 sts)

Continue even until sleeve measures approximately 19 (18¾, 18¼,

---

The sense of being well-dressed gives a feeling of inward tranquility.

—C.F. Forbes

My Favorite Sweater

My favorite sweater is aging,
wearing thin from use and travel.
The yarn has lost its soft texture,
one sleeve has begun to ravel.
The time has come to replace it—
a thought I can hardly bear.
But this much-loved, worn-out sweater
is one I can no longer wear.
While I'm crocheting a new one
I think I'll make one for you.
Maybe, like mine, it will become
your favorite sweater, too.

down from shoulders. Sew in sleeve between markers and sew in place. Sew sleeve and side seams.

Neckline Trim

Rnd 1: With smaller hook, attach A at shoulder seam, ch 1, work 78 sc evenly sp around neckline opening, sl st to join in beg sc, fasten off.

Neck Band

Row 1: With smaller hook and A, ch 20, sc in 2nd ch from hook, sc in each rem ch across, turn.

Row 2: Ch 1, working in back lps only, sc in each st across, turn.

Rep Row 2 until piece, when slightly stretched, fits around neckline opening, leaving a length of yarn, fasten off.

Sew last row to opposite side of foundation ch.

Placing seam of neck band at center back and working through back lps only of Rnd 1 of neckline trim sew neck band in place. ✂

17½, 17) inches from beg, ending after a Row 4 or 10 pattern row, fasten off.

Finishing

Sew shoulder seams. Place markers 8½ (9, 9½, 9½, 10) inches

Family Foot Warmers

Designs by Janet Rehfeldt

Big or small, here are some cozy, colorful socks to fit everyone's feet! Patterns give instructions to fit virtually any-size foot, and can be made in any color combination to suit a variety of tastes!

Skill Level: Intermediate

Size

Adult's: Length to fit foot; bottom of foot to cuff 8 inches; circumference of leg and foot 7¾ (8½, 9¼, 10, 10½) inches

Child's: Length to fit foot; bottom of foot to cuff 5 inches; circumference of leg and foot 5½ (6¼, 6¾, 7¼) inches

Toddler's: 6–18 (18–24) months; bottom of foot to cuff 3 inches; circumference of leg and foot 4¼ (4¾) inches

Materials

- Regia 4-ply sock yarn (50 gram balls): Adults: 2 (2, 2, 2) balls ringel atlantik #5045 (MC), 100 yds royal blue #540 (CC), Child: 1 (1, 1, 1) ball clown #5048 (MC), 50 yds yellow #612 (CC) Toddler: 50 yds papillon #5025 (MC), 15 yds off-white #600 (CC)

- Size D/3 crochet hook or size needed to obtain gauge

- Yarn markers

- Yarn needle

Gauge

3 shells = 1 inch; 25 sc sts = 4 inches; foot pattern 28 rnds = 4 inches
Check gauge to save time.

Pattern Notes

Weave in loose ends as work progresses.

Do not join rnds with a sl st unless otherwise stated.

Socks will stretch in length and width approximately 1 to 1½ inches.

Pattern Stitches

Foundation dc: Ch 3, yo hook, insert hook in first ch, *yo, draw up a lp, yo, draw through 1 lp on hook (ch-1 made), yo, draw through 2 lps on hook, yo, draw through last 2 lps on hook, yo, insert hook into front most lp and bottom hump of ch at base of dc just made *, rep from * to *.

Shell: [Sc, ch 1, sc] in indicated st.

Adult Socks

Cuff

Foundation rnd: With CC, work 48 (52, 56, 60, 64) foundation dc sts (beg ch-3 counts as first dc), sl st in top of beg ch-3 to join.

Rnd 1: Fpdc around first dc in rnd directly below, bpdc around next dc in rnd directly below, [fpdc around next dc directly below, bpdc around next dc directly below] rep around, sl st to join in top of first post st, change to MC. (48, 52, 56, 60, 64 sts)

Rnd 2: [Fpdc around next fpdc, bpdc around next bpdc] rep around, sl st to join in top of first post st.

Rnd 3: Rep Rnd 2.

Leg

Rnd 1: Shell in first st, sk next st, [shell in next st, sk next st] rep around. (24, 26, 28, 30, 32 shells)

Rnd 2: Shell in each ch-1 sp of each shell around.

Rep Rnd 2 until from beg including cuff piece measures 5 inches.

Rnd 3: Sc in each sc around, sk all ch-1 sps. (48, 52, 56, 60, 64 sc)

Rnd 4: Shell in first sc, sk next sc, [shell in next st, sk next st] rep around.

Rnd 5: Sk all ch-1 sps, sc in each of next 24 (24, 26, 26, 26) sc sts, change to CC, turn, drop MC but do not fasten off.

Heel

Row 1 (WS): Ch 1, sc in first sc, sc in each sc across, turn. (24, 24, 26, 26, 26 sc)

Row 2: Ch 1, sc in each sc across, turn.

Rep Row 2 until heel flap measures 2¾ inches ending with a WS row.

Heel turn

Row 1 (RS): Ch 1, sc in first sc, [sc dec over next 2 sc] twice, [sc in each of next 5 (5, 6, 6, 6) sc, {sc dec over next 2 sc} twice] twice, sc in last sc, turn. (18, 18, 20, 20, 20 sc)

Row 2: Ch 1, sc in first sc, [sc dec over next 2 sc] twice, sc in each sc across to last 5 sc, [sc dec over next 2 sc] twice, sc in last sc, turn. (14, 14, 16, 16, 16 sc)

Row 3: Ch 1, sc in each of next 5 (5, 6, 6, 6) sc, [sc dec over next 2 sc] twice, sc in rem sc across, turn. (12, 12, 14, 14, 14 sc)

Row 4: Ch 1, sc in first sc, sc dec over next 2 sc, sc in each sc across to last 3 sc, sc dec over next 2 sc, sc in last sc, turn. (10, 10, 12, 12, 12 sc)

Gusset

Rnd 1 (RS): Work across 10 (10, 12, 12, 12) heel sts, work 17 sc

sts evenly along left edge of heel flap, place a marker in last sc, sc in each of next 24 (28, 30, 34, 38) sc sk all ch-1 sps along front foot sts, work 17 sc sts evenly along right side edge of heel flap and place a marker in first sc on right side of heel, fasten off CC. (68, 72, 76, 80, 84 sts)

Rnd 2 (dec rnd): From Rnd 5 of leg pick up dropped MC, work 12 (14, 15, 17, 18) shells across front foot sts to gusset marker, [sc dec over next 2 sc] twice, sc around heel sts to next gusset marker, [sc dec over next 2 sc] twice and move markers with each rnd. (64, 68, 72, 76, 80 sts)

Rnd 3: Sc in each sc across foot front sk all ch-1 sps, sc in each sc around back of foot.

Continue with MC, rep Rnds 2 and 3, dec 4 sts on each dec rnd until

48 (52, 56, 60, 64) sts rem, ending with Rnd 3, remove gusset markers

Foot

Rnd 1: [Shell in next st, sk next st] rep around foot, place a marker for beg of rnd.

Rnd 2: Sc in each sc around, sk all ch-1 sps around foot.

Rep Rnds 1 and 2 for established pattern until foot measures 2 inches from longest toe ending with Rnd 2.

Shape toe

Fold sock making sure that heel is centered to back of foot. Place markers at each side edge and move markers as work progresses to keep at side edges of sock. Change to CC, fasten off MC.

Rnd 1: Sc in each sc to 2 sts prior to first marker, sc dec over next 2 sts, sc in next st, sc dec over next 2 sts, sc in each sc to 2 sts prior to next marker, sc dec over next 2 sc, sc in next sc, sc dec over next 2 sc. (44, 48, 52, 56, 60 sc)

Rnd 2: Sc in each sc to 2 sts prior to first marker, sc dec over next 2 sc, sc in next sc, sc dec over next 2 sc, sc in each sc to 2 sts prior to next marker, sc dec over next 2 sts, sc in next st, sc dec over next 2 sts. (40, 44, 48, 52, 56 sc)

Rnd 3: Sc in each sc around.

Rep Rnds 2 and 3 until 24 (24, 28, 28, 28) sts rem, leaving a length of yarn, fasten off. Sew toe opening closed.

Child's Socks
Cuff
Foundation rnd: With CC, work 32 (36, 40, 44) foundation

dc sts (beg ch-3 counts as first dc), sl st to join in top of beg ch-3.

On 32 (36, 40, 40) sts continue cuff as for adult sock.

Leg

Rnd 1: Rep Rnd 1 of adult sock. (16, 18, 20, 22 shells)

Rnd 2: [Shell in ch-1 sp of next shell] rep around.

Rep Rnd 2 until sock from beg measures 3½ inches.

Rnd 3: Rep Rnd 3 of adult sock. (32, 36, 40, 44 sc)

Rnd 4: Rep Rnd 4 of adult sock.

Rnd 5: Sk all ch-1 sps, sc in each of next 16 (16, 18, 18) sc sts, change to CC, turn, drop MC but do not fasten off.

Heel

Row 1 (WS): Ch 1, sc in each of next 16 (16, 18, 18) sc, turn.

Row 2: Ch 1, sc in each sc across, turn.

Rep Row 2 until heel flap measures 1½ inches ending with a RS row.

Heel turn

Row 1 (WS): Ch 1, sc in first sc, [sc dec over next 2 sc] twice, sc in each of next 2 (2, 3, 3) sc, sc dec over next 2 sc, sc in each of next 2 (2, 3, 3) sc, [sc dec over next 2 sc] twice, sc in last sc, turn. (11, 11, 13, 13 sc)

Row 2: Ch 1, sc in first sc, sc dec over next 2 sc, sc in each of next 1 (1, 2, 2) sc sts, sc dec over next 2 sc, sc in each of next 2 (2, 3, 3) sc, sc dec over next 2 sc, sc in last sc, turn. (8, 8, 10, 10 sc)

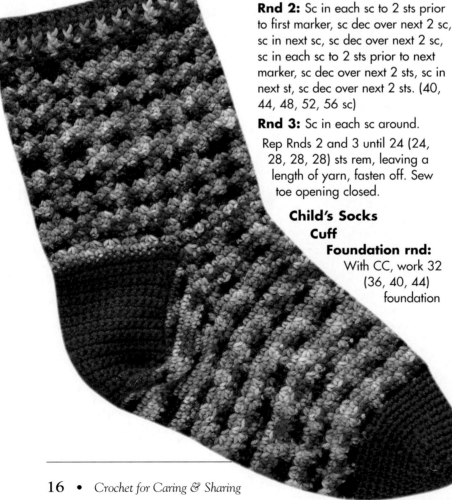

Row 3: Ch 1, sc in first sc, sc dec over next 2 sc, sc in each sc across to last 3 sc, sc dec over next 2 sc, sc in last sc, turn. (6, 6, 8, 8 sc)

Gusset

Rnd 1: Sc across 6 (6, 8, 8) heel sts, work 11 sc evenly along left side edge of heel flap, place marker in last sc, sc in each of 16 (20, 22, 26) sc across foot front sk all ch-1 sps, work 11 sc evenly sp along right side edge of heel flap, place a marker in first sc on right side of heel to mark gusset, fasten off CC. (44, 48, 52, 56 sc)

Rnd 2: Pick up dropped MC at foot front, work 8 (10, 11, 13) shells across front foot sts to gusset marker, sc dec over next 2 sts, sc around heel sts to next gusset marker, sc dec over next 2 sts, move markers as work progresses. (42, 46, 50, 54 sts)

Rnd 3: Sc in each sc across foot front, sk all ch-1 sps, sc in each sc around back of foot.

Continue with MC, rep Rnds 2 and 3, dec 2 sts on each dec rnd (1 at each marker) until 32 (36, 40, 44) sts rem, ending with a Rnd 3, remove gusset markers.

Foot

Rep Rnds 1 and 2 of adult sock on 32 (36, 40, 44) sts until foot measures 2 inches less than longest toe.

Shape toe

Rep the same as adult sock on 32 (36, 40, 44) sts, dec until 16 (16, 20, 20) sts rem, fasten off and sew toe opening closed.

Toddler Socks

Cuff

Foundation rnd: With CC, work 26 (30) foundation dc sts (beg ch-3 counts as first dc) sl st in top of beg ch-3 to join.

Working on 26 (30) sts, rep as for adult cuff.

Leg

Rnd 1: Shell in first st, sk next st, [shell in next st, sk next st] rep around. (13, 15 shells)

Rnd 2: Shell in each ch-1 sp of each shell around.

Rnd 3: Sc in each sc around, sk all ch-1 sps. (26, 30 sc)

Rnd 4: Rep Rnd 1.

Rnd 5: Sc in each of next 12 (12) sc sts, sk all ch-1 sps, change to CC, turn, drop MC, do not fasten off.

Heel

Working on 12 (12) sts, follow adult heel until flap measures ¾ inch ending with a RS row.

Heel turn

Note: When only 1 number is in pattern it applies to both sizes.

Row 1 (WS): Ch 1, sc in first sc, [sc dec over next 2 sc] twice, sc in each of next 2 sc, [sc dec over next 2 sc] twice, sc in last sc, turn. (8 sc)

Row 2: Ch 1, sc in first sc, sc dec over next 2 sc, sc in each of next 2 sc, sc dec over next 2 sc, sc in last sc, turn. (6 sc)

Row 3: Ch 1, sc in first sc, [sc dec over next 2 sc] twice, sc in last sc, turn. (4 sc)

Gusset

Rnd 1: Sc across 4 heel sts, work 7 sc evenly along side edge of heel flap, place marker to mark gusset, sc in each of next 14 (18) sc across foot front sk all ch-1 sps, work 7 sc evenly sp along opposite edge of heel flap, place marker in first sc to mark gusset, fasten off CC. (32, 36 sc)

Rnd 2: Pick up dropped MC at foot front, work 7 (9) shells across front foot sts to gusset marker, sc dec over next 2 sts, sc around heel sts to next gusset marker, sc dec over next 2 sts, move markers as work progresses. (30, 34 sts)

Rnd 3: Sc in each sc across foot front sk all ch-1 sps, sc in each sc around back of foot.

Rep Rnds 2 and 3, dec 2 sts on each dec rnd (1 at each side of gusset) until 26 (30 sts) rem, ending with Rnd 3, remove markers.

Foot

Work as for adult on 26 (30) sts until foot measures approximately 2½–3 (3½–4) inches from back of heel or 1 inch less than longest toe.

Shape toe

Work as for adult sock on 26 (30) sts, dec until 14 sts rem, fasten off, sew toe opening closed. ✄

Young Miss Winter Warmer Set

Designs by Maria Merlino

The scarf, mittens and pert beret in this cozy winter warmer set each feature a different predominant color of white, purple or luscious lavender, yet all combine beautifully into a smartly-styled, coordinated set. The charming tassel doll accent on the beret adds a whimsical touch that's sure to delight a young girl's fancy!

Skill Level: Beginner

Size

Beret: 20 inch circumference

Scarf: 7½ x 48 inches

Mittens: 4 x 7¾ inches

Materials

- Caron Sayelle worsted weight yarn: 8½ oz white #0301 (A), 3½ oz each lilac #0335 (B) and dark lavender #0388 (C)
- Sizes F/5 and I/9 crochet hooks or sizes needed to obtain gauge
- 5-inch cardboard
- 6-inch cardboard
- Yarn marker
- Tapestry needle

Gauge

Larger hook, 5 sc = 1½ inches; 5 sc rnds = 1½ inches; 5 hdc rows = 2 inches; 3 groups of 2 hdc = 2 inches

Smaller hook, 4 sc = 1 inch; 4 sc rnds = 1 inch

Check gauge to save time.

Pattern Notes

Weave in loose ends as work progresses.

Do not join rnds unless otherwise stated. Use marker to mark rnds.

To change color in last step of last hdc, work hdc until 3 lps are on hook, drop working color, pick up next color and draw through rem 3 lps on hook.

Pattern Stitches

Pc: 4 hdc in same st, draw up a lp, remove hook, insert hook in first hdc of 4-hdc group, pick up dropped lp and draw through st on hook, ch 1 to lock.

Beg pc: Ch 2, 3 hdc in same st, draw up a lp, remove hook, insert hook in top of beg ch-2, pick up dropped lp and draw through st on hook, ch 1 to lock.

Beg V-st: [Ch 4 (counts as first dc, ch 1), dc] in same st.

V-st: [Dc, ch 1, dc] in same st.

Beret

Rnd 1: With larger hook and B, ch 2, 7 sc in 2nd ch from hook. (7 sc)

Rnd 2: 2 sc in each sc around. (14 sc)

Rnd 3: [Sc in next sc, 2 sc in next sc] rep around. (21 sc)

Rnd 4: [Sc in each of next 2 sc, 2 sc in next sc] rep around. (28 sc)

Rnd 5: [Sc in each of next 3 sc, 2 sc in next sc] rep around. (35 sc)

Rnd 6: [Sc in each of next 4 sc, 2 sc in next sc] rep around. (42 sc)

Rnd 7: [Sc in each of next 5 sc, 2 sc in next sc] rep around. (49 sc)

Rnd 8: [Sc in each of next 6 sc, 2 sc in next sc] rep around. (56 sc)

Rnd 9: [Sc in each of next 7 sc, 2 sc in next sc] rep around. (63 sc)

Rnd 10: [Sc in each of next 8 sc, 2 sc in next sc] rep around. (70 sc)

Rnd 11: Sc in each sc around.

Rnd 12: [Sc in each of next 9 sc, 2 sc in next sc] rep around. (77 sc)

Rnd 13: [Sc in each of next 10 sc, 2 sc in next sc] rep around. (84 sc)

Rnd 14: Rep Rnd 11.

Rnd 15: [Sc in each of next 11 sc, 2 sc in next sc] rep around. (91 sc)

Rnd 16: [Sc in each of next 12 sc, 2 sc in next sc] rep around. (98 sc)

Rnds 17–19: Rep Rnd 11.

Rnd 20: [Sc in each of next 5 sc, sc dec over next 2 sc] rep around. (84 sc)

Rnd 21: [Sc in each of next 4 sc, sc dec over next 2 sc] rep around. (70 sc)

Rnd 22: [Sc in each of next 3 sc, sc dec over next 2 sc] rep around. (56 sc)

Rnd 23: [Sc in each of next

12 sc, sc dec over next 2 sc] rep around. (52 sc)

Rnd 24: [Sc in each of next 11 sc, sc dec over next 2 sc] rep around. (48 sc)

Rnds 25 & 26: Rep Rnd 11. At the end of Rnd 26, fasten off.

Rnd 27: Attach C with sc in any st, sc in each sc around. (48 sc)

Rnd 28: Sc in each sc around,

changing to A in last step of last sc, drop C, do not fasten off.

Rnd 29: Beg pc in next st, sc in next st, [pc in next st, sc in next st] rep around, changing to C in last step of last sc, fasten off A. (24 pc; 24 sc)

Rnd 30: Sk beg pc, 2 sc in next sc, [sk pc, 2 sc in next sc] rep around. (48 sc)

Rnd 31: Rep Rnd 11.

Rnd 32: Sl st in each st around, fasten off.

Tassel Doll

Working from outside of skein, wrap A evenly 60 times around 5-inch cardboard. Cut one end of lps and remove from cardboard. Cut 2 lengths of A each 8 inches long. With first length, tie a double knot around center of bundle of yarn, and then tie another double knot approximately 1 inch above first double knot. To form head, cut a 6-inch length of B and tie a knot approximately ¾ inch below first knot. For arms, separate 12 pieces of yarn on each side of yarn bundle and braid each group, secure end of each arm with a 6-inch length of B. For waist, cut a 6-inch length of B and tie approximately 1 inch below head. For skirt, trim bottom even across. Trim knotted ends even.

Attach C in Rnd 1 of beret with a sl st, ch 25, sl st in 1 inch lp at top of doll, sl st in each ch across ch-25, sl st in Rnd 1 of beret, fasten off. Tack ch to Rnd 15 of beret.

Scarf

Row 1: With larger hook and A, ch 22, 2 hdc in 4th ch from hook, [sk next ch, 2 hdc in next ch] 9 times, turn. (10 groups 2 hdc)

Row 2: Ch 2, [sk 2 hdc, 2 hdc in sp between hdc groups] 9 times, sk 2 hdc, 2 hdc in end sp, turn. (10 groups 2 hdc)

Rows 3–7: Rep Row 2. At the end of last rep, change to C in last st, drop A.

Rows 8 & 9: Rep Row 2. At the end of last rep, change to A, fasten off C.

Rows 10 & 11: Rep Row 2. At the end of last rep, change to B in last st, drop A.

Rows 12 & 13: Rep Row 2. At the end of last rep, change to A, fasten off B.

Rows 14–97: Rep Row 2. At the end of last rep, change to B, drop A.

Rows 98 & 99: Rep Row 2. At the end of last rep, change A, fasten off B.

Rows 100 & 101: Rep Row 2. At the end of last rep, change to C, drop A.

Rows 102 & 103: Rep Row 2. At the end of last rep, change to A, fasten off C.

Rows 104–110: Rep Row 2. At the end of last rep, fasten off.

Fringe

Wrap A around 6-inch cardboard 6 times for each group of fringe. Fold 6 strands in half, insert hook from WS, draw bundle through at fold to form a lp on hook, draw cut ends through lp on hook, pull tightly to secure. Attach 6 groups of fringe evenly sp across each end. Trim ends even.

Mitten

Make 2

Rnd 1: With smaller hook and C, ch 30, sl st to join to form a ring, ch 1, sc in each ch around. (30 sc)

Rnds 2–6: Sc in each sc around.

Rnd 7: 2 sc in next st, sc in next st, 2 sc in next st (beg gusset for thumb), sc in next 27 sc. (32 sc)

Rnd 8: 2 sc in next sc, sc in each of next 3 sc, 2 sc in next sc, sc in next 27 sc. (34 sc)

Rnd 9: 2 sc in next sc, sc in each of next 5 sc, 2 sc in next sc, sc in next 27 sc. (36 sc)

Rnd 10: 2 sc in next sc, sc in each of next 7 sc, 2 sc in next sc, sc in next 27 sc. (38 sc)

Rnd 11: 2 sc in next sc, sc in each of next 9 sc, 2 sc in next sc, sc in next 27 sc. (40 sc)

Rnd 12: 2 sc in next sc, sc in each of next 11 sc, 2 sc in next sc, sc in next 27 sc. (42 sc)

Rnd 13: Sc in next sc, sk next 14 sc (thumb opening), sc in each of next 27 sc. (28 sc)

Rnd 14: Sc dec over next 2 sc, sc in each of next 24 sc, sc dec over next 2 sc. (26 sc)

Rnd 15: Sc dec over next 2 sc, sc in each of next 22 sc, sc dec over next 2 sc. (24 sc)

Rnds 16–21: Sc in each sc around.

Rnds 22–25: Sc around, dec 4 sc evenly sp on each rnd. At the end of Rnd 25, sl st in next st, leaving a length of yarn, fasten off. (8 sc) Sew opening closed.

Thumb

Rnd 1: With smaller hook, attach C with sc in first sk sc of Rnd 12, sc in same sc as first sc, sc in each of next 12 sc, 2 sc in next sc. (16 sc)

Rnd 2: Sc dec over next 2 sc, sc in each of next 12 sc, sc dec over next 2 sc. (14 sc)

Rnd 3: Sc dec over next 2 sc, sc in each of next 10 sc, sc dec over next 2 sc. (12 sc)

Rnds 4 & 5: Sc in each sc around.

Rnd 6: [Sc dec over next 2 sc] 6 times, sl st in next st, leaving a length of yarn, fasten off. (6 sc) Sew opening closed.

Wrist Trim

Rnd 1: With smaller hook, attach B in opposite side of foundation ch above thumb on side of mitten, ch 1, sc in same ch as beg ch-1, sc in each of next 29 chs, sl st to join in beg sc. (30 sc)

Rnd 2: Beg V-st in same st as joining, sk next st, [V-st in next st, sk next st] rep around, sl st to join in 3rd ch of beg ch-4, draw up a lp of A, drop B. (15 V-sts)

Rnd 3: Sl st into ch-1 sp of V-st, beg pc in same ch-1 sp, sc in sp between next 2 dc, [pc in next ch-1 sp of V-st, sc in sp between next 2 dc] rep around, sl st to join in top of beg pc, draw up a lp of B, fasten off A. (15 pc; 15 sc)

Rnd 4: Sl st into next sc, ch 1, 2 sc in same sc, sk next pc, [2 sc in next sc, sk next pc] rep around, sl st to join in beg sc. (30 sc)

Rnd 5: Beg V-st in same sc as joining, sk next sc, [V-st in next sc, sk next sc] rep around, join in 3rd ch of beg ch-4, fasten off. (15 V-sts). ✄

Puzzle Sweater

Designs by Bendy Carter

An intriguing, jigsaw design slip-stitched on top of a simple, single crochet sweater makes this cute kids' pullover easy to make and a fun fashion accent for a child's winter wardrobe!

Skill Level: Intermediate

Size: Child's size 8 with sizes 10 and 12 in parentheses.

Chest measurements: 27 (28½, 30) inches

Finished chest measurement: 33 (34½, 36) inches

Materials

• Coats & Clark Red Heart Kids worsted weight yarn (4 oz multi): 4 (4, 5) skeins beach #2940 for boys and bikini #2945 for girls (MC), 5 oz black #2012 (CC)

• Size H/8 crochet hook or size needed to obtain gauge

• Size G/6 crochet hook

• 4 yarn markers

• Yarn needle

Gauge

With larger hook, 10 sc = 3 inches; 12 sc rows = 3 inches

Check gauge to save time.

Pattern Notes

Weave in loose ends as work progresses.

Join rnds with a sl st unless otherwise stated.

Each vertical line of each diagram is a sc st.

Pattern Stitch

Surface sl st: Leaving a slight tail on yarn, ch 1, remove hook from lp, holding yarn on WS, insert hook RS to WS, pick up dropped lp and draw through to RS, [insert hook in next sp between sts, yo, draw up a lp and draw through to RS and through st on hook] rep as indicated in diagram to form puzzle pieces.

Back

Row 1 (RS): With larger hook and CC, ch 56 (60, 62), sc in 2nd

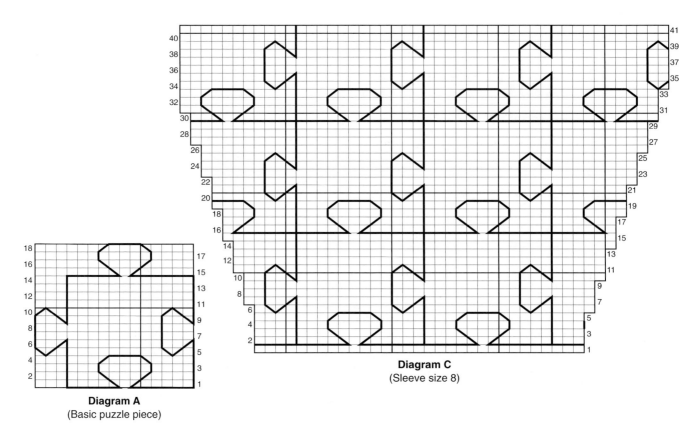

Diagram A
(Basic puzzle piece)

Diagram C
(Sleeve size 8)

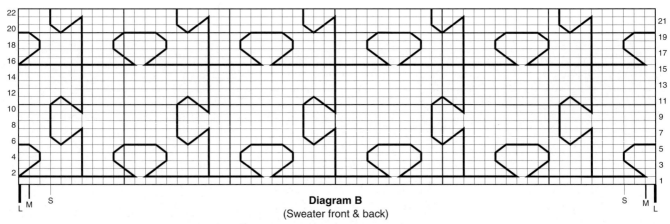

Diagram B
(Sweater front & back)

ch from hook, sc in each rem ch across, changing to MC in last ch, fasten off CC, turn. (55, 59, 61 sc)

Row 2: Ch 1, sc in each of next 51 (53, 54) sc, place a marker, sc in each rem 4 (6, 7) sc, turn.

Row 3: Ch 1, sc in each sc across, turn.

Rep Row 3 until piece measures 16½ (17¾, 19¾) inches from beg.

Neck shaping
Ch 1, sc in each of next 19 (20, 21) sc, fasten off; sk next 17 (19, 19) sc,

attach MC in next sc, ch 1, beg in same sc as beg ch-1, sc in each of next 19 (20, 21) sc, fasten off.

Front
Work same as for back until front has 9 (10, 10) sc rows less than back.

First neck shaping
Ch 1, sc in each of next 25 (27, 28) sc, turn.

Rep Row 3 of back until front is same length as back, *at same time,* dec 2 sc sts at neck edge on next 2

rows, then 1 st at neck edge on next 2 (3, 3) rows, fasten off.

Second neck shaping
Sk next 5 sc sts, attach MC in next sc, rep as for first neck shaping.

Sleeve
Make 2

Row 1 (RS): With larger hook and CC, ch 33, sc in 2nd ch from hook, sc in each rem ch across,

Continued on page 30

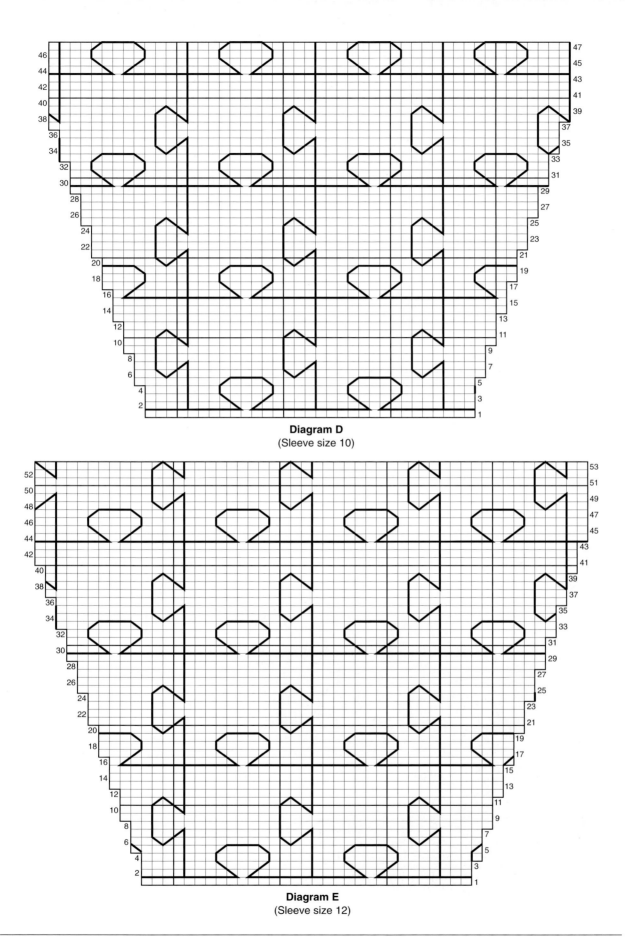

Diagram D
(Sleeve size 10)

Diagram E
(Sleeve size 12)

Convertible Mittens

Designs by Kathleen Stuart

The whole family can keep their hands toasty warm in these cozy mittens that open up to reveal fingerless gloves! This feature comes in very "handy" when regular gloves or mittens make it difficult to pick up and hold small items.

Skill Level: Beginner

Size
Child's: 2½ inches palm width
Adult's: 3 inches palm width

Materials
- Worsted weight yarn: 3 (5) oz MC
- Size G/6 crochet hook or size needed to obtain gauge
- Yarn needle
- Yarn marker

Gauge
Palm, 5 sts and 5 rnds = 1 inch
Check gauge to save time.

Pattern Notes
Weave in loose ends as work progresses.

Do not join rnds unless otherwise stated.

Right Palm

Rnd 1: Ch 30 (36), sl st to join to form a ring, ch 3 (counts as first dc), dc in each ch around, sl st to join in top of beg ch-3. (30, 36 dc)

Rnds 2–5 (8): Ch 2 (counts as first dc), fpdc around each of next 2 sts, [bpdc around next st, fpdc around each of next 2 sts] rep around, sl st to join in 2nd ch of beg ch-2.

Rnd 6 (9): Sc in same st as sl st, sc in each of next 3 (4) sts, 2 sc in next st, [sc in each of next 4 (5) sts, 2 sc in next st] rep around. (36, 42 sc)

Rnds 7–13 (10–19): [Sc in front lp of next st, sc in back lps of next st] rep around. (36, 42 sc)

Rnd 14 (20): Ch 6, sk next 10 sts (thumb opening), [sc in front lp of next st, sc in back lp of next st] rep around.

Rnd 15 (21): Sc in each of next 6 chs, [sc in front lp of next st, sc in back lp of next st] rep around.

Rnds 16 (22 & 23): [Sc in front lp of next st, sc in back lp of next st] rep around. (32, 38 sc)

Rnd 17 (24): Working in back lps only, sc in each st around. (32, 38 sc)

Rnds 18 & 19 (25–27): [Sc in front lp of next st, sc in back lp of next st] rep around.

Right Fingerless Glove
First finger

Rnd 1: Sc in each of next 4 (5) sts of Rnd 19 (27), ch 3, sk all sts to last 4 sts of same rnd, sc in each of last 4 sts.

Rnd 2: Sc in each of next 4 (5) sts, sc in each of next 3 chs, sc in each of next 4 sts. (11, 12 sc)

Rnds 3 & 4 (3–6): Sc in each st around. At the end of last rep, sl st in next st, fasten off.

Second finger

Rnd 1: Sl st in 4th (5th) st of Rnd 19 (27), sc in each of next 4 (5) sts,

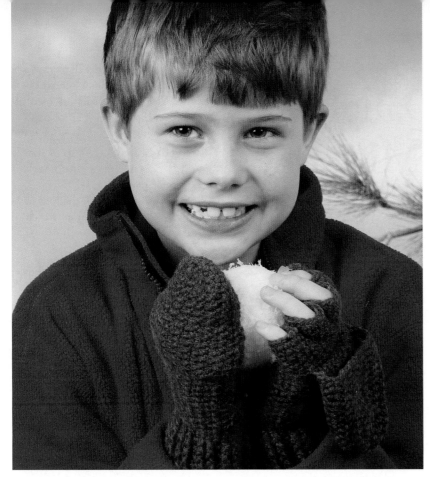

ch 3, sc in last rem 4 (5) sts of Rnd 19 (27), sc 3 sts into base of ch-3 of previous finger. (14, 16 sc)

Rnds 2–4 (2–6): Sc in each sc around. At the end of last rep, sl st in next st, fasten off.

Third finger

Rnd 1: Sl st in 8th (10th) st of Rnd 19 (27), sc in each of next 4 (5) sts, ch 3, sc in last rem 4 (5) sts of Rnd 19 (27), sc 3 sts into base of ch-3 of previous finger. (14, 16 sc)

Rnds 2–4 (2–6): Sc in each sc around. At the end of last rep, sl st in next st, fasten off.

Fourth finger

Rnd 1: Sl st in 12th (15th) st of Rnd 19 (27), sc in last rem 8 (9) sts of Rnd 19 (27), sc 3 sts into base of ch-3 sp of previous finger. (11, 12 sc)

Rnds 2 & 3 (2–5): Sc in each sc around. At the end of last rep, fasten off.

Right Thumb

Rnd 1: Attach yarn in first sk st of Rnd 13 (19), sc in same st, sc

in each of next 9 sts, work 6 sc across base of ch-6 sp of Rnd 14 (20). (16 sc)

Child thumb

Rnd 2: Sc in each sc around. (16 sc)

Rnd 3: [Sc in each of next 6 sc, sc dec over next 2 sc] twice. (14 sc)

Rnds 4–10: Rep Rnd 2.

Rnd 11: [Sc dec over next 2 sc] 7 times, sl st in next st, leaving a length of yarn, fasten off. (7 sc)
Weave rem length through sts, pull to close opening and secure.

Adult thumb

Rnds 2–13: Sc in each sc around. (16 sc)

Rnd 14: [Sc in each of next 2 sts, sc dec over next 2 sts] rep around. (12 sc)

Rnd 15: [Sc in next st, sc dec over next 2 sts] rep around, sl st in next st, leaving a length of yarn, fasten off. (8 sc)

Right Mitten

Rnd 1: With palm facing down

and thumb on the left, sl st in front lp of 2nd to last st of Rnd 16 (23), ch 19 (23), sl st in front lp in the 19 (23rd) st of Rnd 16 (23), sc in same st, sc in front lp of next 12 (14) sts on Rnd 16 (23), sc in each ch around. (32, 38 sc)

Rnds 2–11 (2–17): [Sc in front lp of next st, sc in back lp of next st] rep around. (32, 38 sc)

Note: *Rnd 18 is for adult mitten only. Then continue on with pattern for both sizes.*

Rnd 18: Working in pattern, sc in first st, [sc in each of next 4 sts, sc dec over next 2 sts] rep around, ending with sc in last st. (32 sc)

Rnd 12 (19): Working in pattern, sc in first st, [sc in each of next 3 sts, sc dec over next 2 sts] rep around, ending with sc in last st.

Rnd 13 (20): Working in pattern, sc in first st, [sc in each of next 2 sts, sc dec over next 2 sts] rep around, ending with sc in last st. (20 sc)

Rnd 14 (21): Working in pattern, sc in first st, [sc in next st, sc dec over next 2 sts] rep around, ending with sc in last st, sl st in next st, leaving a length of yarn, fasten off. (14 sc)

Continued on page 31

Warm Hands, Warm Heart

*Children in shelters go out to play
the same as my kids do.
Their mothers warm cold fingers
and kiss cold faces, too.
This winter I'll be crocheting
to keep homeless children warm—
New mittens, hats and scarves
to withstand each flurry and storm.
This year while the kids make snowmen,
their mothers' hearts will glow
to know that in the freezing cold
they'll be warm from head to toe.*

Mother-Daughter Hats & Mittens

Designs by Sheila Leslie

From baby to Grandma, all the ladies in the family can sport stylish hats and mittens with this fun, easy pattern that makes sizes for toddler, child and adult simply by using different yarn weights!

Skill Level: Beginner

Size

Toddler's hat: 17–18 inches

Girl's hat: 19–20 inches

Ladies' hat: 21–22 inches

Materials

- Toddlers: Coats & Clark Red Heart Soft worsted weight yarn: 4 oz white #7001, Girls:

Coats & Clark Red Heart Super Saver worsted weight yarn: 5½ oz pale plum #579, Ladies: Bernat Illusions: 6 oz lilac hues #27959

- Size H/8 crochet hook or size needed to obtain gauge

- Yarn markers

- Yarn needle

Gauge

Toddlers, 9 sc = 2 inches; girls, 4 sc = 1 inch; ladies, 3 sc = 1 inch
Check gauge to save time.

Pattern Notes

Weave in loose ends as work progresses.

Do not join rnds unless otherwise stated. Use a yarn marker to mark rnds.

Ch-3 counts as first dc throughout.

Hat

Rnd 1: Starting at top of hat with appropriate yarn, ch 2, 6 sc in 2nd ch from hook, place marker and move as rnds progress. (6 sc)

Rnd 2: Work 2 sc in each sc around. (12 sc)

Rnd 3: [Sc in next sc, 2 sc in next sc] rep around. (18 sc)

Rnd 4: [Sc in each of next 2 sc, 2 sc in next sc] rep around. (24 sc)

Rnd 5: [Sc in each of next 3 sc, 2 sc in next sc] rep around. (30 sc)

Rnd 6: [2 sc in next sc, sc in each of next 4 sc] rep around. (36 sc)

Rnd 7: [Sc in each of next 5 sc, 2 sc in next sc] rep around. (42 sc)

Rnd 8: [2 sc in next sc, sc in each of next 6 sc] rep around. (48 sc)

Rnd 9: [Sc in each of next 7 sc, 2 sc in next sc] rep around. (54 sc)

Rnd 10: [2 sc in next sc, sc in each of next 8 sc] rep around. (60 sc)

Rnd 11: Sc in each sc around.

Rnd 12: [Sc in each of next 5 sc, 2 sc in next sc] rep around. (70 sc)

Rnds 13–16: Rep Rnd 11.

Rnd 17: Sl st in next st, ch 3, [dc, ch 1, 2 dc] in same st as beg ch-3, sk next 2 sts, sc in next st, sk next st, [{2 dc, ch 1, 2 dc} shell in next st, sk next 2 sts, sc in next st, sk next st] rep around, join in 3rd ch of beg ch-3. (14 shells)

Rnd 18: Sl st into ch-1 sp of shell, [ch 3, 1 dc, ch 1, 2 dc] in same ch-1 sp, sc in next sc, [{2 dc, ch 1, 2 dc} in next ch-1 sp of shell, sc in next sc] rep around, join in 3rd ch of beg ch-3.

Rnds 19–21: Rep Rnd 18.

Rnd 22: Sl st into ch-1 sp of shell, [ch 3, 1 dc, ch 1, 2 dc] in same ch-1 sp, dc in next sc, [{2 dc, ch 1, 2 dc} in next ch-1 sp of shell, dc in next sc] rep around, join in 3rd ch of beg ch-3.

Rnd 23: Ch 1, sc in each dc around, join in beg sc. (70 sc)

Rnds 24 & 25: Rep Rnd 11.

Rnd 26: [Ch 1, sl st in next sc] rep around, ending with ch 1, join in beg sl st, fasten off.

Toddler & Girls Mittens

Cuff

Rnd 1: With appropriate yarn, ch 24, sl st to join to form a ring, ch 3, dc in each ch around, join in 3rd ch of beg ch-3. (24 dc)

Rnd 2: Ch 3, fpdc around next dc, [dc in next dc, fpdc around next dc] rep around, ending with dc in same st as beg ch-3, join in 3rd ch of beg ch-3. (25 sts)

Rnd 3: Ch 3, [dc, ch 1, 2 dc] in same st as beg ch-3, sk next 2 sts, sc in next st, sk next st, [{2 dc, ch 1, 2 dc} in next st, sk next 2 sts, sc in next st, sk next st] rep around, join in 3rd ch of beg ch-3. (5 shells)

Rnds 4–6: Rep Rnd 18 of hat. At the end of Rnd 6, fasten off.

Hand

Rnd 1: Attach yarn in opposite side of foundation ch, ch 1, work 24 sc around.

Rnd 2: [2 sc in next sc] twice, sc in each of next 22 sc. (26 sc)

Rnd 3: Sc in next sc, [2 sc in next

sc] twice, sc in each of next 11 sc, [2 sc in next sc] twice, sc in each of next 10 sc. (30 sc)

Rnd 4: [2 sc in next sc] twice, sc in next sc, [2 sc in next sc] twice, sc in each of next 25 sc. (34 sc)

Rnd 5: Sc in each sc around.

Rnd 6: Sc in next sc, ch 3, sk next 7 sts (thumb opening), sc in each of next 26 sc.

Rnd 7: Sc in each sc and each ch around.

Rnds 8–10: Rep Rnd 5. (30 sc)

Rnd 11: Sc around, dec 1 st at each thumb side and little finger side. (28 sc)

Rnd 12: Rep Rnd 5.

Rnds 13–16: [Rep Rnds 11 and 12] twice. (24 sc)

Rnd 17: [Sc in each of next 6 sc, dec 1 sc over next 2 sc] rep around. (21 sc)

Rnd 18: Rep Rnd 5.

Rnd 19: [Sc in next sc, dec 1 sc over next 2 sc] rep around. (14 sc)

Rnd 20: Rep Rnd 5.

Rnd 21: [Dec 1 sc over next 2 sc] rep around. (7 sc)

Rnd 22: [Dec 1 sc over next 2 sc] 3 times, sl st in next st, leaving a length of yarn, fasten off.

Gather rem sts of Rnd 22, draw opening closed and secure.

Thumb

Rnd 1: Attach yarn in first sk st of Rnd 5, ch 1, sc in same st as beg ch-1, sc in each of next 6 sts, sc in side edge of Rnd 6, sc in each of next 3 chs. (11 sc)

Rnd 2: Sc in each sc around.

Rnd 3: Rep Rnd 2.

Rnd 4: Sc in each of next 4 sc, dec 1 sc over next 2 sc, sc in each of next 5 sc. (10 sc)

Rnds 5 & 6: Rep Rnd 2.

Continued on page 31

Chill Chasers Hat & Scarf Set

Designs by Joyce Messenger

Chase away the chill with this extra-cozy scarf and hat that work up quickly and easily with a double-ended crochet hook and soft, worsted yarn. Make a set for a special boy or girl in his or her favorite colors for a delightful holiday gift!

Skill Level: Beginner

Size

Scarf: 7½ x 36 inches, excluding fringe

Hat: 15½ inches in diameter x 8 inches long

Materials

- Caron Simply Soft worsted weight yarn: 8 oz each MC and CC
- Size K/10½ double-ended crochet hook or size needed to obtain gauge
- Size I/9 crochet hook
- Yarn needle

Gauge

Scarf, horizontal panels = 3½ inches; vertical panels = 2 inches; Hat, horizontal panels = 2 inches; vertical panels = 1¼ inches

Check gauge to save time.

Pattern Notes

Weave in loose ends as work progresses.

Use double-ended hook throughout unless otherwise stated.

Pattern Stitches

Fpsc: Insert hook front to back to front again around vertical post of st, yo, draw up a lp, yo, draw through 2 lps on hook.

Bpsc: Insert hook back to front to back again around vertical post of st, yo, draw up a lp, yo, draw through 2 lps on hook.

Scarf

Horizontal Panel

Row 1: With MC, ch 28, working through back lps only and keeping all lps on hook, insert hook in 2nd ch from hook, yo and draw a lp through, [insert hook in next ch, yo, draw up a lp] rep across, drop MC, turn, slide sts to opposite end. (27 lps on hook)

Row 2: With CC make a sl knot on hook and draw through first lp on hook, [yo, draw through 2 lps on hook] rep across until 1 lp rem on hook, do not turn.

Row 3: Sk first vertical bar, [insert hook under next vertical bar, yo, draw up a lp] rep across, drop CC, turn, slide sts to opposite end.

Row 4: Pick up MC, yo, draw through first lp on hook, [yo, draw through 2 lps on hook] rep across until 1 lp rem on hook, do not turn.

Row 5: Sk first vertical bar, [draw up a lp through next vertical bar] rep across, drop MC, turn, slide sts to opposite end.

Row 6: Pick up CC, yo, draw through first lp on hook, [yo, draw through 2 lps on hook] rep across until 1 lp rem on hook, do not turn.

Row 7: Sk first vertical bar, [draw up a lp through next vertical bar] rep across, drop CC, turn, slide sts to opposite end.

Rep Rows 4–7 until 6 patterns are completed, ending with Row 4, fasten off CC and MC.

Vertical Panel

Row 1: With MC, ch 8, working through back lps of ch only, draw up a lp in 2nd ch from hook, draw up a lp in each of next 5 chs, insert hook in next ch and 2nd vertical bar of horizontal section, yo, draw up a lp, drop MC, turn, slide sts to opposite end. (7 lps on hook)

Row 2: With CC make a sl knot on hook, draw through first lp on hook, [yo, draw through 2 lps on hook] rep across until 1 lp rem on hook, do not turn.

Row 3: Insert hook in next vertical bar of horizontal panel and 2nd vertical bar of working section, yo, draw up a lp, [insert hook in next vertical bar, yo, draw up a lp] rep across, drop CC, turn, slide sts to opposite end.

Row 4: Pick up MC, yo, draw through first lp on hook, [yo, draw through 2 lps on hook] rep across, do not turn.

Row 5: Sk first vertical bar, [insert hook in next vertical bar, yo, draw up a lp] 6 times, insert hook in last vertical bar and next bar of horizontal section, yo, draw up a lp, drop MC, turn, slide sts to opposite end.

Row 6: Pick up CC, yo, draw through first lp on hook, [yo, draw through 2 lps on hook] rep across, do not turn.

Rep Rows 3–6 across horizontal edge, ending with a Row 4.

For next horizontal panel, with MC, pick up 27 lps across vertical section and then rep horizontal panel.

Continue to rep panels until 6 panels each, then rep horizontal panel.

Trim

Row 1: With desired color and I hook, attach yarn in side edge of scarf, working across long edge of scarf, ch 1, [fpsc around next st, bpsc around next st] rep across edge, fasten off.

Rep trim on opposite edge of scarf.

Fringe

Cut 2 strands each 8 inches long of MC and CC, insert hook in end of scarf, fold strands in half, draw strands through at fold to form a lp on hook, draw cut ends through lp on hook, pull gently to secure. Rep fringe across each end of scarf.

Hat

Horizontal Panel

Row 1: With MC, ch 65, rep Row 1 of scarf. (64 lps on hook)

Work scarf horizontal panel until panel measures 2 inches.

Vertical Panel

Work vertical panel of scarf across edge of horizontal panel.

Horizontal Panel

Row 1: With MC, pick up 64 lps across vertical panel. (64 lps on hook)

Work scarf horizontal panel until panel measures 2 inches.

Vertical Panel

Work vertical panel of scarf across edge of horizontal panel.

Horizontal Panel

Row 1: With MC, pick up 64 lps across vertical panel. (64 lps on hook)

Rows 2 & 3: Rep Rows 2 and 3 of scarf.

Continue in pattern of scarf, working dec on pattern Rows 4 and 6 of pattern by working yo, draw through 3 lps instead of 2 across each dec row, ending with a Row 4, leaving a length of each color yarn, fasten off. (32, 16, 8 sts)

Weave rem lengths through top of hat, pull to close opening, secure and sew side seam.

Make a 2-inch pompom and attach to top of hat. ✄

Pretty in Plum Scarf & Ski Band

Continued from page 8

back lp only, sc in next st, leaving a length of yarn, fasten off.

With tapestry needle, sew Rnd 30 to opposite side of foundation ch.

Pompom

Cut 2 cardboard 2½-inch circles, cut 1-inch-in-diameter circle from the center of each circle. Thread tapestry needle with 2 yds orchid yarn and wind yarn around and through the center of 2 circles. With 8 yds violet, continue winding yarn around circles. Cut through the outer lps between 2 circles and separate slightly. Tie a length of violet yarn around the center between cardboard circles and knot securely. Remove cardboard circles, fluff pompom and attach to front of ski band opposite the sewn seam. ✄

North Country Caps

Continued from page 9

Row 37: Rep Row 8. (30 sc)
Rows 38–41: Rep Row 2.
Row 42: Rep Row 8. (24 sc)

Rows 43–47: Rep Row 2.
Row 48: Rep Row 8. (18 sc)
Rows 49–55: Rep Row 2.
Row 56: Rep Row 8. (12 sc)
Rows 57–66: Rep Row 2.
Row 67: Rep Row 8, fasten off. (6 sc)

With matching yarn, sew brim and cap seam. Fold brim upward onto cap.

Tassel

Cut 2 lengths of CC yarn and set aside. Wrap CC around cardboard until desired thickness. Pass a length under bundle of wrapped yarn at center top, tie ends securely tog and knot. Cut opposite end of tassel strands and remove cardboard. Wrap 2nd length of yarn around tassel approximately 1½ inch from top of tassel. Trim ends as desired. Attach tassel to Row 67 of cap. ✄

Puzzle Sweater

Continued from page 22

changing to MC in last ch, fasten off CC, turn. (32 sc)

Row 2: Ch 1, work 28 sc, place a marker, sc in each of next 4 sc, turn.

Row 3: Ch 1, sc in each sc across, turn.

[Rep Row 3] 2 (1, 0) times.

Row 4: Ch 1, sc in each sc across to last sc, 2 sc in last sc, turn.

Row 5: Rep Row 4.

Rows 6 & 7: Rep Row 3.

Rep Rows 4–7 until sleeve has a total of 47 (50, 53) sc sts across.

Rep Row 3 until a total of 42 (48, 54) sc rows are completed, fasten off.

Puzzle Design

Note: *Using diagrams as a guide, work puzzle design on each sleeve, back and front.*

With RS facing, with CC and larger hook, insert hook at marker, beg with bottom right corner of puzzle piece, surface ch st one puzzle piece (Diagram A). Add additional puzzle pieces to sweater in same manner until entire sweater is worked and pieces fit tog in puzzle format.

First 23 rows of back and front are shown in Diagram B, each sweater size has its own individual diagram for sleeve.

Finishing

Sew shoulder seams. Fold sleeve in half lengthwise at center, position center of sleeve to shoulder seam and sew sleeve in place. Sew side and sleeve seams.

Bottom Ribbing

Rnd 1 (RS): With smaller hook, attach CC at seam, ch 2, working around post of sc sts of Row 1, [fpdc around post of next st, bpdc around post of next st] rep around, join in 2nd ch of beg ch-2.

Rnd 2: Ch 2, [fpdc around fpdc, bpdc around bpdc] rep around, join in 2nd ch of beg ch-2.

Rep Rnd 2 until ribbing from beg measures 2 inches, fasten off.

Sleeve Ribbing

Rep bottom ribbing around each sleeve opening.

Neckline Ribbing

Rnd 1 (RS): With larger hook, attach CC at shoulder seam, ch 1, sc evenly sp around neckline opening, join in beg sc.

Rnd 2: With smaller hook, ch 2, [fpdc around next sc, bpdc around next sc] rep around, join in 2nd ch of beg ch-2.

Rnd 3: Ch 2, [fpdc around fpdc, bpdc around bpdc] rep around, join in 2nd ch of beg ch-2.

Rep Rnd 3 until ribbing from beg measures 1 inch, fasten off. ✄

Convertible Mittens

Continued from page 25

Weave rem length through sts, pull to close opening and secure.

Left Palm

Note: *Both mittens could be worked as the right mitten, but we found that due to the nature of sc rnds, that off-setting the fingerless gloves a few sts for the left hand made the left hand glove more comfortable.*

Rnds 1–19 (1–27): Rep Rnds 1–19 (1–27 of right palm).

Left Fingerless Glove
First finger

Rnd 1: Sc in first 8 (9) sts of Rnd 19 (27), ch 3.

Rnd 2: Sc in each of next 8 (9) sc, sc in each of next 3 chs. (11, 12 sc)

Rnds 3 & 4 (3–6): Sc in each sc around. At the end of last rep, sl st in next st, fasten off.

Second finger

Rnd 1: Sl st in 8th (9th) st of Rnd 19 (27), sc in next 4 (5) sts of Rnd 19 (27), ch 3, sc in last rem 4 (5) sts of Rnd 19 (27), sc 3 sts into base of ch-3 of previous finger. (14, 16 sc)

Rnds 2–4 (2–6): Sc in each st around. At the end of last rep, sl st in next sc, fasten off.

Third finger

Rnd 1: Sl st in 12th (14th) st of Rnd 19 (27), sc in next 4 (5) sts of Rnd 19 (27), ch 3, sc in last rem 4 (5) sts of Rnd 19 (27), sc 3 sts into base of ch-3 of previous finger. (14, 16 sc)

Rnds 2–4 (2–6): Sc in each st around. At the end of last rep, sl st in next st, fasten off.

Fourth finger

Rnd 1: Sl st in 16th (19th) st of Rnd 19 (27), sc in last rem 8 (9) sts of Rnd 19 (27), sc 3 sts into base of ch-3 of previous finger. (11, 12 sc)

Rnds 2 & 3 (2–5): Sc in each st around. At the end of last rep, sl st in next st, fasten off.

Left Thumb

Rep right thumb.

Left Mitten

Rnd 1: With palm facing down and thumb on the right, sl st in front lp of 19th (23rd) st of Rnd 16 (23), ch 19 (23), sl st in front lp in the 7th (9th) st of Rnd 16 (23), sc in same st, sc in front lp of next 12 (14) sts on Rnd 16 (23), sc in each ch around. (32, 38 sc)

Rnds 2–14 (2–21): Rep Rnds 2–14 (2–21) of right mitten. ✂

> *To wear the cloak of compassion is to be clothed in beauty.*
>
> —Unknown

Mother-Daughter Hats & Mittens

Continued from page 27

Rnd 7: [Dec 1 sc over next 2 sc] 5 times, sl st in next st, leaving a length of yarn, fasten off. (5 sc)

Gather rem sts of Rnd 7, draw opening closed and secure.

Ladies Mittens
Cuff

Rnds 1–6: With appropriate yarn, rep Rnds 1–6 of toddler and girls cuff.

Hand

Rnds 1–3: With appropriate yarn, rep Rnds 1–3 of toddler and girls hand. (30 sc)

Rnd 4: [2 sc in next sc] twice, sc in next sc, [2 sc in next sc] twice, sc in each of next 12 sc, [2 sc in next sc] twice, sc in each of next 11 sc. (36 sc)

Rnd 5: Sc in each sc around.

Rnd 6: Sc in next st, ch 4, sk next 7 sts (thumb opening), sc in each of next 28 sc.

Rnd 7: Sc in each sc and each ch around. (33 sc)

Rnds 8–10: Rep Rnd 5.

Rnd 11: Sc around, dec 1 st at each thumb side and little finger side. (31 sc)

Rnd 12: Rep Rnd 5.

Rnds 13–22: Rep Rnds 11 and 12. (21 sc)

Rnd 23: [Sc in next sc, dec 1 sc over next 2 sc] rep around. (14 sc)

Rnd 24: [Dec 1 sc over next 2 sc] rep around. (7 sc)

Rnd 25: [Dec 1 sc over next 2 sc] 3 times, sl st in next sc, leaving a length of yarn, fasten off.

Gather rem sts of Rnd 25, draw opening closed and secure.

Thumb

Rnd 1: Attach yarn in first sk st of Rnd 5, ch 1, sc in same st as beg ch-1, sc in each of next 6 sts, sc in side edge of Rnd 6, sc in each of next 4 chs, sc in side edge of Rnd 6. (13 sc)

Rnd 2: Sc in each sc around.

Rnd 3: Rep Rnd 2.

Rnd 4: Sc in each of next 5 sts, dec 1 sc over next 2 sc, sc in each of next 6 sc. (12 sc)

Rnd 5: Rep Rnd 2.

Rnd 6: [Sc in each of next 4 sc, dec 1 sc over next 2 sc] rep around. (10 sc)

Rnds 7 & 8: Rep Rnd 2.

Rnd 9: [Dec 1 sc over next 2 sc] 5 times, sl st in next st, leaving a length of yarn, fasten off.

Gather rem sts of Rnd 9, pull to close opening, secure. ✂

All-Around Afghans

Cozy afghans, whether made as loving gifts for family and friends or as special accents for our own home decor, are always appreciated for their decorative appeal and functional versatility. They warm the body and beautify the home, and touch the hearts of all who receive them, whatever the occasion, whatever the reason.

*Compassion is a
network of invisible
threads that weave
a blanket of love
around many lives.*

—Unknown

Boxed Polka Dots

Design courtesy of Caron International

As beautiful as it is warm, the subtle shades, delicate textures and extra-soft yarn in this delightful afghan create a cozy confection that will add a touch of sophisticated style to any home decor.

Skill Level: Beginner

Size: 64 x 46 inches, excluding fringe

Materials
- Caron Simply Soft worsted weight yarn: 42 oz off-white #2602 (A), 24 oz English rose #2646 (B), 12 oz soft pink #2614 (C)
- Size H/8 crochet hook or size needed to obtain gauge
- Yarn needle

Gauge
7 dc = 2 inches

Check gauge to save time.

Pattern Notes
Weave in loose ends as work progresses.

Afghan is crocheted vertically.

Ch-3 counts as first dc throughout.

All fpdc and bpdc are worked around the post of indicated sts 2 rows previous.

Always sk the sc st directly behind fpdc or in front of bpdc.

Afghan
Row 1 (RS): With A, ch 227, dc in 4th ch from hook, dc in each rem ch across, changing to C in last st, turn. (225 dc)

Row 2: Ch 1, sc in each st across, changing to B in last st, turn.

Row 3: Ch 1, sc in first st, [fpdc around next st 2 rows previous, sc in next st, bpdc around next st 2 rows previous, sc in next st] rep across, changing to A in last st, turn.

Row 4: Ch 3, dc in each st across, changing to C in last st, turn.

Rows 5–10: Rep Rows 2–4, omitting color change at the end of Row 10.

Rows 11–13: Continuing with A, rep Row 4, changing to C at the end of Row 13.

[Rep Rows 2–13] 9 times.

[Rep Rows 2–10] once. At the end of last rep, fasten off.

Fringe
Fringe is worked across ends of afghan rows, each fringe consists of 4 lengths of off-white each 21 inches long and is spaced by 3 groups of fringe every 2 inches.

Holding 4 strands tog, fold in half, insert hook in row end, draw strands through at fold to form a lp on hook, draw cut ends through lp on hook, pull gently to secure. Trim ends even. ✄

Hunter's Lodge

Design by Melissa Leapman

Warm earth colors and rich autumn hues make the perfect color palette for this ruggedly handsome, woven afghan that's just right for a cozy cabin, or the ideal accent for a library or den.

Skill Level: Beginner

Size: 50 x 74 inches, excluding fringe

Materials

• Patons Classic Wool worsted weight yarn: 11 skeins chestnut brown #231 (A), 3 skeins each forest green #241 (B), maize #203 (C), rich red #207 (D), old gold #204 (E) and paprika #238 (F)

• Size I/9 crochet hook or size needed to obtain gauge

• Blunt tapestry needle

Gauge

3 sc = 1 inch

Check gauge to save time.

Pattern Note

Weave in loose ends as work progresses.

Stripe Pattern

[4 rows A, 2 rows B, 4 rows A, 2 rows C, 4 rows A, 2 rows D, 4 rows A, 2 rows E, 4 rows A, 2 rows F] rep for stripe pattern.

Afghan

Row 1: With A, ch 184, sc in 2nd ch from hook, sc in each of next 2 chs, [ch 1, sk next ch, sc in each of next 3 chs] rep across, turn.

Row 2: Ch 1, sc in each of next 3 sc, [ch 1, sk next ch-1 sp, sc in each of next 3 sc] rep across, turn.

Working in stripe pattern, rep Row 2 until afghan measures from beg 74 inches, ending after a rep of 4 rows of A, fasten off.

Weave

Note: Each weave consists of

8 strands of the same color woven through ch-1 sps vertically on afghan.

With RS facing, leaving 6 inches at beg and end, weave 8 strands of yarn through ch-1 sps vertically working the same weave pattern on each weave. Work the following sequence of color weave, [B, C, D, E, F] rep across afghan. Add additional strands of matching fringe to rem 6-inch lengths. Trim fringe even. ✂

Let Freedom Ring

Design by Carolyn Pfeifer

Strips of simple granny motifs worked in vintage Americana colors create the old-time look of this patriotic afghan. Display your pride in our country's heritage while remembering the valiant efforts of those who have faithfully served to protect our freedoms.

Skill Level: Beginner

Size: 46 x 58 inches, excluding fringe

Materials

- Coats & Clark Red Heart Super Saver worsted weight yarn (8 oz per skein): 2 skeins each Aran #313, burgundy #376 and soft navy #387
- Size H/8 crochet hook or size needed to obtain gauge
- Yarn needle

Gauge

Each square is approximately 2¾ inches

Check gauge to save time.

Pattern Notes

Weave in loose ends as work progresses.

Join rnds with a sl st unless otherwise stated.

Ch-3 counts as first dc throughout.

Solid Granny Square

Note: *Make 168 squares with Aran, 105 with burgundy.*

Rnd 1 (RS): Ch 4, join to form a ring, ch 3, 2 dc in ring, ch 3, [3 dc in ring, ch 3] 3 times, join in 3rd ch of beg ch-3.

Rnd 2 (RS): Sl st in each of next 2 dc and into next ch-3 sp, [ch 3, 2 dc in same sp, ch 3, 3 dc] in same ch-3 sp, ch 1, [{3 dc, ch 3, 3 dc} in next ch-3 sp, ch 1] 3 times, join in 3rd ch of beg ch-3, fasten off.

Soft Navy Granny Square

Make 84

Rnd 1: With Aran, ch 4, join to form a ring, ch 3, 2 dc in ring, ch 3, [3 dc in ring, ch 3] 3 times, join in 3rd ch of beg ch-3, fasten off.

Rnd 2: Attach soft navy in any ch-3 sp, [ch 3, 2 dc, ch 3, 3 dc] in same ch-3 sp, ch 1, [{3 dc, ch 3, 3 dc} in next ch-3 sp, ch 1] 3 times, join in 3rd ch of beg ch-3, fasten off.

Assembly

Matching sts, sew squares tog in 17 strips of 21 squares each as follows: 8 strips of 21 squares each of Aran, 5 strips of 21 squares each of burgundy and 4 strips of 21 squares each of soft navy.

Sew the 17 strips tog beg with burgundy, [Aran, soft navy, Aran, burgundy] 4 times.

Fringe

Fringe is worked in each st of each end of afghan. For each square, cut 18 strands of matching color 7 inches long. Fold 2 strands in half, insert hook in st, draw strands through at fold to form a lp on hook, draw cut ends through lp on hook, pull ends to secure.

Trim ends even. Lightly steam press afghan as needed. ✂

Forgotten Heroes

Those who have been wounded
While fighting for our country,
So often seem forgotten
By Americans too busy.
Our veterans appreciate
A visit from you and me.
It only takes an afternoon,
But what a blessing we can be!
My friends and I are crocheting
Afghans from granny squares
To give to those who valiantly served
And show them someone still cares.

Soldier, rest! Thy warfare is o'er,
dream of fighting fields no more.
Sleep the sleep that knows not breaking,
morning of toll, nor night of waking.

—Sir Walter Scott

Windmills & Stars

Design by Dot Drake

This versatile design looks great on either side, whether you prefer whimsical windmills or delicate stars. Make the motifs in the same colors throughout for a more sophisticated look, or use many different colors for a patchwork effect.

Skill Level: Intermediate

Size: 52 x 70 inches

Materials

- Worsted weight yarn: 12 oz black, 6 oz each pink, light rose, dark rose, pale green, medium green, dark green, pale blue, medium blue, navy blue, pale lavender, medium lilac and lavender
- Size G/6 crochet hook or size needed to obtain gauge
- Yarn needle

Gauge

Motif = 8 inches; 4 dc = 1 inch; 2 dc rnds = 1¼ inches

Check gauge to save time.

Pattern Notes

Weave in loose ends as work progresses.

Join rnds with a sl st unless otherwise stated.

Ch-3 counts as first dc throughout.

Make 50 motifs with 4 in light and dark, 4 in light and medium, 4 in medium and dark for each set of colors, plus 2. Do not use black in any color combination of motifs.

Join motifs as work progresses in Rnd 9, beg with a row of 6 motifs, then [5 motifs, 6 motifs] 4 times.

Pattern Stitches

2-dc cl: [Yo, insert hook in ch-3 sp, yo, draw up a lp, yo, draw through 2 lps on hook] twice in same ch-3 sp, yo, draw through all 3 lps on hook.

Beg 2-dc cl: Ch 2, dc in same sp.

Motif

Make 50

Rnd 1 (RS): With light color, ch 4, dc in 4th ch from hook, ch 12, sl st in top of last dc, [2 dc in same ch as previous dc sts, ch 12, sl st in top of last dc] 5 times, join in 4th ch of beg ch-4, fasten off. (6 ch-12 lps; 12 dc)

Rnd 2: Draw up a lp of darker color in first dc of previous rnd, ch 3, dc in same st, holding ch-12 lps forward, work 2 dc in each dc around, join in 3rd ch of beg ch-3. (24 dc)

Rnd 3: Ch 3, dc in same st, dc in next dc, [2 dc in next dc, dc in next dc] rep around, join in 3rd ch of beg ch-3. (36 dc)

Rnd 4: Ch 3, dc in same st, dc in each of next 2 sts, *ch 3, dc in each of next 2 sts **, 2 dc in each of next 2 sts, dc in each of next 2 sts, rep from * around, ending last rep at **, 2 dc in next dc, join in 3rd ch of beg ch-3, draw up a lp, remove hook, do not fasten off. (48 dc; 6 ch-3 sps)

Rnd 5: Draw up a lp of light color in first ch-3 sp, beg 2-dc cl, [ch 3, 2-dc cl] twice in same ch-3 sp, *ch 2, [3 dc, ch 3, sl st in top of last dc, 3 dc] in next ch-12 lp, ch 2 **, 2-dc cl in next ch-3 sp, [ch 3, 2-dc cl] twice in same ch-3 sp, rep from * around, ending last rep at **, join in 2nd ch of beg cl, fasten off.

Rnd 6: Pick up dropped lp of dark color, ch 3, dc in next dc, *working over ch-2 sp of previous rnd and into dc sts of Rnd 4, dc in each of next 2 dc, 3 sc in each of next 2 ch-3 sps, working over ch-2 sp of previous rnd and into dc sts of Rnd 4, dc in each of next 2 dc **, dc in each of next 4 dc of Rnd 4, rep from * around, ending last rep at **, dc in each of next 2 dc, join in 3rd ch of beg ch-3.

Rnd 7: Ch 1, sc in each dc and each sc around, join in beg sc. (84 sc)

Rnd 8: With dark color, ch 3, remove hook, attach light color in next st with a sc, holding dark ch-3 to front, with light color, ch 3, [sc in next sc, ch 3, remove hook, holding light color ch-3 to front, pick up dark color, sc in next sc, ch 3, remove hook, holding dark color ch-3 to front, pick up light color] rep around, join, fasten off.

Rnd 9 (first motif): Attach black in any ch-3 sp of dark color, ch 1, sc in same ch-3 sp, ch 3, sk next light color ch-3 sp, [sc in next dark color ch-3 sp, ch 3, sk next light color ch-3 sp] rep around, join in beg sc, fasten off. (42 ch-3 sps)

Rnd 9 (rem motifs): Rep as for Rnd 9 of first motif, except along one side of motif, join 7 ch-3 sps

---

Loving and being loved brings a warmth and richness to life that nothing else can bring.

—Oscar Wilde

to previous motif with, sc in dark ch-3 sp of working motif, [ch 1, sc in ch-3 sp of adjacent motif, ch 1, sc in next dark ch-3 sp on working motif] 7 times.

Border

Rnd 1: Attach black in any ch-3 sp, ch 1, sc in same ch-3 sp, ch 3, [sc in next ch-3 sp, ch 3] rep around, join in beg sc.

Rnd 2: Sl st into next ch-3 sp, ch 3, 2 dc in same ch-3 sp, work 3 dc in each ch-3 sp around, except sk the ch-3 sp at each inside corner, join in 3rd ch of beg ch-3.

Rnd 3: Ch 1, sc in each dc around, except sk 4 dc at each inside corner (2 dc on each side of inner corner), join in beg sc.

Rnd 4: Working with various left-over colors and black, rep Rnd 8 of motif, sk 6 sc at each inside corner (3 sc on each side of inner corner), join, fasten off. ✂

Aspen Twist

Design by Glenda Winkleman

Simple, one-piece styling and velvety-soft, bulky yarn worked with a large hook make this cozy afghan a quick and easy weekend project. The addition of woven, twisted cables in contrasting colors creates a distinctive, striped design.

Skill Level: Beginner

Size: 45 x 64 inches

Materials
- Coats & Clark Red Heart Light & Lofty bulky yarn: 42 oz café au lait #9334, 13½ oz aspen #9313
- Size M/13 crochet hook or size needed to obtain gauge
- Yarn needle

Gauge

4 sc = 2 inches; 4 rows = 2 inches
Check gauge to save time.

Pattern Notes

Weave in loose ends as work progresses.

Join rnds with a sl st unless otherwise stated.

Afghan

Row 1: With café au lait, ch 130, sc in 2nd ch from hook, sc in each rem ch across, turn. (129 sc)

Row 2: Ch 1, sc in first sc, [ch 1, sk next sc, sc in next sc] rep across, turn. (64 sc; 64 ch-1 sps)

Row 3: Ch 1, sc in first sc, [ch 1, sk next ch-1 sp, sc in next sc] rep across, turn.

Row 4: Ch 1, sc in first sc, [sc in next ch-1 sp, sc in next sc] rep across, turn. (129 sc)

Rows 5–94: Rep Rows 2–4. At the end of Row 94, fasten off.

Woven Strip

Make 16

With aspen, ch 195, fasten off.

Each strip is woven horizontally through ch-1 sps of every other group of Rows 2 and 3 of afghan.

With RS facing, start first strip at right edge of afghan in Row 2, draw strip up through first ch-1 sp of Row 2, insert strip down through next corresponding ch-1 sp above in Row 3, [insert strip up through next free ch-1 sp of Row 2 and down through next free ch-1 sp of Row 3] rep across, secure beg and ending of strip, weave in loose ends.

*Sk next 4 rows of afghan, working in next 2 sets of ch-1 sps (rep of Rows 2 and 3 of pattern), draw strip up through first ch-1 sp, insert strip down through next corresponding ch-1 sp directly above, [insert strip up through next free ch-1 sp of row below and down through next ch-1 sp directly above] rep across, secure beg and end, weave in loose ends. Rep from * until all strips are woven into afghan.

Border

Rnd 1 (RS): Attach aspen in top right corner sc, ch 3 (counts as first dc), dc in next st, ch 3, sl st in top of last dc, *[dc in each of next 2 sts, ch 3, sl st in top of last dc] rep across to last st, [2 dc, ch 3, sl st in last st] in last st, dc in end of each of next 2 rows, ch 3, sl st in last dc, [dc in end of next row, sk next row, dc in end of next row, ch 3, sl st in top of last dc] rep across to last row, [2 dc, ch 3, sl st in last dc] in last st, rep from * around, join in 3rd ch of beg ch-3, fasten off. ✄

Aurora

Design by Rosalie DeVries

Like vibrant paintings in the nighttime sky, the vivid color patterns of celestial auroras are re-created in the rich hues of this beautiful afghan that works up easily in large motifs.

Skill Level: Advanced

Size: 50 x 60 inches

Materials

- Coats & Clark Red Heart Super Saver worsted weight

- yarn: 24 oz each gemstone #959 and monet print #310

- Size I/9 crochet hook or size needed to obtain gauge

- Yarn needle

Gauge

Motif = 12 x 12 inches; 4 sts = 1 inch

Check gauge to save time.

Pattern Notes

Weave in loose ends as work progresses.

Entire afghan is worked on RS.

At start of Rnd 2 through border, ch 1, draw up lp, insert hook through first ch.

Join rnds with a sl st unless otherwise stated.

Motifs are joined tog as work progresses 4 x 5 motifs.

When joining motifs, insert hook from back to front through lps of finished motifs.

Pattern Stitch

Dtr: Yo hook 3 times, insert hook in indicated st, yo, draw up a lp, [yo, draw through 2 lps on hook] 4 times.

Motif

Make 20

Rnd 1 (RS): With gemstone, ch 9, join to form a ring, [ch 4, 6 dc in 4th ch from hook, sk 2 chs of ring, sl st in next ch] 3 times with last sl st in base of first beg ch-4, fasten off. (21 sts)

Rnd 2: Draw up a lp of monet print in top of first ch-4, [sc in each of next 3 dc, hdc in next dc, dc in next dc, 4 tr in next dc, sc in top of next ch-4] rep around, join with sl st in drawn up lp. (30 sts)

Rnd 3: [Ch 4, 6 dc in 4th ch from hook, sk next 2 sts of Rnd 2, sl st in next st] 10 times with 10th sl st in drawn up lp, fasten off.

Rnd 4: Draw up a lp of gemstone in top of first ch-4 of Rnd 3, [sc in each of next 3 dc, hdc in next dc, dc in next dc, tr in next dc, sc in top of next ch-4] rep around, join with sl st in drawn up lp. (70 sts)

Rnd 5: [Ch 4, 3 dc, 1 tr, 1 dtr in 4th ch from hook, sk next 4 sts of Rnd 4, sl st in next st] 14 times, with 14th sl st in first ch of first ch-4, fasten off. (84 sts)

Rnd 6: Draw up a lp of monet print in top of first ch-4 of Rnd 5, [sc in each of next 2 sts, hdc in next st, dc in next st, 2 tr in next st, sc in top of next ch-4] rep around, join with sl st in drawn up lp. (98 sts)

Rnd 7: Ch 1, [sc in each of next 3 sts, hdc in next st, dc in next st, tr in next st, ch 4, sl st in same st as last tr, sc in next st] rep around, join with sl st in ch-1, fasten off.

Rnd 8: Draw up a lp of gemstone in first ch of last ch-4 of Rnd 7, *tr in each of next 4 sts, dc in each of next 2 sts, hdc in next st **, sc in first ch of next ch-4, rep from * around, ending last rep at **, join with sl st in drawn up lp, fasten off.

Rnd 9: Draw up a lp of monet print in any sc of Rnd 8, sc in next 8 sts, *hdc in each of next 3 sts, dc in each of next 3 sts, tr in each of next 2 sts, dtr in each of next 2 sts, [ch 1, dtr in same last st] twice (this creates corner of motif), dtr in next st, tr in each of next 2 sts, dc in each of next 3 sts, hdc in each of next 3 sts, sc in each of next 9 sts, rep from * around, join with sl st in drawn up lp, fasten off.

Rnd 10 (first motif only): Draw up a lp of gemstone in first ch-1 of corner, *ch 2, sc in next ch-1 sp, [ch 3, yo hook, insert hook before last sc made and hdc, sk next st, sc in next st] rep across to next corner, sc in next ch-1 sp, rep from * around, ending with join with sl st in drawn up lp, fasten off.

Rnd 10 (joining for rem motifs): Draw up a lp of gemstone in first ch-1 sp of corner, *ch 2, sc in next ch-1 sp, [ch 3, yo hook, insert hook before last sc made and hdc, sk next st, sc in next st] rep across to next ch-1 corner sp, [ch 2, sc in next ch-1 sp, ch 1, sc in next corresponding lp of previous motif, ch 1, yo hook, insert hook before last sc of working motif and hdc, sk next st of working motif, sc in next st] rep across to next corner ch-1 sp (for 2nd side joining, rep from * once, complete working motif as indicated in Rnd 10 for first motif only, fasten off.

Corner Inserts

Note: *Work corner inserts in*

open sps as they are formed while joining motifs.

Rnd 1 (RS): Draw up a lp of monet print in a ch-2 corner lp of motif center, *ch 4, 4 dc and 1 tr in 4th ch from hook, sl st in side of next sc motif joining, ch 4, 4 dc and 1 tr in 4th ch from hook, sl st in next ch-2 lp of next motif corner, rep from * around, join with sl st in drawn up lp, fasten off.

Rnd 2: Draw up a lp of gemstone in 4th ch of a ch-4 of Rnd 1, sc in 4th ch of each ch-4 around, join with sl st in drawn up lp, fasten off.

Border

Rnd 1 (RS): Draw up a lp of monet print in any corner ch-2 lp, ch 3, 4 dc in same ch-2 lp, sc in next lp, *ch 3, yo hook, insert hook behind last sc and complete as hdc, rep from * to lp before next ch-2 motif corner lp, ch 3, yo hook, insert hook behind last sc and complete as hdc, sc in next ch-2 lp, 7 dc in side of sc that joins motifs, sc in next lp, rep from * to last motif corner ch-2 lp, 5 dc in corner ch-2 lp, sc in next lp, rep from * around, join with sl st in top of first ch-3, fasten off.

Rnd 2: Draw up a lp of gemstone in first dc of 5-dc corner, ch 3, hdc in first ch of ch-3, sc in next dc, *ch 3, yo hook, insert hook behind last sc and complete as hdc, sc in next dc, rep from * to 5th dc, [ch 3, yo hook, insert hook behind last sc and complete as hdc, sc in next lp] rep across to lp before 7-dc, ch 3, yo hook, insert hook behind last sc and complete as hdc, dc in next sc, ch 3, yo hook, insert hook behind last sc and complete as hdc, sk 2 dc, sc in next dc, ch 3, yo hook, insert hook behind last sc and complete as hdc, sk next dc, sc in next dc, ch 3, yo hook, insert hook behind last sc and complete as hdc, dc in next sc, ch 3, yo hook, insert hook behind last sc and complete as hdc, sc in next lp, rep from * to first dc of next corner, rep from * around, join with sl st in drawn up lp, fasten off.

Rnd 3: Draw up a lp in any lp of Rnd 2, working around afghan in reverse sc (left to right), ch 2, [reverse sc in next lp, ch 2] rep around, join with sl st in drawn up lp, fasten off. ✂

Fireside Chat

Design by Dot Drake

Settle down by a cozy fire with a cup of hot cocoa and a good book, or enjoy quiet conversation with someone special, wrapped in this handsome hearthside warmer that features a striking herringbone-style pattern.

Do you not stay at home of evenings? Do you not love a cushioned seat in a corner by the fireside, with your slippers on your feet?

—Oliver Wendell Holmes

Skill Level: Intermediate

Size: 52 x 60 inches

Materials

- Coats & Clark Red Heart TLC Heathers light worsted weight yarn (5 oz per skein): 6 skeins light mulberry #2451, 5 skeins mulberry #2452
- Size I/9 crochet hook or size needed to obtain gauge
- Yarn needle

Gauge

4 sc = 1½ inches; 4 sc rows = 1½ inches

Check gauge to save time.

Pattern Notes

Weave in loose ends as work progresses.

Join rnds with a sl st unless otherwise stated.

Carry yarn not in use along side edge of afghan.

Pattern Stitches

Long dc (long dc): Yo hook, insert hook in indicated st, yo, draw up a lp level with working row, [yo, draw through 2 lps on hook] twice, sk sc directly under long dc.

Afghan

Row 1 (WS): With light mulberry, ch 146, sc in 2nd ch from hook, sc in each rem ch across, drop light mulberry, turn. (145 sc)

Row 2 (RS): Draw up a lp of mulberry, ch 1, sc in each sc across, turn.

Row 3 (WS): Rep Row 2, drop mulberry, turn.

Row 4 (RS): Draw up a lp of light mulberry, ch 1, sc in first sc, sc in next sc, long dc in 4th sc from end 3 rows below, *sc in next sc, long dc in same st as last long dc **, sc in next sc, sk next 2 sc 3 rows below and long dc in next sc, sc in next sc, sk next 2 sc 3 rows below and long dc in next sc rep from * across, ending last rep at **, sc in each of next 2 sc, turn. (24 sets V-shape long dc; 23 single long dc)

Row 5 (WS): Ch 1, sc in each sc and each long dc across, drop light mulberry, turn. (145 sc)

Row 6 (RS): Draw up a lp of mulberry, ch 1, sc in first sc, [long dc in next sc 3 rows below, sc in next sc] rep across, turn. (72 long dc; 73 sc)

Row 7 (WS): Ch 1, sc in each sc and each long dc across, drop mulberry, turn.

Row 8 (RS): Draw up a lp of light mulberry, ch 1, sc in first sc, sc in next sc, sk first long dc directly below of Row 6, work next long dc in center between 2 strands of long dc directly below of Row 6, *sc in next sc, long dc in same sp as last long dc **, sc in next sc, long dc in sc 3 rows below between 2 long dc sts of Row 6, sc in next sc, long dc in center between 2 strands of long dc directly below of Row 6, rep from * across, ending last rep at **, sc in each of next 2 sc, turn.

Rep Rows 5–8 until afghan measures 58 inches, ending with a Row 8, do not fasten off light mulberry. Fasten off mulberry.

Border

Rnd 1 (RS): Ch 1, sc evenly sp around outer edge, working 3 sc in each corner, join in beg sc.

Rnd 2 (RS): Ch 1, sc in same sc, ch 4, sl st in 3rd ch from hook, dc in next sc, sk next sc, [sc in next sc, ch 4, sl st in 3rd ch from hook, dc in next sc, sk next sc] rep around, join in beg sc, fasten off. ✁

Vineyard in the Valley

Design by Anne Halliday

The rich hues of lush grapes and the soft, misty colors of a valley vineyard are captured in the subtle beauty of this charming granny-style afghan that works up easily in quick-to-stitch strips.

Skill Level: Beginner

Size: 50½ x 69½ inches

Materials

- Coats & Clark Red Heart Super Saver worsted weight yarn:
- 21 oz Aran #313, 18 oz dark plum #533, 6 oz light sage #631, 3 oz light plum #531
- Size I/9 crochet hook or size needed to obtain gauge
- Yarn needle

Gauge

Rnds 1–3 of square = 4 inches
Check gauge to save time.

Pattern Notes

Weave in loose ends as work progresses.

Join rnds with a sl st unless otherwise stated.

Ch-3 counts as first dc throughout.

Afghan Strip

Make 6

Square

Make 16

Rnd 1 (RS): With light plum, ch 4, 2 dc in 4th ch from hook, ch 3, [3 dc in same ch, ch 3] 3 times, join in 4th ch of beg ch-4, fasten off. (12 dc; 4 ch-3 sps)

Rnd 2 (RS): Attach Aran in any corner ch-3 sp, ch 3, [2 dc, ch 3, 3 dc] in same ch-3 sp, ch 1, *[3 dc, ch 3, 3 dc] in next corner ch-3 sp, ch 1, rep from * twice, join in 3rd ch of beg ch-3, fasten off. (24 dc; 4 corner ch-3 sps; 4 ch-1 sps)

Rnd 3 (RS): Draw up a lp of dark plum in any corner ch-3 sp, ch 3, [2 dc, ch 3, 3 dc] in same ch-3 sp, ch 1, 3 dc in next ch-1 sp, ch 1, *[3 dc, ch 3, 3 dc] in next ch-3 corner sp, ch 1, 3 dc in next ch-1 sp, ch 1, rep from * twice, join in 3rd ch of beg ch-3, fasten off.

With dark plum, whipstitch 16 squares tog to form a strip, beg and ending in center corner chs and sewing through 2 lps of each st.

Strip Border

Rnd 1 (RS): Draw up a lp of dark plum in any corner ch-3 sp, ch 1, [sc, ch 3, sc] in corner ch-3 sp, *ch 1, sk next dc, sc in next dc, ch 1, [sc in next ch-1 sp, ch 1, sk next dc, sc in next dc, ch 1] rep across to next corner ch-3 sp **, [sc, ch 3, sc] in corner ch-3 sp, rep from * around, ending last rep at **, join in beg sc.

Rnd 2 (RS): Sl st into corner ch-3 sp, ch 1, *[sc, ch 3, sc] in corner ch-3 sp, ch 1, [sc in next ch-1 sp, ch 1] rep across to next corner ch-3 sp, rep from * around, join in beg sc, fasten off.

Rnd 3 (RS): Draw up a lp of Aran in any corner ch-3 sp, ch 3, [2 dc, ch 3, 3 dc] in same corner ch-3 sp, *ch 1, sk next ch-1 sp, [3 dc in next ch-1 sp, ch 1, sk next ch-1 sp] rep across to next corner ch-3 sp **, [3 dc, ch 3, 3 dc] in next corner ch-3 sp, rep from * around, ending last rep at **, join in 3rd ch of beg ch-3, fasten off.

Rnd 4 (RS): Draw up a lp of light sage in corner ch-3 sp, ch 3, [2 dc, ch 3, 3 dc] in same sp, *ch 1, [3 dc in next ch-1 sp, ch 1] rep across to next corner ch-3 sp **, [3 dc, ch

The Afghan Givers

*In sacks and boxes people brought
The yarn that they had saved.
No matter how small, we used every scrap
That our dear neighbors gave.
An afghan grew from our granny squares.
Then we had two, then four.
As bags of yarn kept pouring in
We crocheted more and more.
Then came the day to deliver our work
To lonely folks we knew.
The afghans brightened their dreary days
And warmed them through and through.*

3, 3 dc] in next corner ch-3 sp, rep from * around, ending last rep at **, join in 3rd ch of beg ch-3, fasten off.

Rnd 5 (RS): With Aran, rep Rnd 4. With Aran whipstitch strips tog, beg and ending in center corner chs and sewing through 2 lps of each st.

Edging

Rnd 1 (RS): Attach Aran in corner ch-3 sp at top right, ch 1, *[sc, ch

2, sc] in corner ch-3 sp, ch 1, sk next dc, sc in next dc, ch 1, [sc in next ch-1 sp, ch 1, sk next dc, sc in next dc, ch 1] 6 times, [sc in next ch sp, ch 1] twice, sk next dc, sc in next dc, ch 1, [{sc in next ch-1 sp, ch 1, sk next dc, sc in next dc, ch 1} 6 times] 5 times, [sc, ch 3, sc] in corner ch-3 sp, ch 1, sk next dc, sc in next dc, ch 1, [sc in next ch-1 sp, ch 1, sk next dc, sc in next dc, ch 1] rep across to next corner ch-3 sp,

rep from * around, join in beg sc.

Rnd 2 (RS): Sl st into corner ch-2 sp, ch 1, *[sc, ch 2, sc] in corner ch-2 sp, ch 1, [sc in next ch-1 sp, ch 1] rep across to next corner ch-2 sp, rep from * around, join in beg sc.

Rnd 3 (RS): *[Sl st, ch 2, sl st] in corner ch-2 sp, ch 1, [sl st in next ch-1 sp, ch 1] rep across to next corner ch-2 sp, rep from * around, join in same st as first sl st, fasten off. ✄

Dream Catcher

Design by Rosalie DeVries

A creative combination of shell and inverted shell stitches creates this beautiful pattern of enchanting webs that are sure to capture only sweet dreams!

Skill Level: Intermediate

Size: 51 x 62 inches

Materials

- Coats & Clark Red Heart Super Saver worsted weight

yarn: 27 oz black #312 (A), 25 oz monet print #310 (B), 4 oz frosty green #661 (C)

- Size I/9 crochet hook or size needed to obtain gauge
- Yarn needle

Gauge

3 rows = 2½ inches; 5 sts = 1½ inches

Check gauge to save time.

Pattern Notes

Weave in loose ends as work progresses.

Join rnds with a sl st unless otherwise stated.

When drawing up the first lp on all rows excluding first, make lp on hook, ch 1, draw lp through st and insert hook through first lp.

First ch-3 and last ch-3 of shells are counted as dc st.

Pattern Stitch

Shell: Sl st into indicated st, ch 3 (counts as first dc), 3 dc in same st, ch 3 (counts as 5th dc), sl st in same st as last dc. (5 dc shell)

Inverted shell: [Yo, insert hook in next indicated st, yo, draw up a lp, yo, draw through 2 lps on hook] 5 times, yo, draw through all 6 lps on hook.

Afghan

Row 1: With A, ch 4, 3 dc in 4th ch from hook, ch 3, sl st in same ch as last dc, [ch 9, 3 dc in 4th ch from hook, ch 3, sl st in same ch as last dc] 26 times, fasten off, turn. (27 shells)

May the dreams you hold dearest be those which come true, and the kindness you spread keep returning to you.

—Irish Blessing

Row 2: Draw up a lp of B in center dc of 5-dc shell, *[ch 3, 3 dc in same dc, ch 3, sl st] in same dc for shell **, sl st in next 2 dc, inverted shell over next 5 chs of Row 1, sl st in each of next 3 dc, rep from * across, ending last rep at **, fasten off, turn.

Row 3: Draw up a lp of A in center dc of 5-dc shell, [ch 3, 3 dc in same dc, ch 3, sl st] in same dc, not counting sl st at base of ch-3, sl st in next 2 dc, *inverted shell in next 5 sts (2 sl sts, top of inverted shell directly below and next 2 sl sts), sl st in each of next 3 dc, [ch 3, 3 dc in same dc, ch 3, sl st] in same dc **, sl st in next 2 dc, rep from * across, ending last rep at **, fasten off, turn.

Row 4: With B, rep Row 3.

Row 5: With A, rep Row 3.

Row 6: With C, rep Row 3.

Rows 7–21: Rep Rows 5 and 4 alternately.

Rows 22–69: Rep Rows 6–21.

Row 70: Rep Row 6.

Rows 71–74: Rep Rows 5 and 4.

Row 75: Draw up a lp of A in first dc of 5-dc shell, *sl st in each of next 5 dc **, inverted shell over next 5 sts, rep from * across, ending last rep at **, do not fasten off, turn.

Border

Rnd 1: Ch 1, sc in each st across edge of Row 75, 4 sc over end dc of Row 75, 3 sc over end dc of each row to last row, 4 sc over end dc of last row, sc evenly sp across opposite side of Row 1, 4 sc over side edge of Row 1, 3 sc over end of each row to last row, 4 sc over end dc of Row 75, join in beg sc, fasten off, turn.

Rnd 2: Draw up a lp of B in last sc of previous rnd, working in reverse around afghan (right to left), ch 3, sk next sc, [reverse sc in next sc, ch 2, sk next sc] rep around outer edge, join with sl st in same st as beg ch-3, sl st into center of next ch sp.

Rnd 3: Continue working in reverse around afghan, ch 3, [reverse sc in next ch lp, ch 2] rep around, join with sl st in same ch sp as beg ch-3.

Rnd 4: Sl st into center of next ch sp, ch 1, *insert hook from back to front of next lp, sl st in next ch lp, insert hook from front to back of next lp, sl st in lp, rep from * around, join with sl st in beg ch-1.

Rnd 5: Ch 1, reverse sc in each sl st around, sl st to join in beg ch-1, fasten off. ✄

1

Cuddly Comforts

F ew things are more delightful to observe than a child's limitless imagination at work when he or she is engaged in carefree, playtime fun. In this charming collection of projects chosen especially for kids, cuddly stuffed animals beg to be hugged and games bring squeals of delight. A cozy sleeping bag, snuggly blanket and soft pillows provide comforting places for nestling, and little playbooks hold stories and toys to enchant a child's curiosity. These kid-pleasing projects are sure to delight every lucky child who receives them!

We find delight in the beauty and happiness of children that makes the heart too big for the body.

—Ralph Waldo Emerson

Toss & Twist Game

Design by Bendy Carter

Kids of all ages will giggle with delight at the comical contortions they find themselves in with this captivating game of twists and turns! The game mat can also be used as a decorative rug or extra-cozy blanket.

Skill Level: Intermediate

Size

Rug: 51 x 58 inches

Block: 6 inches square

Materials

- Coats & Clark Kids worsted weight yarn (5 oz per skein): 3 skeins each red #2390, blue #2845, yellow #2230 and green #2677
- Coats & Clark Red Heart Super Saver worsted weight yarn (8 oz per skein): 7 skeins black #312
- Fiberfill
- Sizes G/6 and N/15 crochet hooks or sizes needed to obtain gauge
- Yarn needle

Gauge

Smaller hook, 15 sc = 4 inches; 16 rows = 4 inches; larger hook 13 sc = 7½ inches; 14 rows = 7½ inches

Check gauge to save time.

Pattern Notes

Weave in loose ends as work progresses.

Join rnds with a sl st unless otherwise stated.

Rug is crocheted with 3 strands of yarn held tog throughout.

Pattern Stitch

Surface ch st: With RS of black solid side facing, with indicated color make a sl knot on hook, draw up a lp, remove hook, insert hook from RS, holding yarn lp on WS, pick up dropped lp, draw through to RS, [insert hook in next indicated st, yo, draw lp through to RS and through lp on hook] rep to complete letter, ending after letter is completed, leaving a 3-inch length of yarn, insert hook and draw strand completely through lp on hook, insert hook from WS and draw rem length through to WS and secure.

To Play the Game

Game requires 1 caller and 2 or more players.

The caller rolls both blocks and calls out what is on top. One block tells which hand or foot to use. The other block gives the color. The first player places the hand or foot (whichever is called) on whichever color is called, on the rug. If the block shows "Either Foot" or "Either Hand," the player has a choice of which foot or hand

to move (right or left). If the block shows red and blue, or green and yellow, the player has a choice of which color to move on. Then the caller rolls the blocks for the 2nd player. The caller continues rolling the blocks for each player until all players have had a turn. The caller then starts over with the first player. Game play continues until everyone is "out" except one person. A player is "out" if any body part touches the rug other than hands and feet. The remaining player is the winner!

Game Block

Make 2

Solid side

Note: *Make 6 black and 1 each with red, blue, yellow and green.*

Row 1: With hook size G, ch 19, sc in 2nd ch from hook, sc in each rem ch across, turn. (18 sc)

Rows 2–18: Ch 1, sc in each sc across, turn.

Row 19: Ch 1, sc in each sc across.

Rnd 20: Ch 1, working down side edge in ends of rows, sc in each of next 9 rows, sc dec over next 2 rows, sc in each of next 8 rows, ch 1 to turn corner, working in opposite side of foundation ch, sc in each of next 18 chs, ch 1 to turn corner, sc in each of next 9 rows, sc dec over next 2 rows, sc in each of next 8 rows, ch 1 to turn corner, sc in each of next 18 sc, ch 1, join in beg sc, fasten off.

Surface lettering

Using diagrams as a guide and colors as indicated on each solid block, work surface ch st on each block.

With black, using assembly diagram as a guide, sc sides tog to form a block, stuffing with fiberfill before closing.

Multicolored sides

Note: *Make 1 with black with blue (color 1) and red (color 2). Make 1 with black with green (color 1) and yellow (color 2).*

I will not play tug o' war.
I'd rather play hug o' war.
Where everyone hugs instead of tugs,
Where everyone giggles and rolls on the rug.
Where everyone kisses, and everyone grins,
Where everyone cuddles, and everyone wins.

—Shel Silverstein

Row 1 (RS): With hook size G and black, ch 19, sc in 2nd ch from hook, sc in each rem ch across, turn. (18 sc)

Row 2: Ch 1, with black work 9 sc, changing to color 1 in last step of 9th sc, sc in each of next 9 sc, turn.

Row 3: With color 1, ch 1, sc in each of next 9 sc, changing to black in last step of 9th sc, sc in each of next 9 sc, turn.

Rows 4–9: Rep Rows 2 and 3. At the end of Row 9, fasten off color 1 only.

Row 10: With black, ch 1, sc in each sc across, turn.

Row 11: Ch 1, with black work 9 sc, changing to color 2 in last step of 9th sc, sc in each of next 9 sc, turn.

Row 12: With color 2, ch 1, sc in each of next 9 sc, changing to black in last step of 9th sc, sc in each of next 9 sc, turn.

Rows 13–18: Rep Rows 11 and 12. At the end of Row 18, fasten off color 2 only.

Row 19: With black, ch 1, sc in each sc across.

Rnd 20: Rep Rnd 20 of solid side. With black, using assembly diagram as a guide, sc block sides tog, stuffing with fiberfill before closing.

Rug
Base outline
Row 1 (RS): With hook size N and 3 strands of black, ch 86, sc in 2nd ch from hook, sc in each rem ch across, turn. (85 sc)

Row 2: Ch 1, sc in each sc across, turn.

Rows 3–5: Rep Row 2.

Row 6: Ch 1, sc in each of next 6 sc, turn. (6 sc)

Rows 7–18: Ch 1, sc in each of sc across section, turn. At the end of Row 18, fasten off.

[Sk next 13 sc of Row 5, attach 3 strands of black in next sc, ch 1, sc in same sc as beg ch-1, sc in each of next 6 sc (7 sc) turn. Rep Rows 7–18, fasten off at the end of last rep] 3 times.

Sk next 13 sc of Row 5, attach 3 strands of black in next sc, ch 1, sc in same sc as beg ch-1, sc in each of next 5 sc, turn. Rep Rows 7–18, turn at the end of Row 18.

Row 19: Ch 1, sc in each of next 6 sc, [ch 13, sc in each of next 7 sc of next column] 3 times, ch 13, sc in each of next 6 sc of end column, turn.

Row 20: Ch 1, sc in each sc and each ch across, turn. (85 sc)

[Rep Rows 2–20] 4 times.

[Rep Rows 2–5] once, fasten off.

Edging
Rnd 1 (RS): With N hook, attach 3 strands of black in any corner, ch 1, [{sc, ch 1, sc} in corner st, sc evenly sp across edge] rep around, join in beg sc.

Rnd 2: Ch 1, sc in each sc around, working [sc, ch 1, sc] in each corner ch-1 sp, join in beg sc, fasten off.

Square
Note: *Make 5 each red, blue, yellow and green.*

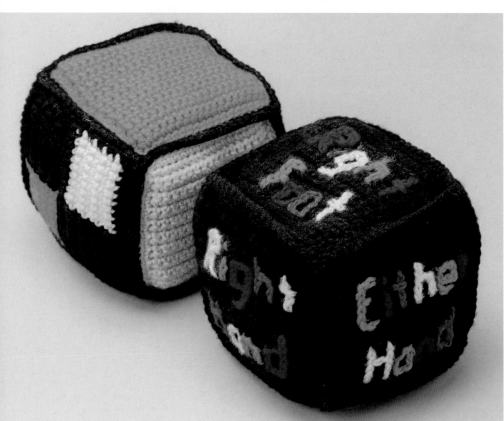

Row 1: With hook size N and 3 strands of yarn, ch 14, sc in 2nd ch from hook, sc in each rem ch across, turn. (13 sc)

Rows 2–14: Ch 1, sc in each sc across, turn. At the end of Row 14, fasten off.

Rnd 15: To attach square to rug outline opening, using diagram as a guide and same color yarn as square, insert hook in corner of square, yo, draw up a lp, insert hook in corner of outline of rug opening, yo, draw up a lp and draw through lp on hook, *insert hook in next st on square, yo, draw up a lp and draw through st on hook, insert hook in next st on outline of rug opening, yo, draw up a lp and draw through st on hook, rep from * around, join in beg st, fasten off. ✂

Assembly Diagram
Solid Black Block Sides

Assembly Diagram
Multicolored & Solid Color Block Sides

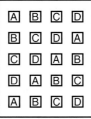

Rug
Square Placement

MULTICOLORED & SOLID COLOR COLOR KEY
A=Red
B=Blue
C=Yellow
D=Green
E=Red & Blue
F=Yellow & Green

RUG COLOR KEY
A=Red
B=Blue
C=Yellow
D=Green

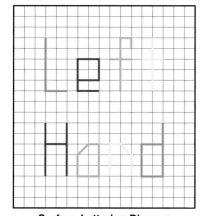

Surface Lettering Diagram
Block Side A

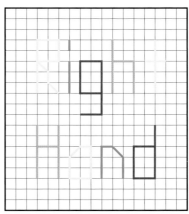

Surface Lettering Diagram
Block Side B

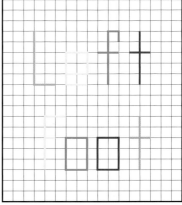

Surface Lettering Diagram
Block Side C

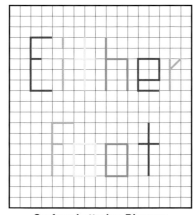

Surface Lettering Diagram
Block Side D

Surface Lettering Diagram
Block Side E

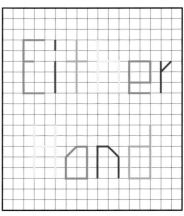

Surface Lettering Diagram
Block Side F

Play With Me Bear

Design by Michele Wilcox

When it's time to sleep, he'll snuggle close beside you, but when it's time to play, he's ready with games for hours of fun!

Skill Level: Beginner

Size: 21 inches tall

Materials

- Bernat Berella 4 worsted weight yarn: 7 oz each true taupe #1012 and light tapestry gold #8886, 6 oz soft teal #1205, 2 oz natural #8940, small amount each geranium #8929, black #8994, soft taupe #1011
- Sizes G/6 and J/10 crochet hooks or sizes needed to obtain gauge
- 2 (1-inch) black buttons
- Fiberfill
- Yarn marker
- Tapestry needle

Gauge

With J hook and 2 strands of yarn, 6 sc = 2 inches; 5 sc rnds = 2 inches
Check gauge to save time.

Pattern Notes

Weave in loose ends as work progresses.

Sharing Cuddles

Every child needs something cuddly
To tote wherever she goes—
A snuggly pillow or blanket
To soften all life's blows.
A crocheted dolly or teddy
Is the perfect little friend
To comfort a frightened toddler
And bring her fears to an end.
Not every child has a mother
To cradle her tenderly.
So I hope my crocheted cuddly toys
Can give a tiny tot security.

Do not join rnds unless otherwise stated. Use yarn marker to mark rnds.

Bear

Head

Rnd 1 (RS): With hook size J and 2 strands of true taupe, ch 2, 6 sc in 2nd ch from hook. (6 sc)

Rnd 2: 2 sc in each sc around. (12 sc)

Rnd 3: [Sc in next sc, 2 sc in next sc] rep around. (18 sc)

Rnd 4: [Sc in each of next 2 sc, 2 sc in next sc] rep around. (24 sc)

Rnd 5: Sc in each sc around.

Rnd 6: [Sc in each of next 3 sc, 2 sc in next sc] rep around. (30 sc)

Rnd 7: [Sc in each of next 4 sc, 2 sc in next sc] rep around. (36 sc)

Rnds 8–16: Rep Rnd 5.

Rnd 17: [Sc in each of next 4 sc, sc dec over next 2 sc] rep around. (30 sc)

Rnd 18: [Sc in each of next 3 sc, sc dec over next 2 sc] rep around. (24 sc)
Stuff head with fiberfill.

Rnd 19: [Sc dec over next 2 sc] rep around. (12 sc)

Rnd 20: Rep Rnd 5, changing to 2 strands of light tapestry gold in last sc, fasten off true taupe.

Body

Rnd 21: Rep Rnd 5.

Rnd 22: Rep Rnd 2. (24 sc)

Rnd 23: Rep Rnd 6. (30 sc)

Rnd 24: Rep Rnd 5.

Rnd 25: Rep Rnd 7. (36 sc)

Rnds 26–28: Rep Rnd 5.

Rnd 29: [Sc in each of next 5 sc, 2 sc in next sc] rep around. (42 sc)

Rnds 30–32: Rep Rnd 5, changing to 2 strands of soft teal in last sc, fasten off light tapestry gold.

Rnds 33 & 34: Rep Rnd 5.

Rnd 35: [Sc in next sc, 2 sc in next sc] 4 times, sc in each of next 26 sc, [2 sc in next sc, sc in next sc] 4 times. (50 sc)

Rnds 36–41: Rep Rnd 5.

Rnd 42: [Sc in next sc, sc dec over next 2 sc] 4 times, sc in each of next 26 sc, [sc dec over next 2 sc, sc in next sc] 4 times. (42 sc)

Rnd 43: [Sc in next sc, sc dec over next 2 sc] 4 times, sc in each of next 18 sc, [sc dec over next 2 sc, sc in next sc] 4 times. (34 sc)

Rnd 44: [Sc in each of next 4 sc, sc dec over next 2 sc] twice, sc in each of next 10 sc, [sc dec over next 2 sc, sc in each of next 4 sc] twice. (30 sc)

Rnd 45: [Sc in each of next 3 sc, sc dec over next 2 sc] rep around. (24 sc)
Stuff body with fiberfill.

Rnds 46 & 47: [Sc dec over next 2 sc] rep around. (6 sc)

At the end of Rnd 47, leaving a length of yarn, fasten off. Weave rem length through sts, draw tightly to close opening and secure.

Ear
Make 2

Rnd 1: With hook size J and true taupe, ch 2, 6 sc in 2nd ch from hook. (6 sc)

Rnd 2: 2 sc in each sc around. (12 sc)

Rnds 3–6: Sc in each sc around. At the end of last rep, sl st in next sc, leaving a length of yarn, fasten off.

Fold Rnd 6 flat across, sew opening closed and sew ears to top of head.

Snout

Rnd 1: With hook size J and 2 strands soft taupe, ch 2, 6 sc in 2nd ch from hook. (6 sc)

Rnd 2: 2 sc in each sc around. (12 sc)

Continued on page 74

County Fair Sleeping Bag

Design by Brenda Stratton

Bright carnival colors and Ferris Wheel-style motifs bring to mind the fun of a county fair in this cozy sleeping bag made with its own built-in pillow! Worsted yarn, worked in dimensional motifs on the front and double-stranded single crochet on the back, makes this delightful design both durable and easy to care for.

Skill Level: Beginner

Size

Small (ages 3–6) approximately 27½ x 49½ inches

Large (ages 7–10) approximately 33 x 55 inches

Materials

- Coats & Clark Red Heart Classic worsted weight yarn (3 oz per skein): 16 skeins jockey red #902, 3 skeins each black #12 and white #1, 2 skeins emerald green #676, 1 skein each yellow #230 and skipper blue #848
- Sizes G/6 and K/10½ crochet hooks or sizes needed to obtain gauge
- ⅓ yd ¼-inch polyester quilt batting
- Fiberfill
- Sewing needle
- Yellow and white sewing threads
- 35 (48) ⅜-inch round domed black shank buttons
- Straight pins
- Yarn needle

Gauge

With G hook, motif = 5½ inches square; 2 strands of yarn and K hook, 3 sc = 1 inch; 3 sc rows = 1 inch

Check gauge to save time.

Pattern Notes

Weave in loose ends as work progresses.

Join rnds with a sl st unless otherwise stated.

Ch-3 counts as first dc throughout.

Pattern Stitches

Pc: 4 dc in indicated st, draw up a lp, remove hook, insert hook in first dc of 4-dc group, pick up dropped lp and draw through st on hook, ch 1 to lock.

Beg pc: Ch 3, 3 dc in same st, draw up a lp, remove hook, insert hook in 3rd ch of beg ch-3, pick up dropped lp, draw through st on hook, ch 1 to lock.

Reverse hdc: Working from left to right with relaxed tension, ch 2, yo hook, insert hook in next st to the right, yo, draw up a lp, yo, draw through all 3 lps on hook.

Front
Motif
Make 35 (48)

Rnd 1 (RS): With yellow and G hook, ch 5, join to form a ring, ch 3, 15 dc in ring, join in 3rd ch of beg ch-3, fasten off. (16 dc)

Rnd 2: Attach skipper blue in any dc, ch 3, 2 dc in same dc, ch 1, sk 1 dc, [3 dc in next dc, ch 1, sk 1 dc] 7 times, join in 3rd ch of beg ch-3, fasten off. (24 dc)

Rnd 3: Attach jockey red in first dc of any 3-dc group, ch 1, sc in same dc, sc in each of next 2 dc, *working over ch-1 sp of previous rnd, 2 dc in next sk dc of Rnd 1 **, sc in each of next 3 dc, rep from * around, ending last rep at **, join in beg sc. (40 sts)

Rnd 4: Ch 1, sc in each sc around, join in beg sc, fasten off. (40 sc)

Rnd 5: Attach white in any sc, beg pc in same st, *ch 2, sk 1 sc **, pc in next sc, rep from * around, ending last rep at **, join in top of beg pc, fasten off. (20 pc)

Rnd 6: Attach emerald green in ch-2 sp, ch 4 (counts as first tr), [2 tr, ch 2, 3 tr] in same ch-2 sp, *[2 dc, hdc] in next ch-2 sp, [hdc, 2 sc] in next ch-2 sp, [2 sc, hdc] in next ch-2 sp, [hdc, 2 dc] in next ch-2 sp **, [3 tr, ch 2, 3 tr] in next ch-2 sp, rep from * around, ending last rep at **, join in 4th ch of beg ch-4, fasten off. (72 sts)

Rnd 7: Working in back lps for this

---

*There never was
a child so lovely
but his mother was glad
to get him to sleep.*

—Ralph Waldo Emerson

rnd only, attach black in first ch of corner ch-2 sp, ch 1, 2 sc in same ch, ch 1, 2 sc in next ch, *sc in each st across to next corner ch-2 sp **, 2 sc in first ch, ch 1, 2 sc in next ch, rep from * around, ending last rep at **, join in beg sc, fasten off. (88 sc; 4 ch-1 sps)

Button center

With sewing needle and yellow thread, place a black shank button through opening at center of Rnd 1 of motif and invisibly sew button securely from underside of motif.

Joining

With G hook and black yarn, holding WS of motifs tog and working through both lps, sl st motifs tog in a grid of 5 x 7 (6 x 8) motifs.

Edging

Rnd 1 (RS): With G hook, attach black yarn in any sc on outer edge, ch 1, sc evenly sp around outer edge, working 3 sc in each corner, join in beg sc, fasten off.

Top border

Row 1 (RS): With G hook, attach black in top left corner of front, work reverse hdc across top edge only, fasten off.

Back

Row 1 (RS): With K hook and 2 strands of jockey red, ch 84 (100), sc in 2nd ch from hook, sc in each rem ch across, turn. (83; 99 sc)

Row 2: Ch 1, sc in each sc across, turn.

Rep Row 2 until piece measures 49½ (55) inches. At the end of last rep, fasten off.

Pillow Panel

Rep instruction for back until piece measures 9½ inches, fasten off.

Bottom pillow border

Holding pillow panel upside down, with G hook, attach black in first free st at left bottom edge of panel, work reverse hdc across edge of panel, fasten off.

Pillow insert

Using pillow panel as a guide cut 2 pieces of quilt batting ¼ inch larger on all sides. With white sewing thread and needle, holding both pieces tog, allowing a ⅜-inch seam allowance, sew around 3 sides, if necessary trim seams, then turn right side out and stuff with fiberfill taking care to smooth it out as work progresses, do not overstuff. On rem open edge, turn ⅜-inch seam under and whipstitch closed.

Assembly

Note: *Use care while working with straight pins to remove all as work progresses.*

Place WS of pillow panel and RS of back tog evenly at top edge, pin in place along top and sides, then pin bottom edge of pillow panel to back, aligning work evenly.

With G hook and 1 strand of jockey red, working through sts just before bottom pillow border, sl st bottom edge of pillow panel to back, removing pins across the bottom edge as work progresses.

Place WS of front and RS of back tog evenly at bottom edge and pin in place along bottom and sides, aligning evenly, leaving top opening free.

With RS facing and G hook, attach black in bottom left side, working through all thicknesses work reverse hdc evenly sp around outer edge, working 3 reverse hdc in each corner st and insert pillow form between pillow panel and back before opening is closed across last edge, join in beg st, fasten off. ✄

Li'l Friends Sleeping Bags

Designs by Kathy Weese

Even our smallest playtime friends deserve a cozy place to sleep, too! These quick-to-stitch, miniature sleeping bags are made in two different sizes to perfectly fit 11½-inch fashion dolls and small stuffed animals.

Skill Level: Beginner

Size: Sleeping bags vary from 7 inches to 13½ inches

Materials
- Worsted weight yarn: 1–3 oz desired MC, small amount CC
- Sizes G/6 and D/3 crochet hooks or sizes needed to obtain gauge
- Straight pins
- 3 (¾-inch) silk flowers
- Hot-glue gun
- Yarn needle

Gauge

With G hook, 7 sc = 2 inches; 4 sc rows = 1 inch

Check gauge to save time.

Pattern Notes

Weave in loose ends as work progresses.

Join rnds with a sl st unless otherwise stated.

Great way to use up scrap amounts of yarn, use several scrap amounts to make sleeping bags.

Small Sleeping Bag

Row 1 (RS): With hook size G and MC, ch 16, sc in 2nd ch from hook, sc in each rem ch across, turn. (15 sc)

Row 2: Ch 1, sc in each sc across, turn.

Rows 3–46: Rep Row 2. At the end of last rep, fasten off.

Assembly

Fold RS up last row to 10th row from the top of piece and pin in place. Attach MC or CC at top right edge through both thicknesses of last row, ch 1, sc in same st, sc evenly sp to top right corner, work 3 sc in corner st, sc in each st across top edge, 3 sc in left top corner, sc evenly sp down side edge to the folded area, working through both thicknesses, sc evenly sp to bottom corner, fasten off. Attach yarn through both thicknesses at bottom right corner, ch 1, sc in same st, sc through both thicknesses evenly sp to top of folded edge, working across opening of sleeping bag, sc in each sc across, sl st in left edge, fasten off. Remove straight pins.

Medium Sleeping Bag

Row 1 (RS): With hook size G and MC, ch 21, sc in 2nd ch from hook, sc in each rem ch across, turn. (20 sc)

Rows 2–52: Rep Row 2 of small sleeping bag.

Continued on page 75

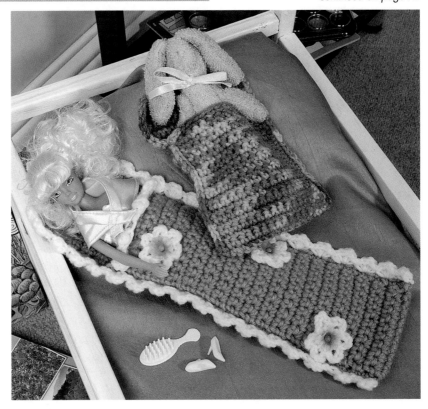

Kitty & Puppy Neck Nuzzlers

Designs by Michele Wilcox

These adorable furry friends will gently hug your neck to keep you company or chase away the chill on cold, winter days. Fluffy, bulky yarn makes them oh-so-soft and cuddly—you'll never want to put them down!

Skill Level: Beginner

Size
Kitty: 31 inches long
Puppy: 29 inches long

Materials
- Coats & Clark Red Heart Light & Lofty yarn: 9 oz each onyx #9312 and café au lait #9334, small amount cloud #9311
- Size 3 pearl cotton: small amounts of each peach and blue
- Small amount brown worsted weight yarn
- Size P/16 crochet hook or size needed to obtain gauge
- 1 bag poly-pellets
- Fiberfill
- 1 pair each white and black panty hose
- Yarn marker
- Sewing needle and thread
- Tapestry needle

Gauge
2 sc rnds = 1 inch; 2 sc = 1 inch
Check gauge to save time.

Pattern Notes
Weave in loose ends as work progresses.

Do not join unless otherwise indicated, use a marker to mark rnds.

Join rnds with a sl st unless otherwise stated.

Nylon Stocking Preparation
This step is done with both the kitty and puppy. Cut the legs from the panty hose, insert one leg into the other. Fill double nylon stocking with 16-oz pellets. Place pellet filled stocking on flat surface, measure from tip of toe 18 inches, sew across this area to close opening. Cut off excess stocking.

Kitty

Head
Rnd 1: With onyx, ch 2, 6 sc in 2nd ch from hook. (6 sc)
Rnd 2: [Sc in next sc, 2 sc in next sc] rep around. (9 sc)
Rnd 3: Sc in each sc around.
Rnd 4: 2 sc in each sc around. (18 sc)
Rnd 5: Rep Rnd 3.
Rnd 6: [Sc in each of next 5 sc, 2 sc in next sc] rep around. (21 sc)
Rnds 7 & 8: Rep Rnd 3. Stuff head with fiberfill.
Rnd 9: [Sc in next sc, sc dec over next 2 sc] rep around. (14 sc)
Rnd 10: [Sc dec over next 2 sc] rep around, sl st in next sc, leaving a length of yarn, fasten off. (7 sc)
Weave rem length through sts, draw opening closed and secure.

Facial Features
With pearl cotton, embroider blue satin st eyes, peach satin st nose and with peach work mouth with straight sts.

Ear
Make 2
Rnd 1: With onyx, ch 2, 4 sc in 2nd ch from hook. (4 sc)
Rnd 2: 2 sc in each sc around. (8 sc)
Rnd 3: Sc in each sc around, sl st in next st, leaving a length of yarn, fasten off.
Do not stuff ears with fiberfill. Fold Rnd 3 flat across and sew opening closed, sew to top of head.

Body
Rnd 1: With onyx, ch 2, 6 sc in 2nd ch from hook. (6 sc)
Rnd 2: 2 sc in each sc around. (12 sc)
Rnd 3: [Sc in next sc, 2 sc in next sc] rep around. (18 sc)
Rnds 4–36: Sc in each sc around.
At the end of Rnd 36, insert panty hose pellet bag.

Because they are children, and for no other reason, they have dignity and worth simply because they are.

—Unknown

Rnd 37: [Sc in next sc, sc dec over next 2 sc] rep around. (12 sc)

Rnd 38: [Sc dec over next 2 sc] 6 times, sl st in next st, leaving a length of yarn, fasten off. Weave rem length through sts, draw opening closed and secure.

Sew head to top edge of body over Rnds 3–5.

Leg

Note: *Make 2 legs with onyx only and 2 legs with Rnds 1–3 with cloud and Rnds 4–12 with onyx.*

Rnd 1: Ch 2, 6 sc in 2nd ch from hook. (6 sc)

Rnd 2: 2 sc in each sc around. (12 sc)

Rnd 3: Sc in each sc around.

Rnd 4: Sc in each sc around.

Rnd 5: [Sc dec over next 2 sc] rep around. (6 sc)

Rnds 6–12: Rep Rnd 4. At the end of Rnd 12, sl st in next st, leaving a length of yarn, fasten off.

Do not stuff legs. Sew 2 legs to each end of body.

Tail

Rnd 1: With cloud, ch 2, 6 sc in 2nd ch from hook. (6 sc)

Rnds 2–6: Sc in each sc around. At the end of Rnd 6, sl st in next st, fasten off.

Rnd 7: Attach onyx, sc in each sc around.

Rnds 8–12: Sc in each sc around. At the end of Rnd 12, sl st in next st, fasten off.

Do not stuff tail. Sew tail to back body slightly above back legs.

Puppy

Head

Rnd 1: With café au lait, ch 2, 6 sc in 2nd ch from hook. (6 sc)

Rnd 2: Sc in each sc around.

Rnd 3: [Sc in next sc, 2 sc in next sc] rep around. (9 sc)

Rnd 4: [2 sc in next sc] 6 times, sc in each of next 3 sc (mark these 3 sc with a scrap of yarn as bottom of head). (15 sc)

Rnd 5: Rep Rnd 2.

Rnd 6: [Sc in next sc, 2 sc in next sc] 6 times, sc in each of next 3 sc. (21 sc)

Rnds 7–10: Rep Rnd 2.

Rnd 11: [Sc in next sc, sc dec over next 2 sc] rep around. (14 sc) Stuff head with fiberfill.

Rnd 12: [Sc dec over next 2 sc] 7 times, sl st in next sc, leaving a length of yarn, fasten off. Weave rem length through sts, draw opening closed.

Facial Features

With brown yarn, embroider satin st eyes and nose, embroider mouth with straight sts.

Ear

Make 2

Rnds 1–3: Rep Rnds 1–3 of head. (9 sc)

Rnds 4–6: Sc in each sc around.

Rnd 7: [Sc in next sc, sc dec over next 2 sc] 3 times, sl st in next st, leaving a length of yarn, fasten off.

Do not stuff ear. Sew Rnd 7 of ear flat and sew to side of head.

Body

Rnds 1–38: With café au lait, rep Rnds 1–38 of Kitty.

Continued on page 75

Harry the Horned Lizard

Design by Beverly Mewhorter

Despite being known for a tough hide and sharp horns, this little lizard is really just an old softie made with fluffy worsted yarn and fiberfill stuffing. Harry is sure to delight the hearts of all little boys who love reptiles!

Skill Level: Beginner

Size: 11 inches long

Materials

- Lion Brand Homespun worsted weight yarn: 2 oz adirondack #319
- Size K/10½ crochet hook or size needed to obtain gauge
- Fiberfill
- 9mm animal eyes
- Hot-glue gun
- Yarn needle

Gauge

3 sc = 1 inch

Check gauge to save time.

Pattern Notes

Weave in loose ends as work progresses.

Join rnds with a sl st unless otherwise stated.

Body

Top

Rnd 1: ch 2, 10 sc in 2nd ch from hook, join in beg sc. (10 sc)

Rnd 2: Ch 1, 2 sc in each sc around, join in beg sc. (20 sc)

Rnd 3: Ch 1, sc in each sc around, join in beg sc.

Rnd 4: Ch 1, sc in first sc, [2 sc in next sc, sc in next sc] rep around, join in beg sc. (30 sc)

Rnd 5: Rep Rnd 3.

Rnd 6: Ch 1, [sc in each of next 5 sc, {sc in next sc, ch 2, sl st in top of last sc, sc in same sc} 10 times] twice, join in beg sc, fasten off.

Bottom

Rnds 1–5: Rep Rnds 1–5 of top. At the end of Rnd 5, leaving a length of yarn, fasten off.

Sew Rnd 5 of bottom to Rnd 5 of top stuffing with fiberfill before closing.

Tail

Rnd 1: Ch 2, 3 sc in 2nd ch from hook, join in beg sc. (3 sc)

Rnd 2: Ch 1, 2 sc in each sc around, join in beg sc. (6 sc)

Rnd 3: Ch 1, sc in each sc around, join in beg sc.

Rnds 4–6: Rep Rnd 3.

Rnd 7: Ch 1, sc in first sc, [2 sc in next sc, sc in next sc] rep around, join in beg sc. (9 sc)

Rnd 8: Rep Rnd 3.

Rnd 9: Rep Rnd 7, fasten off. (13 sc)

Stuff tail and sew to body across 5 sc of Rnd 6.

Back Ridge

Ch 25, sc in 2nd ch from hook, sc in

each rem ch across, leaving a length of yarn, fasten off.

Sew back ridge down center of top of body to tip of tail.

Head

Rnd 1: Ch 2, 4 sc in 2nd ch from hook, join in beg sc. (4 sc)

Rnd 2: Ch 1, sc in each sc around, join in beg sc.

Rnd 3: Ch 1, 2 sc in each sc around, join. (8 sc)

Rnd 4: Rep Rnd 2.

Rnd 5: Ch 1, sc in each of next 2 sc, [2 sc in next sc, sc in each of next 2 sc] twice, join in beg sc. (10 sc)

Rnds 6 & 7: Rep Rnd 2, stuff head with fiberfill.

Rnd 8: Ch 1, [sc dec over next 2

sc] rep around, join in beg sc, leaving a length of yarn, fasten off. (5 sc)

Sew head to opposite end of body across 5 sc of Rnd 6.

Head crown

Ch 9, sc in 2nd ch from hook, ch 3, sl st in top of sc, [sc in next ch, ch 3, sl st in top of sc] rep across, ending with sc in last sc, leaving a length of yarn, fasten off.

Sew crown to top of head over Rnd 6.

Eyebrow
Make 2

Ch 3, sl st in 2nd ch from hook, sl st in next ch, leaving a length of yarn, fasten off.

Sew in front of crown at a slight angle. Glue eyes below eyebrows.

Mouth ridge
Make 2

Ch 10, leaving a length of yarn, fasten off. Sew to each side of face.

Leg
Make 4

Rnd 1: Ch 2, 7 sc in 2nd ch from hook, join in beg sc. (7 sc)

Rnds 2–6: Ch 1, sc in each sc around, join in beg sc.

Rnd 7: Ch 1, sc in each of next 2 sc, [sl st in next sc, ch 3, sl st in 2nd ch from hook, sl st in next ch, sl st in same sc] 3 times (toes), sc in each of next 2 sc, join in beg sc, leaving a length of yarn, fasten off.

Stuff lightly and sew opening closed. Sew 2 legs to each side of body to Rnd 5 of bottom body. ✄

Before There Was Fiberfill

By Rose Pirrone

Imagine this, if you will … the pillow or cute toy you have just crocheted is ready to be stuffed. But, first you have to cut into small pieces the old clothing, socks, sweaters and scraps of wool materials that were saved solely for the purpose of using for stuffing.

This was a common method used as late as the 1960s. Back then, we didn't have the luxury of going to the store to purchase ready-to-use stuffing like those available today.

From the 1940s on, nylon stockings were also used as stuffing material, although during the World War II years, nylons were very scarce. Cut-up nylon stockings were softer and more lightweight than other clothing items. Usually, relatives and neighbors helped by saving their cast-off nylons because it took a lot of stockings to stuff a pillow or toy.

As time passed, other materials became available on the market. Cotton batting replaced old clothing, and it was used as we use synthetic fiberfill today. However, it was often very coarse and discolored. I even remember removing what appeared to be seed hulls stuck in the batting.

Absorbent cotton rolls such as those still available in drug stores today were also sometimes used for stuffing. It seems to me that the size of the package has shrunk considerably, and the cost, even taking into consideration the difference in dollar value between then and now, would make it very expensive to use today.

Kapok, another natural material, was a more luxurious type of stuffing. It was softer and silkier-feeling than the cotton batting. Dacron was one of the first washable synthetic fillings, similar to polyester fiberfill,

to appear on the market.

Later, foam rubber became available by the piece or in pillow forms that were either two or three inches thick, or knife-edged—the predecessor of today's pillow forms. Anyone who has used shredded rubber or latex foam for stuffing pillows or toys will remember how messy a task that was. The pieces seemed to have a life of their own and clung to everything. Shredded foam rubber also has a tendency to disintegrate.

Today, we are fortunate to have soft, easy-to-use, packaged polyester fiberfill and ready-made, cloth-covered, fiber-filled pillow forms available in various sizes and shapes. Yes, we've come a long way in the fine art of stuffing, and our old clothing can now be saved from the scissors to be donated for our neighbors in need.

Fun-Time Play Books

Designs by Karen Isak

These whimsical play books, created in three colorful designs, work up easily in small amounts of worsted weight yarn. Each holds a child-size storybook and small toy for sharing some reading fun and imaginative play with the little ones in your life!

Skill Level: Beginner

Size: 5 x 5 inches

Materials

- Worsted weight yarn: 2 oz each turquoise, yellow, brown, 1 oz each red and white, small amounts pink, green
- Size G/6 crochet hook or size needed to obtain gauge
- Embroidery floss: small amounts of black, red and white
- 3 story books each 3¼ x 2¾ inches
- Fiberfill
- Tapestry needle
- Yarn needle

Gauge

7 sc = 2 inches; 4 sc rows = 1 inch
Check gauge to save time.

Pattern Notes

Weave in loose ends as work progresses.

Join rnds with a sl st unless otherwise stated.

Basic Book

Make 2

Row 1: Ch 17, sc in 2nd ch from hook, sc in each rem ch across, turn. (16 sc)

Rows 2–11: Ch 1, sc in each sc across, turn.

Row 12: Ch 1, sc dec over next 2 sc, sc in each sc across to last 2 sc, sc dec over next 2 sc, turn. (14 sc)

Rows 13–18: Rep Row 12. (2 sc)

Row 19: Ch 1, sc dec over next 2 sc, do not turn. (1 sc)

Rnd 20: Ch 1, sc evenly sp around outer edge, join in beg sc, do not turn.

Rnd 21: Working in back lps only, ch 1, sc in each st around, join in beg sc, do not turn.

Rnd 22: Ch 1, sc in each sc around, join in beg sc, do not turn.

Rnds 23–26: Rep Rnds 21 and 22. At the end of Rnd 26, leaving a length of yarn, fasten off.

With yarn needle and rem length, sew Rnd 26 to inside of piece forming a ridge and stuffing with fiberfill as work progresses.

Holding book sections tog, sew back seam from bottom upward 10 sts. Cut 2 lengths of yarn and attach to each edge of book opening. To close book, tie ends in a bow.

Fish Book

With turquoise, make basic book.

Wave

Row 1: With white, ch 16, sc in 2nd ch from hook, *ch 6, sl st in 2nd ch from hook, [sc dec over next 2 chs] twice **, sc in each of next 3 chs of foundation ch, rep from * across, ending last rep at **, sl st in last ch, leaving a length of yarn, fasten off. Sew wave to front of book

Fish

Make 3

Row 1: With yellow, ch 2, 2 sc in 2nd ch from hook, turn. (2 sc)

Row 2: Ch 1, 2 sc in first sc, sc in next sc, turn. (3 sc)

Row 3: Ch 1, sc in first sc, 2 sc in next sc, sc in next sc, turn. (4 sc)

Rows 4–6: Ch 1, sc in each sc across, turn.

Row 7: Ch 1, [sc dec over next 2 sc] twice, turn. (2 sc)

Row 8: Ch 1, [sc dec over next 2 sc] twice. (2 sc)

Rnd 9: Sl st in side edge of Row 8, sl st in side edge of each of next 7

Do you know what it is to be a child? It is to believe in love, to believe in beauty, to believe in belief; it is to turn lowness into loftiness and nothing into everything, for each child has its own fairy godmother in its soul.

—Francis Thompson

rows, sl st in opposite side of foundation ch, sl st in side edge of each of next 8 rows, sl st in top of Row 8, fasten off. (18 sl sts)

Using photo as a guide, with black embroidery floss, embroider with straight sts face and gills on two of the fish.

Note: *Rnd 10 is worked on a single fish for cover and then holding rem 2 fish tog and working through both thicknesses, rep Rnd 10, stuffing lightly with fiberfill before closing.*

Rnd 10: Working in back lps only of sl sts of Rnd 9, draw a lp of pink in sl st worked in top of Row 8, [sc, 2 dc, sc] in next st, sl st in each of next 15 sts, [sc, 2 dc, sc] in next st, sl st in same starting st, fasten off.

Sew single fish to front of cover.

With yellow, leaving a length at beg, ch 12, leaving a length of yarn, fasten off.

Holding fish to inside of back section of book, sew ch-12 to book to hold fish in place.

Book Holder

Row 1: With turquoise, ch 20, dc in 5th ch from hook, [ch 2, sk next 2 chs, dc in next ch] rep across, turn.

Row 2: Ch 5 (counts as first dc, ch 2), dc in next dc, [ch 2, dc in next dc] rep across, turn.

Row 3: Rep Row 2, fasten off.

Sew to front inside section of book and insert book.

Flower Book

With yellow, make basic book.

Fence

Make 2

Row 1: With white, ch 4, 2 sc in 2nd ch from hook, sc in each of next 2 chs, turn. (4 sc)

Row 2: Ch 1, sc in each of next 3 sc, turn. (3 sc)

Row 3: Ch 1, 2 sc in first sc, sc in each of next 2 sc, turn. (4 sc)

Rows 4–15: Rep Rows 2 and 3. At the end of Row 15, do not turn.

Row 16: Working across bottom of fence, ch 1, sc in each of next 15 rows, ch 1, working on opposite side of foundation ch, sc in each of next 3 sts, leaving a length of yarn, fasten off.

Sew a fence to the front cover and 2nd fence to inside of front section. Use inside fence section to insert book into.

Cover Flower

For stem, with green, ch 12, leaving a length of yarn, fasten off. Sew centered to cover of book with bottom edge below top edge of fence.

For leaves, with green, ch 8, leaving a length of yarn, fasten off. Sew centered over stem in V-shape.

Rnd 1: With white, ch 2, 7 sc in 2nd ch from hook, join in beg sc, fasten off.

Rnd 2: Attach red with a sl st in any sc, [ch 3, sl st in next sc] rep around, fasten off.

With black embroidery floss, embroider eyes and smiley mouth over Rnd 1 of flower. Sew flower to cover at top of stem.

Flower Baby

Stem

Rnd 1: With green, ch 2, 7 sc in 2nd ch from hook, join. (7 sc)

Rnds 2–8: Ch 1, sc in each sc around, join in beg sc. At the end of Rnd 8 leaving a length of yarn, fasten off.

Row 9: For leaf, attach green in side edge of Rnd 5 with a sl st, 2 sc and sl st in same st, fasten off. Rep leaf on opposite edge of Rnd 5.

Stuff stem with fiberfill, sew top opening closed.

Flower center

Make 2

Rnd 1: With white, ch 2, 7 sc in 2nd ch from hook, join in beg sc. (7 sc)

Rnd 2: Ch 1, 2 sc in each sc around, join in beg sc, fasten off. (14 sc)

With length of black embroidery

floss, embroider eyes and smiley face on one flower center.

Petals

Rnd 3: Holding both flower centers tog and working through both thicknesses, attach red, ch 1, [2 sc in same st, sl st in next st] rep around, join, fasten off.

Sew flower to top of stem.

With green, ch 12, leaving a length of yarn, fasten off. Secure ch to center back book section; insert flower baby into holder.

Gingerbread Book

With brown, make basic book.

Candy Cane

Make 2

Holding 1 strand of each red and white tog, ch 15, fasten off.

Using photo as a guide, with a length of yarn sew to front in cane shape at a slight angle crossing canes at center.

Icing

Attach white at end of Row 12 on edge of front of book and working upward around arch of book to opposite edge of Row 12 in zigzag fashion, ch 1, sc in same st, [ch 2, catching lp of st near end of ch-2, sc over st] rep across arch, fasten off.

Gingerbread Doll

Make 2

Row 1: Starting at top of head, with brown, ch 5, sc in 2nd ch from hook, sc in each rem ch across, turn. (4 sc)

Row 2: Ch 1, 2 sc in first sc, sc in each of next 2 sc, 2 sc in next sc, turn. (6 sc)

Row 3: Ch 1, sc in each sc across, turn.

Row 4: Ch 1, [sc dec over next 2 sc] 3 times, turn. (3 sc)

Row 5: Rep Row 3.

Row 6: Ch 1, 2 sc in first sc, sc in next sc, 2 sc in last sc, turn. (5 sc)

Row 7: Ch 1, 2 sc in first sc, sc in each of next 3 sc, 2 sc in last sc, turn. (7 sc)

Row 8: Sl st in each of next 3 sc, ch 1, sc in same sc as last sl st, sc in each of next 2 sc, turn. (3 sc)

Row 9: Rep Row 6. (5 sc)

Row 10: Ch 1, [sc, dc] in first sc, [dc, sc] in next sc, sl st in next sc, [sc, dc] in next sc, [dc, sc, sl st] in last sc, fasten off.

Working on front section, with white embroider floss, embroider white eyes and 2 cross-sts over body. With red embroidery floss, embroider smiley mouth.

Rnd 11: Holding front and back tog, working through both thicknesses and stuffing with fiberfill as work progresses, sl st around outer edge, fasten off.

With brown ch 12, leaving a length of yarn, fasten off.

Secure ch-12 to inside back of book at center. Insert gingerbread doll into holder.

Book Holder

Rows 1–3: With white, rep Rows 1–3 of fish book holder and sew to inside of front of book. Insert book into holder. ✄

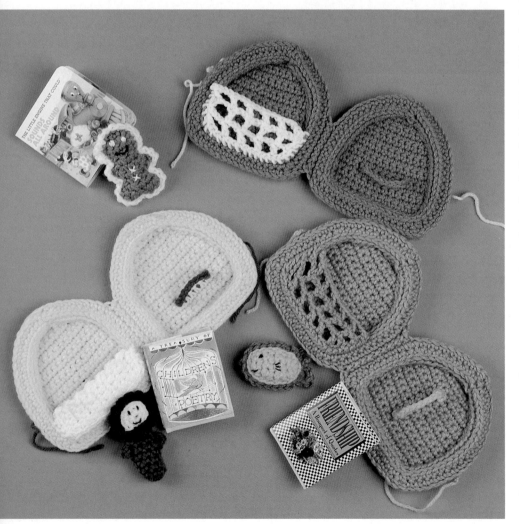

Who takes the child by the hand, takes the mother by the heart.

—Danish Proverb

Crayon Box Afghan & Pillows

Designs by Janet Rehfeldt

A simple stitch pattern worked in bold, colorful stripes creates the kid-pleasing design in this cheerful blanket and three matching pillows that are sure to brighten a child's world with rainbow visions!

Skill Level: Beginner

Size

Afghan: 42 x 52 inches

Round pillow: 14 inches in diameter

Bolster pillow: 14 inches long

Square pillow: 14 inches square

Materials

- Coats & Clark Red Heart Kids worsted weight yarn: 18 oz crayon #2930 (MC), 14 oz blue #2845 (CC1), 9 oz each green #2677 (CC3) and red #2390 (CC4), 5 oz orange #2252 (CC2)
- Sizes H/8, J/10 and K/10½ crochet hooks or sizes needed to obtain gauge
- ½-inch button
- 14-inch square pillow form
- 14-inch bolster pillow form
- 14-inch round pillow form
- 5 (3-inch) plastic canvas circles
- Straight pins
- Tapestry needle
- Long tapestry needle

Gauge

With J hook, 3 esc = 1 inch; 2 esc rows = 1 inch

Check gauge to save time.

Pattern Notes

Weave in loose ends as work progresses.

Join rnds with a sl st unless otherwise stated.

Afghan is crocheted vertically.

Work all sl sts loosely, making sure the width across top of sl sts are the same as the st on previous row.

Loosely carry multicolor (crayon) up side edge of afghan, as this will make fewer ends to be woven into afghan. Do not carry solid colors up side edge of afghan.

Work the following color sequence for afghan: CC1, MC, CC2, MC, CC3, MC, CC4 and MC.

Pattern Stitch

Extended sc (esc): Insert hook in next st, yo, draw up a lp, yo, draw through first lp on hook, yo, draw through rem 2 lps on hook.

Afghan

Row 1 (RS): With J hook and CC1, ch 148, esc in 2nd ch from hook, esc in each rem ch across, turn. (147 esc)

Row 2: Ch 1, esc in each st across, turn.

Rows 3 & 4: Rep Row 2. At the end of Row 4 change to MC, turn.

Row 5: With K hook, ch 1, working in front lps for this row only, loosely sl st in first st, loosely sl st in each st across. (147 sl sts)

Row 6: Ch 1, working in back lps for this row only of sl sts of previous row, sl st in each st across, turn.

Rows 7–10: Rep Rows 5 and 6. At the end of Row 10, change to next solid color, turn.

Row 11: With hook size J, ch 1, working in front lps for this row only, esc in first sl st, esc in each rem sl st across, turn. (147 esc)

Rows 12–14: Working through both lps of sts, ch 1, esc in each st across, turn. At the end of Row 14, change to MC, turn.

Rep Rows 5–14 in established color sequence until afghan measures 36 inches, ending with CC1, fasten off.

Border

Rnd 1 (RS): With hook size H, attach MC, ch 1, sc evenly around afghan working 3 sc in each corner, 147 sc along each side, 110 sc along top and bottom, join in beg sc.

Rnd 2: Ch 1, working in back lps only, sc in each sc around, working 3 sc through both lps of each center corner sc, join in beg sc, change to CC1.

Rnd 3: Ch 2 (counts as first hdc throughout), working in back lps only, hdc in each sc around, working 3 hdc through both lps of each center corner sc, join in 2nd ch of beg ch-2.

Rnd 4: Ch 2, working through both lps of each hdc, ch 2, hdc in each hdc around, working 3 hdc in each center corner hdc, join in 2nd ch of beg ch-2, change to MC.

Rnd 5: Ch 1, working in back lps only, sc in each st around, working

3 sc through both lps of each center corner st, join in beg sc.

Rnd 6: Rep Rnd 5, change to CC1.

Rnd 7: Ch 1, working in back lps only, sc in each st around, working 3 sc through both lps of each center corner st, join in beg sc.

Rnd 8: Ch 1, working left to right around afghan, reverse sc in each st around, join in beg sc, fasten off.

Round Pillow

Row 1 (RS): With J hook and CC1, ch 46, esc in 2nd ch from hook, esc in each rem ch across, turn. (45 esc)

Rows 2–4: Ch 1, esc in each esc across, turn. At the end of Row 4, change to MC, turn.

Rows 5–10: Rep Rows 5–10 of afghan. At the end of Row 10, change to CC1, turn.

Rows 11–14: Rep Rows 11–14 of afghan. At the end of Row 14, change to MC, turn.

[Rep Rows 5–14] 8 times.

[Rep Rows 5–10] once, fasten off.

Assembly

Lightly block piece to measure 14½ x 31 inches, allow piece to dry.

With tapestry needle, sew short ends of piece tog. Weave a length of yarn through edge of pillow cover, draw tightly to gather edge and secure

The Blanket

The child's eyes are full
of timidity and wonder
As she snuggles under
The blanket of soft wool.
Who knows what she knows
of abandonment and weeping,
This little one now sleeping
'Neath the blanket she holds close?
I hope my gift can offer
Some small amount of pleasure
To this precious little treasure
Who is someone's daughter.

ends. Insert round pillow form and weave another length through rem edge, draw tightly to gather edge and secure ends, do not cut ends. Thread long tapestry needle with rem length, push needle through center of pillow to opposite side, pull slightly to indent pillow center, push needle back through center of pillow, pull to indent slightly and secure ends.

Covered Button
Make 2

Button is worked in quarters over plastic canvas disk with same color yarns as pillow. Thread tapestry needle with double strands approximately 3 yds of solid color yarn. Working from center of a plastic canvas circle, leaving a 5-inch tail at beg, bring needle up through center hole, needle back down through plastic canvas through hole at outer edge, *bring needle back up through the same center hole, put needle back down through next hole at outer edge of circle, continue to sew the yarn up and down through holes until 12 holes on outer edge have been worked *. Working directly opposite the area just completed, rep from * to * forming an hourglass shape with the solid color yarn. Secure yarn ends on underside with a knot. Change to 3 yds of multicolor and work rem 2 sections of button. Thread tapestry needle with 1 yd solid color doubled and whipstitch around outer edge of canvas circle, secure tails to underside center of button, leaving a length to attach to pillow.

Sew a button to center of each side of pillow.

Bolster Pillow

Row 1 (RS): With J hook and CC2, ch 59, esc in 2nd ch from hook, esc in each rem ch across, turn. (58 esc)

Rows 2–4: Ch 1, esc in each esc across, turn. At the end of Row 4, change to MC, turn.

Rows 5–10: Rep Rows 5–10 of afghan. At the end of Row 10 change to CC2, turn.

Rows 11–14: Rep Rows 11–14 of afghan. At the end of Row 14, change to MC, turn.

[Rep Rows 5–14] 5 times.

[Rep Rows 5–10] once, fasten off.

Assembly

Lightly block piece to measure 14 x 21 inches, allow piece to dry.

Sew last row to foundation ch. Weave a length of yarn through side edge of rows, pull to gather opening closed and secure. Insert pillow form and weave another length through side edge of rows, pull to gather opening close and secure.

Make 2 covered buttons with green and multicolor and sew a button to each end of pillow over gathered section.

Square Pillow
Back
Make 1

Row 1 (RS): With J hook and CC4, ch 43, esc in 2nd ch from hook, esc in each rem ch across, turn. (42 esc)

Rows 2–4: Ch 1, esc in each esc across, turn. At the end of Row 4, change to MC, turn.

Rows 5–10: Rep Rows 5–10 of afghan. At the end of Row 10 change to CC4, turn.

Rows 11–14: Rep Rows 11–14 of afghan. At the end of Row 14, change to MC, turn.

[Rep Rows 5–14] 3 times. At the end of last rep, fasten off.

Front
Make 2

Rows 1–15: Rep Rows 1–15 of back.

[Rep Rows 5–14] once.

[Rep Rows 5–10] once, fasten off front, do not fasten off 2nd front, draw up a lp, remove hook.

Assembly
Lightly block pieces, allow pieces to dry.

Assemble pillow with WS tog, place back on flat surface, place first front on top and pin outer corner in place, place 2nd front on top of back overlapping fronts at center and pin outer corners and inner edges through all thicknesses.

Rnd 1 (RS): Pick up dropped lp, ch 1, working through all thicknesses, sc evenly sp around outer edge, working 2 sc in each corner, join in beg sc.

Rnd 2: Ch 1, reverse sc in each sc around outer edge of pillow, join in beg sc, do not fasten off.

Row 3: Working across top opening of front, reverse sc in each st across center of cover, fasten off.

Attach ½-inch button at center on inside of top front half, use natural sp between sts of front bottom to button opening closed.

Make a covered button with red and multicolor yarn. Sew covered button to center front in line with button used to close opening.

Insert pillow form and secure button. ✄

Butterfly Buddy Pillow

Design by Debbie Tabor

Cute as a bug and cuddly as can be, this whimsical little fellow is the perfect companion for playtime fun or naptime dreams!

Skill Level: Intermediate

Size: 14 inches tall

Materials

- Coats & Clark Red Heart Classic worsted weight yarn: 3 oz each tangerine #253 and orange #245, 2 oz black #12, 1 oz each mid brown #339 and white #1, 2 yds parakeet #513
- Size J/10 double-ended crochet hook or size needed to obtain gauge
- Size H/8 crochet hook
- 24 inches ⅛-inch-wide orange ribbon
- Fiberfill
- Yarn marker
- Tapestry needle

Gauge

4 sts = 1 inch; 6 rows = 1 inch
Check gauge to save time.

Pattern Notes

Weave in loose ends as work progresses.

Do not join rnds unless otherwise stated. Use yarn marker to mark rnds.

Wing

Make 2

Row 1: With size J hook and tangerine, ch 62, draw up a lp in 2nd ch from hook, retaining all lps on hook, draw up a lp in each rem ch across, turn. (62 lps on hook)

Row 2: With orange, make a sl knot on hook, yo, draw through first lp on hook, [yo, draw through 2 lps on hook] rep across until 1 lp remains on hook, do not turn.

Row 3: Ch 1, retaining all lps on hook, draw up a lp in top strand of first horizontal bar, draw up a lp in each rem top strand of each horizontal bar across, turn.

Row 4: With tangerine, yo, draw through first lp on hook, [yo, draw through 2 lps on hook] rep across until 1 lp remains on hook, do not turn

Row 5: Rep Row 3.

Row 6: With orange, yo, draw through first lp on hook, [yo, draw through 2 lps on hook] rep across until 1 lp remains on hook, do not turn.

Rows 7–26: Rep Rows 3–6.

Row 27: Rep Row 3.

Row 28: With black, rep Row 2, fasten off black and beg following row with orange.

Rows 29–56: Rep Rows 3–6.

Row 57: Draw up a lp in top strand of first horizontal bar, draw up a lp and draw through st on hook, [insert hook in next horizontal bar, draw up a lp and draw through st on hook] rep across, fasten off.

Body

Row 1: With size J hook and black, ch 29, draw up a lp in 2nd ch from hook, retaining all lps on hook, draw up a lp in each rem ch across, turn. (29 lps on hook)

Row 2: With brown, rep Row 2 of wing.

Row 3: Rep Row 3 of wing.

Row 4: With black, rep Row 4 of wing.

Row 5: Rep Row 3 of wing.

Row 6: With brown, rep Row 6 of wing.

Rows 7–76: Rep Rows 3–6.

Row 77: Rep Row 57 of wing.

Antenna

Make 2

With hook size H and black, ch 20, sl st in 5th ch from hook, working in ch ring, work 2 sc in each ch around (10 sc), sc in each rem ch of antenna, leaving a length of yarn, fasten off.

Foot & Leg

Make 2

Rnd 1: With hook size H and white, ch 4, join to form a ring, ch 1, 8 sc in ring. (8 sc)

Rnd 2: 2 sc in each sc around. (16 sc)

Rnd 3: Sc in each sc around.

Rnds 4–7: Rep Rnd 3.

Rnd 8: Sc in next sc, [sk next sc, sc in each of next 2 sc] 5 times. (11 sc)

Rnd 9: Rep Rnd 3.

Rnd 10: Sc in each of next 2 sc, [sk next sc, sc in each of next 2 sc] 3 times, sl st in next st, fasten off. (8 sc)
Stuff foot lightly with fiberfill.

Rnd 11: Attach black, ch 1, sc in each sc around. (8 sc)

Rnds 12–28: Rep Rnd 3.

Row 29: With foot facing forward, fold leg flat across, working through both thicknessses, work 4 sc across, leaving a length of yarn, fasten off.

Cut orange ribbon in half, lace ribbon through Rnd 3 of foot, cross ribbon ends and lace through Rnd 6; tie ends in a bow, double knot to secure ribbon ends. Trim as desired. With a length of white yarn, tack foot just above laces to leg, knot, fasten off.

Hand & Arm

Make 2

Rnd 1: With hook size H and white, ch 4, join to form a ring, 8 sc in ring. (8 sc)

Rnds 2–5: Sc in each sc around.

Rnd 6: [Sc, dc, tr, dc, sc] in same st for thumb, sc in each rem sc around.

Row 7: With thumb pointing to the side fold piece flat across and working through both thicknesses, ch 1, work 3 sc across, fasten off.

Row 8: Attach black, ch 1, sc in first sc, 2 sc in next sc, sc in last sc, turn. (4 sc)

Rows 9–21: Ch 1, sc in each of next 4 sc, turn. At the end of Row 21, leaving a length of yarn, fasten off.

Assembly

Fold wing in half so stripes are horizontal, with length of black working in the center black row, weave a running stitch and gather slightly or as desired. With WS facing out, with a length of orange weave a running st to close off the outer corners of wing approximately 1 inch

There is no better exercise for the soul than reaching down and lifting a child close to your heart.

—Christina Elizabeth Bublick

from outer edge diagonally across to 1 inch from outer edge. Turn RS out and with hook size H, attach black and working through both thicknesses, sc across the top of wing including corner, down along folded edge of wing and along bottom of wing including corner, ch 3, turn, dc in each sc back around wing, working 2 dc in corner edges as needed, fasten off. Insert fiberfill loosely in both sections of wing, shaping and flattening as work progresses. With a length of orange, weave a running st to gather and close inner edge of wing. Rep the same for 2nd wing.

Fold Row 1 of body to Row 77 and with a length of black sew edge closed to form a tube, knot to secure, weave rem length through sts at end of tube, draw to close opening and secure. Fill body with fiberfill. Weave another length through opposite end of tube, draw opening closed, knot to secure. To form head, weave another length of black yarn about 10 sts down from top to form neck, gather slightly and knot to secure.

With black, whipstitch wing to body side beg just below neck. Rep with

2nd wing on opposite side of body.

Sew legs to bottom of body. With thumb pointing upward, sew arm to body centered between neck and black center gathered stripe of wing.

Sew antennae to center top of head. Tie a soft overhand knot in each antenna close to the base to help antenna stand up.

Facial Features

Using Fig. 1 as a guide, with parakeet, embroider eyes. With white, back st around each eye. With white, embroider back st mouth. ✂

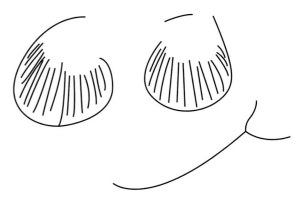

Fig. 1

Play With Me Bear

Continued from page 57

Rnd 3: [Sc in next sc, 2 sc in next sc] rep around. (18 sc)

Rnds 4 & 5: Sc in each sc around. At the end of Rnd 5, sl st in next sc, leaving a length of yarn, fasten off.

Sew snout to head over Rnds 10–16 stuffing with fiberfill before closing.

Facial Features

Using photo as a guide, with black yarn, embroider nose in satin st through center of Rnd 1 and over top of Rnd 2. For mouth, sew straight line centered under nose to the lower side of Rnd 2 and a straight st outward on each side through Rnd 3.

With black, embroider eyes 2¾ inches apart in satin st over Rnds 9 and 10.

Foot & Leg
Make 2

Rnd 1: With hook size J and true taupe, ch 6, sc in 2nd ch from hook, sc in each of next 3 chs, 3 sc in last ch, working on opposite side of foundation ch, sc in each of next 3 chs, 2 sc in same ch as beg sc. (12 sc)

Rnd 2: 2 sc in first sc, sc in each of next 3 sc, [2 sc in next sc] 3 times, sc in each of next 3 sc, [2 sc in next sc] twice. (18 sc)

Rnd 3: [Sc in each of next 2 sc, 2 sc in next sc] rep around. (24 sc)

Rnd 4: Sc in each sc around.

Rnds 5 & 6: Rep Rnd 4.

Rnd 7: Sc in each of next 6 sc, [sc dec over next 2 sc] 6 times, sc in each of next 6 sc. (18 sc)

Rnd 8: Sc in each sc around, changing to 2 strands of soft teal in last sc, fasten off true taupe.

Rnds 9–19: Rep Rnd 4. At the end of Rnd 19, sl st in next st, leaving a length of yarn, fasten off.

Stuff foot and leg with fiberfill. With foot facing forward, fold Rnd 19 flat across and sew opening closed.

With toes pointing forward, sew legs 1-inch apart to center front of body over Rnd 43.

Arm
Make 2

Rnd 1: With hook size J and 2 strands of true taupe, ch 2, 6 sc in 2nd ch from hook. (6 sc)

Rnd 2: 2 sc in each sc around. (12 sc)

Rnd 3: [Sc in each of next 3 sc, 2 sc in next sc] rep around. (15 sc)

Rnds 4–6: Sc in each sc around. At the end of Rnd 6, change to light tapestry gold, fasten off true taupe.

Rnds 7–21: Sc in each sc around. At the end of Rnd 21, sl st in next st, leaving a length of yarn, fasten off.

Stuff arm with fiberfill. Fold Rnd 21 flat and sew across. Sew arm to shoulder area of body.

Collar

Row 1: With hook size G and 1 strand of light tapestry gold, ch 6, sc in 2nd ch from hook, sc in each rem ch across, turn. (5 sc)

Row 2: Ch 1, working in back lps only, sc in each st across, turn.

Rows 3–33: Rep Row 2.

At the end of Row 33, leaving a length of yarn, fasten off. Place collar around neckline, sew ends tog at back neckline.

Waistband

Row 1: Rep Row 1 of collar.

Rows 2–62: Rep Row 2 of collar.

At the end of Row 62, leaving a long length of yarn, fasten off. Place around waistline, sew ends tog at center back, and sew entire edge of waistband to bear.

Arm Cuff
Make 2

Row 1: With hook size G and light tapestry gold, ch 4, sc in 2nd ch from hook, sc in each rem ch across, turn. (3 sc)

Rows 2–26: Rep Row 2 of collar.

At the end of Row 26, leaving a length of yarn, fasten off. Sew cuff to wrist of bear.

Pants Cuff
Make 2

Row 1: With hook size G and 1 strand of soft teal, ch 32, sc in 2nd ch from hook, sc in each rem ch across, turn. (31 sc)

Rows 2 & 3: Ch 1, sc in each sc across, turn.

At the end of Row 3, leaving a length of yarn, fasten off. Sew cuff around bottom of pants.

Tote

Tote Front

Row 1: With hook size G and 1 strand of natural, ch 21, sc in 2nd ch from hook, sc in each rem ch across, turn. (20 sc)

Rows 2–20: Ch 1, sc in each sc across, turn.

Row 21: Ch 1, sc in each sc across, do not turn.

Row 22: Ch 1, work 21 sc down side edge of tote, 20 sc across opposite side of foundation ch, 21 sc up opposite edge of tote, turn. (62 sc)

Row 23: Ch 1, sc in each of next 62 sc, fasten off.

Back

Rows 1–22: Rep Rows 1–22 of front. At the end of Row 22, leaving a length of yarn, fasten off.

Sew the 62 sts of Row 22 of back to Row 23 of front.

Handle
Make 2

Row 1: With hook size G and 1 strand of natural, ch 34, sc in 2nd ch from hook, sc in each rem ch across, fasten off.

Leaving center 7 sc of tote front free,

sew handle to front of tote. Sew 2nd handle in same manner to back.

Car
Row 1: With hook size G and 1 strand of geranium, ch 12, sc in 2nd ch from hook, sc in each rem ch across, turn. (11 sc)

Rows 2 & 3: Ch 1, sc in each sc across, turn.

Row 4: Ch 1, sc dec over next 2 sc, sc in each of next 7 sc, sc dec over next 2 sc, turn. (9 sc)

Row 5: Ch 1, sc dec over next 2 sc, sc in next sc, ch 9, sk next 3 sc, sc in next sc, sc dec over next 2 sc, turn.

Rnd 6: Ch 1, sc in each of next 2 sc, sc in each of next 9 chs, sc in each of next 2 sc, working down side edge, sc in side edge of each row, working 3 sc in bottom corner, sc across opposite side of foundation ch, 3 sc in next bottom corner, sc in each row up opposite side of car, sl st to join in beg sc, leaving a length of yarn, fasten off.

Using photo as a guide, sew car to front of tote. With black yarn, for wheels, sew black buttons to bottom edge of car. ✄

Li'l Friends Sleeping Bags
Continued from page 61

Rep assembly as for small sleeping bag.

Large Sleeping Bag
Row 1 (RS): With hook size G and MC, ch 26, sc in 2nd ch from hook, sc in each rem ch across, turn. (25 sc)

Rows 2–56: Rep Row 2 of small sleeping bag.

Rep assembly as for small sleeping bag.

Fashion Dolls Sleeping Bag
Row 1 (RS): With hook size G and MC, ch 11, sc in 2nd ch from hook, sc in each rem ch across, turn. (10 sc)

Row 2: Ch 1, sc in each sc across, turn.

For medium size sleeping bag, rep Row 2 until 78 rows are completed, fasten off. For large size, rep Row 2 until 84 rows are completed, fasten off.

Rep assembly as for small sleeping bag.

Trim
Row 1 (RS): With hook size D, attach CC with sl st in bottom right edge sc of assembly, ch 1, [sc, 2 dc, sc] in same sc as beg ch-1, [sk 2 sc, {sc, 2 dc, sc} in next sc] rep up side edge, sk only 1 sc at each corner, across top and down opposite side edge to bottom corner, fasten off.

Row 2: With hook size D, attach CC at right edge of sleeping bag opening, ch 1, [sc, 2 dc, sc] in same st as beg ch-1, [sk next 2 sc, {sc, 2 dc, sc} in next sc] 3 times, fasten off.

Flower
Make 3

Rnd 1 (RS): With hook size D and CC, leaving a 2-inch length at beg, ch 5, sl st to join to form a ring, [ch 4, sl st in ring] 6 times, leaving a 2-inch length, fasten off.

Hold flower next to front of sleeping bag, draw rem beg strand through a st and back out to RS, draw ending rem length through st near beg length, knot ends to secure, weave lengths back through front and trim. Glue a silk flower to the center of crocheted flower.

Attach rem flowers in same manner as desired. ✄

Kitty & Puppy Neck Nuzzlers
Continued from page 63

Leg
Make 4

Rnd 1: With café au lait, ch 2, 6 sc in 2nd ch from hook. (6 sc)

Rnd 2: 2 sc in each sc around. (12 sc)

Rnd 3: Sc in each sc around.

Rnd 4: Rep Rnd 3.

Rnd 5: [Sc dec over next 2 sc] rep around. (6 sc)

Rnds 6–12: Rep Rnd 3. At the end of Rnd 12, sl st in next st, leaving a length of yarn, fasten off.

Do not stuff leg. Fold Rnd 12 flat across, sew 2 legs to each end of body.

Tail
Rnd 1: With café au lait, ch 2, 6 sc in 2nd ch from hook. (6 sc)

Rnds 2–11: Sc in each sc around. At the end of Rnd 11, sl st in next st, leaving a length of yarn, fasten off.

Do not stuff tail, fold tail flat across and sew to body slightly above hind legs. ✄

Handy Helpers

The decorative appeal and functional versatility of the helpful projects in this chapter prove that crochet can be pretty as well as practical! You'll find useful patterns for making a variety of holders for small and large items, designs to assist with active, on-the-go schedules, and handy helpers for work and recreation. From purses to pouches or bags to bottle holders, you're sure to find the perfect handy helper for yourself or someone special!

Great opportunities to help others seldom come, but small ones surround us every day.

—Sally Koch

Mini Purselette

Design by Eleanor Albano-Miles

Here's a fashion accessory that's great for keeping spare change or a small lipstick close at hand. Scraps of crochet thread and small metal rings are all it takes to make this trendy little necklace purse!

Skill Level: Beginner

Size: 2¼ x 2¼ inches, excluding fringe

Materials

- Pearl cotton size 5: 50 yds variegated pastels
- Size 0 crochet hook or size needed to obtain gauge
- 2 (1-inch) gold rings
- Yarn needle

Fringe

Cut 30 lengths of cotton each 4 inches long. Working across 15 sc of purse bottom, [fold 2 strands in half, insert hook in sc st, draw fold through st to form a lp on hook, draw cut ends through lp on hook, pull ends slightly to secure] rep fringe in each rem st across bottom. Trim ends even. ✄

Even if it's a little thing, do something for those who have need of help, something for which you get no pay, but simply the privilege of doing it.

—Albert Schweitzer

Gauge

7 sc = 1 inch; 4 sc rows = ½ inch
Check gauge to save time.

Pattern Note

Weave in loose ends as work progresses.

Purse

Make 2

Row 1: Attach cotton to ring, ch 1, work 15 sc over ring, turn. (15 sc)

Rows 2–13: Ch 1, sc in each sc across, turn. At the end of Row 13, fasten off.

Assembly

Rnd 14: Holding both purse pieces tog and working through both thicknesses, attach cotton in side edge of Row 1, ch 1, sc in same row as beg ch-1, sc evenly sp down side edge of row, 2 sc in corner, sc across bottom of purse, 2 sc in corner, sc evenly sp up opposite side of purse, sl st in same st as last sc, ch 150 (neckline strap), sl st in first sc of Rnd 14, fasten off.

Accessory Pockets

Design by Sharon Phillips

Keep your cell phone and eyewear safe and secure in these attractive holders that work up quickly and easily in a simple shell-stitch pattern and sport weight yarn!

Skill Level: Beginner

Size

Cell phone case: 3 x 6 inches

Eyewear case: 3½ x 7½ inches

Materials

- J & P Coats Luster Sheen sport weight yarn (1.75 oz per ball): 2½ oz spa blue #821

- Size F/5 crochet hook or size needed to obtain gauge

- 2 (¾-inch) flower buttons

- Yarn needle

Gauge

6 sts = 1 inch; 4 pattern rnds = 1 inch

Check gauge to save time.

Pattern Notes

Weave in loose ends as work progresses.

Join rnds with a sl st unless otherwise stated.

Ch-3 counts as first dc throughout.

Pattern Stitches

Shell: 3 dc in indicated st.

Beg shell: Ch 3, 2 dc in same st.

Cell Phone Case

Rnd 1: Ch 14, 6 dc in 4th ch from hook, dc in each of next 9 chs, 7 dc in last ch, working on opposite side of foundation ch, dc in each of next 9 chs, join in top of beg ch. (32 dc)

Rnd 2: Ch 1, sc in same st as joining, *sk next st, shell in next st, sk next st **, sc in next st, rep from * around, ending last rep at **, join in beg sc. (8 sc; 8 shells)

Rnd 3: Beg shell in same sc as joining, *sk next dc, sc in next dc, sk next dc **, shell in next sc, rep from * around, ending last rep at **, join in 3rd ch of beg ch-3.

Rnd 4: Sl st into next dc, ch 1, sc in same dc, *sk next dc, shell in next sc, sk next dc **, sc in next dc, rep from * around, ending last rep at **, join in beg sc.

Rnds 5–19: Rep Rnds 3 and 4, ending last rep with Rnd 3. At the end of Rnd 19, turn.

Strap

Row 20: Sl st in next st, ch 2 (counts as first dc for strap for a neater edge), dc in next sc, sk next dc, sc in next dc, sk next dc, shell in next sc, sk next dc, sc in next dc, sk next dc, 2 dc in next sc, sk rem sts of Rnd 19, turn. (7 dc; 2 sc)

Row 21: Ch 1, sc in first dc, [sk next dc, shell in next sc, sk next dc, sc in next dc] twice, sc in top of ch-2, turn. (6 dc; 3 sc)

Row 22: Ch 2, dc in first sc, sk next dc, sc in next dc, sk next dc, shell in next sc, sk next dc, sc in next dc, sk next dc, 2 dc in last sc, turn.

Rows 23–28: Rep Rows 21 and 22.

Row 29: Ch 1, sc in first dc, sk next dc, 2 dc in next sc, sk next dc,

Continued on page 93

Plentiful Pockets Tote

Designs by Shirley Zebrowski

There's room aplenty in this oversized tote designed with numerous handy pockets for tucking in all the necessities! Everything from crafts to kids' essentials fits neatly inside for easy carrying.

Skill Level: Beginner

Size

Tote: 15 x 17 inches, excluding handles

Hook holder: 8 inches square

Materials

- Pop'n worsted weight yarn: 11 oz emerald green, 6 oz purple passion, 5½ oz autumn jewels
- Size H/8 crochet hook or size needed to obtain gauge
- 3 (1-inch) buttons
- Sewing needle and thread
- Straight pins
- Tapestry needle

Gauge

6 sc = 2 inches; 7 sc rows = 2 inches

Check gauge to save time.

Pattern Notes

Weave in loose ends as work progresses.

Join rnds with a sl st unless otherwise stated.

Pattern Stitch

Esc: Insert hook in st, yo, draw up a lp, yo, draw through 1 lp on hook, yo, draw through 2 lps on hook.

Tote

Back

Row 1: With emerald green, ch 48, sc in 2nd ch from hook, sc in each rem ch across, turn. (47 sc)

Row 2: Ch 1, sc in each sc across, turn.

Rows 3–58: Rep Row 2. At the end of Row 58, fasten off.

Front

Rows 1–58: Rep Rows 1–58 of back.

Side

Make 2

Row 1: With purple passion, ch 17 sc in 2nd ch from hook, sc in each rem ch across, turn. (16 sc)

Rows 2–58: Ch 1, sc in each sc across, turn. At the end of Row 58, fasten off.

Bottom

Row 1: With purple passion, ch 48, sc in 2nd ch from hook, sc in each rem ch across, turn. (47 sc)

Rows 2–17: Ch 1, sc in each sc across, turn. At the end of Row 17, fasten off.

Side Pocket

Make 2

Row 1: With autumn jewels, ch 48, esc in 2nd ch from hook, esc in each rem ch across, turn. (47 esc)

Rows 2–14: Ch 1, esc in each esc across, turn. At the end of Row 14, fasten off.

Front Pocket

Row 1: With purple passion, ch 30, esc in 2nd ch from hook, esc in each rem ch across, turn. (29 esc)

Row 2: Ch 1, esc in each esc across, turn.

Rows 3–15: Rep Row 2.

Row 16: Ch 1, esc in each of next 13 esc, ch 3, sk next 3 esc, esc in each of next 13 esc, turn.

Row 17: Ch 1, esc in each of next 13 esc, esc in each of next 3 chs, esc in each of next 13 esc, turn.

Row 18: Ch 1, sc in each esc across, fasten off.

Sew front pocket centered to front with Row 1 of pocket to Row 9 of front. Sew button to front opposite buttonhole of pocket.

Back Pocket

Note: Make 1 each with purple passion and autumn jewels.

Row 1: Ch 18, esc in 2nd ch from hook, esc in each rem ch across, turn. (17 esc)

Rows 2–13: Ch 1, esc in each esc across, turn.

Row 14: Ch 1, esc in each of next 7 esc, ch 3, sk next 3 esc, esc in each of next 7 esc, turn.

Row 15: Ch 1, esc in each of next 7 esc, esc in each of next 3 chs, esc in each of next 7 esc, turn.

Row 16: Ch 1, sc in each esc across, fasten off.

With back facing, sew purple passion pocket to left edge and autumn jewels to right edge. Sew Row 1 of each pocket to Row 7 of back, leaving 4 sts free at each outer edge and 7 sc free at center between pockets. Sew a button opposite each buttonhole of each pocket.

Assembly

Sew bottom and sides to each front and back. Sew a side pocket to each side section.

Top Trim

Rnd 1: Attach autumn jewels in top opening of tote, ch 1, reverse sc evenly sp around top opening, join in beg sc, fasten off.

Handle

Make 2

Row 1: With autumn jewels, ch 48, esc in 2nd ch from hook, esc in each rem ch across, turn.

Rows 2–5: Ch 1, esc in each esc across, turn. At the end of Row 5, fasten off.

Sew each end of handle 3 inches in from outer edge of tote front. Sew 2nd handle in same manner to tote back.

Hook Holder

Body

Row 1: With autumn jewels, ch 25, esc in 2nd ch from hook, esc in each rem ch across, turn. (24 esc)

Rows 2–27: Ch 1, esc in each esc across, turn. At the end of Row 27, fasten off.

Hook Holder

Row 1: With emerald green, ch 25, esc in 2nd ch from hook, esc in each rem ch across, turn. (24 esc)

Rows 2–8: Ch 1, esc in each esc across, turn. At the end of Row 8, fasten off.

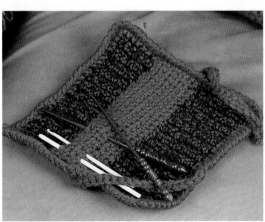

Place hook holder centered on body, secure with straight pins and sew opposite side of foundation ch and Row 8 to body.

Border

Rnd 1: Attach emerald green in any st on outer edge of body, ch 1, sc evenly sp around entire outer edge working through both thicknesses when working in area of hook holder and work 3 sc in each corner, join in beg sc.

Rnd 2: Ch 1, reverse sc in each sc around outer edge, join in beg sc, fasten off.

Closing Cord

Row 1: With emerald green, ch 71, sc in 2nd ch from hook, sc in each rem ch across, fasten off. With body outer side facing, draw end of cord through center row, with

ends even, knot at center. Place hook through hook holder, roll up hook holder and wrap closing cord around and tie ends in a bow. ✂

The Handy Tote

*My friends and I make crocheted totes
For growing families in need,
And fill each bag with children's books
To encourage the kids to read.*

*Some folks say that on car trips
The bag is the first thing they pack.
It keeps the little ones busy
The whole journey there and back.*

*Other moms use the tote bag
To store diapers, bottles and snacks.
They claim there is nothing handier
Than our pretty, crocheted sacks!*

Magic Purple Passion Purse

Design by Darla Fanton

This chic little purse has a fascinating secret! Made with a special, solar-sensitive yarn, you stitch it in white, but take it out in the sun and it magically changes to luscious purple!

Skill Level: Beginner

Size: 7 x 7½ inches

Materials

- DMC Baroque crochet cotton: 200 yds white
- SolarActive craft yarn by SolarActive International: 200 yds purple
- Size F/5 crochet hook or size needed to obtain gauge
- 3 color change pony beads by SolarActive International
- 7-inch white zipper
- 8½ x 15 white lining fabric
- White sewing thread and needle
- Yarn marker
- Yarn needle

Gauge

5 sc = 1 inch; 6 sc rows = 1 inch
Check gauge to save time.

Pattern Notes

Weave in loose ends as work progresses.

Do not join rnds unless otherwise stated. Use a yarn marker to mark first st of each rnd.

Purse Body

Rnd 1: With 1 strand each white and solar active yarn, ch 38, 3 sc in 2nd ch from hook, sc in each of next 35 sc, 3 sc in last sc, working on opposite side of foundation ch, sc in each of next 35 chs. (76 sc)

Rnd 2: Sc in next sc, 2 sc in next sc, sc in each of next 37 sc, 2 sc in next sc, sc in each of next 36 sc. (78 sc)

Rnd 3: Sc in each st around.

Rnds 4–16: Rep Rnd 3.

Rnd 17: Sc in each of next 4 sts, sc in next st, move marker to st just completed, dc in each st around to marker. (78 dc)

Rnd 18: Drop solar active yarn and add a 2nd ball of white cotton (2 strands white cotton), [bpdc around next st, fpdc around next st] rep around.

Rnd 19: Drop 1 strand white cotton and pick up solar active yarn (1 strand each yarn), [fpdc around next st, bpdc around next st] rep around.

Rnd 20: Drop solar active yarn, pick up 2nd strand of white cotton (2 strands white cotton), [bpdc around next st, fpdc around next st] rep around.

Rnds 21–25: Rep Rnds 19 and 20.

Rnds 26–39: Working with 1 strand each solar active yarn and white cotton, rep Rnd 3. At the end of Rnd 39, fasten off.

Handle

Rnd 1: Leaving an 8-inch length at beg of each solar active yarn and

white cotton, ch 8, sl st to join to form a ring, sc in each ch around, do not join. (8 sc)

Rnd 2: Sc in each sc around.

Rep Rnd 2 until handle measures 24 inches, sl st in next st, leaving an 8 inch length, fasten off.

Finishing

Using photo as a guide, using rem lengths at beg and end securely stitch each end of handle to inside of purse at side edges.

With sewing thread, blindstitch zipper in place approximately ¼ inch down from the top of the purse.

For lining, fold fabric in half with short ends touching, sew each side seam using ¼-inch seam allowance. Turn fabric inside out and again sew each side seam using ¼-inch seam allowance. This encases the side seams so there are no raw edges to ravel. Turn top edge under ¼ inch and press, turn again ¼ inch. Stitch top edge of lining to top inside of purse over zipper tapes.

For zipper pull, cut 3 pieces of crochet cotton each 18 inches long. Fold pieces in half and attach through hole in zipper pull using a half hitch. Thread beads on strands and tie a double knot to hold beads in place. ✂

*The best thing to give
to a friend is your heart;
to a child, a good example;
to your parents, deference
and exemplary conduct;
to yourself, respect;
to all men, charity.*

—Lord Balfour

Dainty Scallops Lingerie Bag

Design by Nancy Nehring

Crochet thread, pretty button accents and a bit of mosquito netting combine to create this dainty and versatile Victorian-style lingerie bag. It's great for storing delicate scarves and lingerie articles, protecting nylons from snags or organizing small suitcase items when traveling!

Skill Level: Beginner

Size: 6 x 8½ inches

Materials
- Crochet cotton size 30: 250 yds shaded lavenders
- Size 11 steel crochet hook or size needed to obtain gauge
- 5¾ x 6¾ inches mosquito netting
- 2 (½-inch) flower buttons
- Straight pins
- Tapestry needle

Inside Button Flap
Row 1 (RS): Attach cotton in top edge (short width edge), ch 1, sc in each sc across top edge, turn.

Rows 2–9: Ch 2, hdc in each st across, turn. At the end of Row 9, fasten off.

Bag Body
Row 1 (RS): Attach cotton in bottom edge (opposite end of inside button flap), ch 1, sc in each sc across bottom edge, turn.

Row 2: Ch 2, hdc in each st across, turn.

Rows 3–9: Rep Row 2.

Row 10: Ch 1, sc in each st across, turn.

Row 11 (RS): Ch 1, working in front lps only, sc in each st across, turn.

Continued on page 93

Gauge
14 hdc = 1 inch; 10 hdc rows = 1 inch

Check gauge to save time.

Pattern Notes
Weave in loose ends as work progresses.

Join rnds with a sl st unless otherwise stated.

Ch-2 counts as first hdc throughout.

Mosquito Netting
Note: *Cut mosquito netting along a single row of rectangles on all 4 sides to measurements indicated.*

Rnd 1: Turn under 2 rows (blocks) of netting around outer edge as work progresses, attach cotton in 4th mesh from any corner, work 1 sc in each mesh around outer edge, working 4 sc in each corner mesh, join in beg sc, fasten off.

Water Bottle Holders

Designs by Carol Decker

Walkers, runners, bicyclists, hikers, campers and other people on the go will appreciate having a bottle of refreshing water or juice close at hand. It's easy to carry along in these simple-to-stitch thread bottle holders designed for him and her!

Skill Level: Beginner

Size: Fits up to 33.8-oz water bottles

Materials

- South Maid crochet cotton size 10 (350 yds per ball): 3 balls light peach #424, 1 ball cappuccino #434, 100 yds goldenrod #421, 70 yds purple #458, 50 yds victory red #494
- Size 7 steel crochet hook or size needed to obtain gauge
- Yarn marker
- Yarn needle

Gauge

With size 7 hook, 9 sc = 1 inch; 10 sc rows = 1 inch

Check gauge to save time.

Pattern Notes

Weave in loose ends as work progresses.

Join rnds with a sl st unless otherwise stated.

Ch-3 counts as first dc throughout unless otherwise stated.

Pattern Stitches

Bpsc: Insert hook back to front to back again around vertical post of indicated st, yo, draw up a lp, yo, draw through 2 lps on hook.

Shell: [2 dc, ch 3, 2 dc] in indicated st.

Beg shell: [Ch 3, 1 dc, ch 3, 2 dc] in indicated st.

When a rnd begs with a shell, simply work a beg shell.

Fptr: Yo hook twice, insert hook front to back to front again around vertical post of indicated st, yo, draw up a lp, [yo, draw through 2 lps on hook] 3 times.

Fpsc: Insert hook front to back to front again around vertical post of indicated st, yo, draw up a lp, yo, draw through 2 lps on hook.

Hers

Rnd 1: With light peach, ch 5, join to form a ring, ch 1, 6 sc in ring, do not join. (6 sc)

Rnd 2: 2 sc in each sc around, do not join. (12 sc)

Rnd 3: [Sc in next sc, 2 sc in next sc] rep around, do not join. (18 sc)

Rnds 4–16: Sc around, inc 6 sc evenly sp around, changing position of inc sts on each rnd, do not join. (96 sc)

Rnd 17: [Sc in each of next 6 sc, sc dec over next 2 sc] rep around, do not join. (84 sc)

Rnd 18: Sl st in next st, ch 3, dc in next st, *ch 3, dc in each of next 2 sts, ch 2, sk next 2 sts, sc in next st, [ch 3, sk next st, sc in next st] 5 times, ch 2, sk next 2 sts, dc in each of next 2 sts, ch 3, dc in each of next 2 sts, [ch 2, sk 1 st, tr in next st] twice, ch 2 **, sk next st, dc in each of next 2 sts, rep from * around, ending last rep at **, join in 3rd ch of beg ch-3.

Rnd 19: Sl st into ch-3 sp, *shell in ch-3 sp, ch 3, [sc in next ch-3 sp, ch 3] 5 times, shell in next ch-3 sp, ch 2, sk next ch-2 sp, [tr, ch 5, tr] in next ch-2 sp, ch 2, sk next ch-2 sp, rep from * around, join in 3rd ch of beg ch-3.

Rnd 20: Sl st into ch-3 sp, *shell in ch-3 sp of shell, ch 3, sk next ch-3 sp, [sc in next ch-3 sp, ch 3] 4 times, shell in next shell, ch 2, 9 tr in next ch-5 sp, ch 2, rep from * around, join in 3rd ch of beg ch-3.

Rnd 21: Sl st into ch-3 sp of shell, *shell in ch-3 sp of shell, ch 3, sk next ch-3 sp, [sc in next ch-3 sp, ch 3] 3 times, shell in ch-3 sp of next shell, ch 1, [tr in next tr, ch 1] 9 times, rep from * around, join in 3rd ch of beg ch-3.

Rnd 22: Sl st into ch-3 sp of shell, *shell in ch-3 sp of shell, ch 4, sk next ch-3 sp, sc in next ch-3 sp, ch 3, sc in next ch-3 sp, ch 4, shell in ch-3 sp of next shell, ch 2, [sc in next ch-1 sp, ch 3] 7 times, sc in next ch-1 sp, ch 2, rep from * around, join in 3rd ch of beg ch-3.

Rnd 23: Sl st into ch-3 sp, *shell in ch-3 sp of next shell, ch 5, sc in next ch-3 sp, ch 5, shell in ch-3 sp of next shell, ch 2, [sc in next ch-3 sp, ch 3] 6 times, sc in next ch-3 sp, ch 2, rep from * around, join in 3rd ch of beg ch-3.

Rnd 24: Sl st into ch-3 sp, *shell

in ch-3 sp of shell, [ch 2, tr in next ch-5 sp] twice, ch 2, shell in next ch-3 sp of next shell, ch 3, [sc in next ch-3 sp, ch 3] 6 times, rep from * around, join in 3rd ch of beg ch-3.

Rnd 25: Sl st into ch-3 sp, *shell in ch-3 sp of shell, ch 2, sk next ch-2 sp, [tr, ch 5, tr] in next ch-2 sp, ch 2, shell in ch-3 sp of shell, ch 3, sk next ch-3 sp, [sc in next ch-3 sp, ch 3] 5 times, rep from * around, join in 3rd ch of beg ch-3.

Rnd 26: Sl st into ch-3 sp of shell, *shell in ch-3 sp of shell, ch 2, 9 tr in next ch-5 sp, ch 2, shell in next ch-3 sp of shell, ch 3, sk next ch-3 sp, [sc in next ch-3 sp, ch 3] 4 times, rep from * around, join in 3rd ch of beg ch-3.

Rnd 27: Sl st into ch-3 sp, *shell in ch-3 sp of shell, ch 1, [tr in next tr, ch 1] 9 times, shell in next ch-3 sp of shell, ch 3, sk next ch-3 sp, [sc in next ch-3 sp, ch 3] 3 times, rep from * around, join in 3rd ch of beg ch-3.

Rnd 28: Sl st into ch-3 sp, *shell in ch-3 sp of shell, ch 2, [sc in next ch-1 sp, ch 3] 7 times, sc in next ch-1 sp, ch 2, shell in next ch-3 sp of shell, ch 4, sk next ch-3 sp, sc in next ch-3 sp, ch 3, sc in next ch-3 sp, ch 4, rep from * around, join in 3rd ch of beg ch-3.

Rnd 29: Sl st into ch-3 sp, *shell in ch-3 sp of shell, ch 2, [sc in next ch-3 sp, ch 3] 6 times, sc in next ch-3 sp, ch 2, shell in next ch-3 sp of next shell, ch 5, sc in next ch-3 sp, ch 5, rep from * around, join in 3rd ch of beg ch-3.

Rnd 30: Sl st into ch-3 sp, *shell in ch-3 sp of shell, ch 3, [sc in next ch-3 sp, ch 3] 6 times, shell in next ch-3 sp, [ch 2, tr in next ch-5 sp] twice, ch 2, rep from * around, join in 3rd ch of beg ch-3.

[Rep Rnds 19–30] twice, for longer version, [rep Rnds 19–30] 3 times, then rep Rnds 19–24.

Rnd 31: Ch 1, *bpsc around next 4 dc, [sc in next ch-2 sp, sc in next tr] twice, sc in next ch-2 sp, bpsc

around next 4 dc, ch 2, [bpsc around next sc, ch 1] 5 times, bpsc around next sc, ch 2, rep from * around, mark beg of rnd, do not join.

Rnd 32: *Sc in each of next 13 sc, 2 sc in next ch-2 sp, [sc in next sc, sc in next ch-1 sp] 5 times, sc in next sc, 2 sc in next ch-2 sp, rep from * around, do not join. (84 sc)

Rnd 33: Sc in each sc around, do not join.

Shoulder Strap

Row 34: Sc in each of next 42 sc, turn.

Row 35: Ch 2, sc dec over next 2 sc, sc in each of next 38 sc, sc dec over next 2 sts, turn. (40 sc)

Row 36: Ch 2, sc dec over next 2 sts, sc in each sc across to last 2 sc, sc dec over next 2 sts, turn. (38 sc)

Row 37: Ch 2, sc dec over next 2 sc, sc in each sc across to last 2 sc, sc dec over next 2 sc, turn. (36 sc)

Rep Row 37 until 14 sc rem.

Dec 1 sc at beg of next 2 rows. (12 sc)

[Ch 1, sc in each of next 12 sc, turn] rep until strap measures 30 inches, fasten off.

Attach light peach on opposite edge in next sk st of Rnd 33, beg with Row 34, rep as for first strap. Knot ends of straps tog.

Pineapple Finishing

Row 1: Attach light peach in ch-3 sp of shell before next incomplete pineapple, beg shell in same ch-3 sp, ch 3, sk next ch-3 sp, [sc in next ch-3 sp, ch 3] 5 times, shell in next ch-3 sp of next shell, turn.

Row 2: Ch 4, shell in next ch-3 sp of next shell, ch 3, sk next ch-3 sp, [sc in next ch-3 sp, ch 3] 4 times, shell in next ch-3 sp of shell, turn.

Row 3: Ch 4, shell in next ch-3 sp of next shell, ch 3, sk next ch-3 sp, [sc in next ch-3 sp, ch 3] 3 times, shell in next ch-3 sp of next shell, turn.

Row 4: Ch 4, shell in ch-3 sp of next shell, ch 4, sk next ch-3 sp, sc

in next ch-3 sp, ch 3, sc in next ch-3 sp, ch 4, shell in next ch-3 sp of next shell, turn.

Row 5: Ch 4, shell in ch-3 sp of next shell, ch 5, sc in next ch-3 sp, ch 5, shell in ch-3 sp of next shell, turn.

Row 6: Ch 4, shell in ch-3 sp of next shell, ch 1, tr in each of next 2 ch-5 sps, ch 1, shell in next ch-3 sp of next shell, turn.

Row 7: Ch 4, [shell in ch-3 sp of next shell] twice, turn.

Row 8: Ch 4, *[yo, insert hook in next ch-3 sp, yo, draw up a lp, yo, draw through 2 lps on hook] twice in same ch-3 sp, yo, draw through all 3 lps (dc dec), rep from * in next ch-3 sp, ch 5, sl st in top of first dc dec, leaving a length of cotton, fasten off.

Sew point of pineapple to center ch-2 sp between tr sts at base of same pineapple.

Rep Rows 1–8 over each of rem 3 incomplete pineapple.

His

Rnds 1–17: With cappuccino, rep Rnds 1–17 of hers. (84 sc)

Note: *Beg with Rnd 18, do not fasten off crochet cotton as colors change, carry colors not in use loosely on WS. Simply pick up color as needed and drop to WS when not in use.*

Rnd 18: Attach goldenrod with a sl st in next st, tr in same st as sl st, sc in each of next 3 sts, [tr in next st, sc in each of next 3 sts] rep around, join in first tr.

Rnd 19: With purple, [hdc in tr, hdc in each of next 3 sc] rep around, join in beg hdc.

Rnd 20: With goldenrod, hdc in each of next 2 hdc, *fptr around middle sc 2 rnds below **, hdc in each of next 3 hdc, rep from * around, ending last rep at **, hdc in next st, join in beg hdc.

Rnd 21: With cappuccino, dc in each st around, join in beg dc.

Rnd 22: With victory red, *sc in next dc, ch 1, fpsc around next dc, ch 1, rep from * around, join in beg sc.

Rnd 23: With purple, dc in each ch-1 sp around, join in beg dc.

Rnd 24: With cappuccino, sc in each st around, join in beg sc.

Rnd 25: With cappuccino, sc in each st around, join in beg sc.

Rnd 26: With goldenrod, sc in each of next 2 sts, *fptr around dc directly below (purple rnd) **, sc in each of next 3 sts, rep from * around, ending last rep at **, sc in next st, join in beg sc.

Rnd 27: With goldenrod, *tr in next st, sc in each of next 3 sts, rep from * around, join in beg tr.

Rnd 28: With purple, dc in each st around, join in beg dc.

Rnd 29: With goldenrod, hdc in each of next 2 sts, *fptr around middle sc 2 rnds below **, hdc in each of next 3 sts, rep from * around, ending last rep at **, hdc in next st, join in beg hdc.

Rnd 30: With cappuccino, dc in each st around, join in beg dc.

Rnd 31: Rep Rnd 22.

Rnd 32: Rep Rnd 23.

Rnd 33: With cappuccino, sc in each st around, join in beg sc.

Rnds 34 & 35: With cappuccino, sc in each st around, join in beg sc.

[Rep Rnds 18–35] twice, then rep Rnds 18–25.

Shoulder Strap

Rows 36–38: Rep Rows 34–36 of hers. (38 sc)

Row 39: Ch 2, sc dec over next 2 sts, sc in each st across to last 2 sc, sc dec over next 2 sc, turn. (36 sc)

Rep Row 39 until 14 sc rem.

Dec 1 sc at the beg of next 2 rows. (12 sc)

[Ch 1, sc in each of next 12 sc, turn] rep until strap measures 20 inches, fasten off.

Attach cappuccino in next st of last rnd worked, beg with Row 36, rep 2nd strap the same as first. At the end of 2nd strap, leaving a length of cotton, fasten off. Matching sts, sew ends of straps tog. ✂

Many Textures Tote

Design by Cindy Carlson

This handy bag is made in several dimensional stitch techniques to create a variety of interesting textures throughout. Short or long straps make it versatile to use either as a wheelchair or walker tote, or as a fashionable shoulder purse!

Skill Level: Beginner

Size: 9½ x 10½ inches

Materials

- Worsted weight cotton yarn: 14 oz variegated
- Size G/6 crochet hook or size needed to obtain gauge
- 1-inch brass key ring
- 2 (⅞-inch) buttons for tote
- ⅞-inch button purse
- 1-inch hook-and-loop tape
- Sewing needle and matching thread
- Yarn needle

Gauge

7 sc = 2 inches; 8 sc rows = 2 inches
Check gauge to save time.

Pattern Notes

Weave in loose ends as work progresses.

Join rnds with a sl st unless otherwise stated.

Front

Row 1: Beg at top edge, ch 35, sc in 2nd ch from hook, dc in next ch, [sc in next ch, dc in next ch] rep across, turn. (34 sts)

Rows 2–11: Ch 1, [sc in dc, dc in sc] rep across, turn. (34 sts)

Rows 12–31: Ch 1, sc in each st across, turn. (34 sc) At the end of Row 31, fasten off.

Back

Row 1: Beg at top edge, ch 35, sc in 2nd ch from hook, dc in next ch, [sc in next ch, dc in next ch] rep across, turn. (34 sts)

Rows 2–24: Ch 1, [sc in dc, dc in sc] rep across, turn. At the end of Row 24, fasten off.

Side

Make 2

Row 1: Ch 9, sc in 2nd ch from hook, sc in each rem ch across, turn. (8 sc)

Rows 2–31: Ch 1, sc in each sc across, turn. At the end of Row 31, fasten off.

Bottom

Row 1: Ch 9, sc in 2nd ch from hook, sc in each rem ch across, turn. (8 sc)

Rows 2–32: Ch 1, sc in each sc across, turn. At the end of Row 32, fasten off.

Outer Front Pocket

Row 1: Ch 35, sc in 2nd ch from hook, sc in each rem ch across, turn. (34 sc)

Rows 2–19: Ch 1, working in back lps only, sc in each st across, turn.

Row 20: Ch 1, sc in each sc across, fasten off.

Inside Pocket

Row 1: Ch 35, sc in 2nd ch from hook, sc in each rem ch across, turn. (34 sc)

Rows 2–14: Ch 1, sc in each sc across, turn. At the end of Row 14, fasten off.

Side Pocket

Row 1: Ch 9, sc in 2nd ch from hook, dc in next ch, [sc in next ch, dc in next ch] rep across, turn. (8 sc)

Rows 2–18: Ch 1, [sc in next dc, dc in next sc] rep across, turn. At the end of Row 18, fasten off.

Closing Tab

Row 1: Ch 13, sc in 2nd ch from hook, sc in each rem ch across, turn. (12 sc)

Row 2: Ch 1, sc in each sc across, turn.

Row 3: Ch 3, dc in each sc across, turn.

Row 4: Ch 3, dc in next st, [fpdc around each of next 2 sts, dc in next st] 3 times, dc in next st, turn. (12 sts)

Row 5: Ch 3, dc in next st, [bpdc around each of next 2 sts, dc in next st] 3 times, dc in next st, turn. (12 sts)

It is one of the most beautiful compensations of this life that no man can sincerely try to help another without helping himself.

—Ralph Waldo Emerson

Rows 6–9: Rep Rows 4 and 5.

Row 10: Ch 1, sc in each of next 6 sts, ch 4 (button lp), sc in each of next 6 sts, fasten off.

Key Chain

Row 1: Ch 6, sc in 2nd ch from hook, sc in each rem ch across, turn. (5 sc)

Rows 2–5: Ch 1, sc in each sc across, turn.

Row 6: Ch 1, sc in each of next 2 sc, ch 21, 3 sc in 2nd ch from hook, 3 sc in each rem ch across, sc in each of next 2 rem sc sts of Row 5, fasten off.

Shoulder Strap

Note: *Only make if you are making the purse version.*

Row 1: Ch 7, sc in 2nd ch from hook, sc in each rem ch across, turn. (6 sc)

Rows 2–75: Ch 1, sc in first st, [dc in next st, sc in next st] twice, dc in next st, turn.

Row 76: Ch 1, sc in each st across, fasten off.

Note: *After purse is assembled, sew shoulder strap to each end at top edge of side pieces.*

Assembly

Note: *If making wheelchair or walker tote, work assembly before straps.*

Sew outer front pocket to the front piece making sure that pocket covers only the sc rows on front.

Sew inside pocket to inside of back.

Sew side pocket to side.

Sc the short end of side pocket piece with the pocket opening on top, to bottom short end and then sc the other end of the bottom to the 2nd side piece.

Sew hook-and-loop tape to 3rd row from the top of the 2nd side piece. Sew opposite side of hook-and-loop tape centered over Rows 1–5 of key chain. Attach brass key ring to sc sts at end of curled section of the key chain.

Now holding the pocket side piece with the pocket facing out and opening on top, sc the front and side pieces tog, when you get to the bottom piece continue sc around and sc the other side piece to the front with the key ring inside and at the top. Rep the process with the back piece.

Sew closing tab to center back top of tote. Sew button centered

approximately 2 inches down on front of tote.

Wheelchair or Walker Tote
Button strap

Row 1: Attach yarn with a sl st to side piece, ch 1, sc in same sp, sc in each of next 3 sps, do not work across rem 4 sc, turn. (4 sc)

Rows 2–14: Ch 1, sc in each sc across, turn. At the end of Row 14, fasten off.

Sew a button to center of Row 11 of button strap.

Buttonhole strap

Row 1: Attach yarn with sl st in next st of same side piece, ch 1, sc in same st as beg ch-1, sc in each of next 3 sts, turn. (4 sc)

Rows 2–14: Ch 1, sc in each sc across, turn.

Row 15: Ch 6, sl st in 4th sc at opposite end of row, fasten off.

Rep button strap and buttonhole strap on opposite side. ✄

Chair Pouch

Design by Amy Venditti

Durable crochet nylon creates this sturdy, yet lightweight chair pouch that easily buttons over the arm of a wheelchair, folding patio or beach chair, or even a walker to keep necessities close at hand.

Skill Level: Beginner

Size: 12½ x 12½ inches

Materials

- Crochet nylon (250 yds per roll): 4 rolls MC
- Size I/9 crochet hook or size needed to obtain gauge
- 4 (25mm) buttons
- Sewing needle and matching thread
- Yarn marker
- Tapestry needle

Gauge

4 rows = 1 inch; 4 sts = 1 inch
Check gauge to save time.

Pattern Notes

Weave in loose ends as work progresses.

Work with 2 strands of nylon held together throughout.

Join rnds with a sl st unless otherwise stated.

My Helpers

Some folks I know are bedridden;
Others are wheelchair bound.
I can't be with them all the time
So I leave my helpers around.

A crocheted basket by the bed,
A handy wheelchair pack,
Will help my good friends help themselves
Until I can come back.

Pattern Stitch

Double st (ds): Insert hook in indicated st, yo, draw up a lp, insert hook in next st, yo, draw up a lp, yo, draw through all 3 lps on hook.

Pouch

Rnd 1: With 2 strands of nylon held tog, ch 53, draw up a lp in 3rd ch from hook, draw up a lp in next ch, yo, draw through all 3 lps on hook, [insert hook in same ch as last st, yo, draw up a lp, insert hook in next ch, yo, draw up a lp, yo, draw through all 3 lps on hook] rep across ch and on opposite side of foundation ch, do not join. (100 ds)

Rnds 2–40: [Insert hook in same st as last st, yo, draw up a lp, insert hook in next st, yo, draw up a lp, yo, draw through all 3 lps on hook] rep around. Do not join. (100 ds)

Row 41: [Insert hook in same st as last st, yo, draw up a lp, insert hook in next st, yo, draw up a lp, yo, draw through all 3 lps

on hook] 50 times, turn. (50 ds)

Rows 42–62: Ch 1, ds in each st across, turn. (50 ds)

At the end of Row 62, do not turn.

Note: Rows 63–66 are worked in 5 sections of 4 rows each to create 4 vertical buttonholes.

Rows 63–66: [Ch 1, turn, ds in each of next 5 ds] 4 times, fasten off. Sl st in 6th ds, ch 1, turn, ds in each of next 13 ds, [ch 1, turn, ds in each of next 13 ds] 3 times, fasten off. Sl st in 19th ds, ch 1, ds in each of next 14 ds, [ch 1, turn, ds in each of next 14 ds] 3 times, fasten off. Sl st in 33rd ds, ch 1, turn, ds in each of next 13 ds, [ch 1, turn, ds in each of next 13 ds] 3 times, fasten off. Sl st in next 46th ds, ch 1, ds in each of next 5 ds, [ch 1, turn, ds in each of next 5 ds] 3 times, fasten off.

Row 67: Attach 2 strands of nylon in first section that created buttonholes, ch 1, ds across each of the 5 sections, turn. (50 ds)

Rows 68 & 69: Ch 1, ds in each ds across, turn. (50 ds)

Row 70: Ch 1, reverse sc in each st across, fasten off.

Sew buttons to Row 48 opposite vertical buttonholes.

Drawstring

Attach 2 strands of nylon approximately 50 inches long to side edge of Row 40, insert hook and draw up a lp, ch to end of nylon threads. Rep on opposite edge of Row 40.

Weave each ch length through top edge of front pocket to center of piece, tie ends in a bow. ✂

Southwest Baskets

Designs by Katherine Eng

Bring a bit of Native American beauty to any room in your home with these Southwest-style baskets stitched in worsted weight ombre yarn. They make cozy catchalls for everyday essentials, handy holders for household accessories, decorative servers for tasty treats or pretty containers for home decor accents!

Skill Level: Beginner

Size

Basket No. 1: 5½ x 8 inches
Basket No. 2: 3½ x 7 inches

Materials
- Coats & Clark Red Heart Super Saver worsted weight yarn: 3½ oz each linen #330, buff #334
- Coats & Clark Misty chunky weight yarn: 3½ oz high plains heather multi #2943
- Size H/8 crochet hook or size needed to obtain gauge
- Yarn needle

Gauge

Rnds 1 and 2 = 2¾ inches
Check gauge to save time.

Pattern Notes

Weave in loose ends as work progresses.

Join rnds with a sl st unless otherwise stated.

Ch-3 counts as first dc throughout.

Work with 3 strands of yarn held tog throughout.

Pattern Stitches

Fptr: Yo hook twice, insert hook front to back and to front again around vertical post of indicated st, yo, draw up a lp, [yo, draw through 2 lps on hook] 3 times.

Pc: 4 dc in indicated st, draw up a lp, remove hook, insert hook in top of first dc, pick up dropped lp, draw through st on hook.

Beg pc: Ch 3, 3 dc in same st, draw up a lp, remove hook, insert hook in top of beg ch-3, pick up dropped lp, draw through st on hook.

Shell: 3 dc in indicated st.

Basket No. 1

Rnd 1: With 1 strand each color held tog, ch 5, join to form a ring, ch 1, 10 sc in ring, join in beg sc. (10 sc)

Rnd 2: Ch 1, 2 sc in each sc around, join in beg sc. (20 sc)

Rnd 3: Ch 1, [sc in next sc, 2 sc in next sc] rep around, join in beg sc. (30 sc)

Rnd 4: Ch 1, [2 sc in next sc, sc in each of next 2 sc] rep around, join in beg sc. (40 sc)

Rnd 5: Ch 1, [sc in each of next 9 sc, 2 sc in next sc] 4 times, join in beg sc. (44 sc)

Rnd 6: Ch 1, [sc in each of next 10 sc, 2 sc in next sc] 4 times, join in beg sc. (48 sc)

Rnd 7: Ch 1, sc in each st around, join in beg sc.

Rnds 8 & 9: Rep Rnd 7.

Rnd 10: Ch 3, dc in each st around, join in 3rd ch of beg ch-3.

Rnd 11: Ch 1, sc in first dc, sc in each of next 2 dc, fptr around post of dc directly below, [sc in each of next 3 dc, fptr around post of dc directly below] rep around, join in beg sc. (12 fptr; 36 sc)

Rnd 12: Rep Rnd 10.

Rnd 13: Ch 1, sc in first dc, fptr around post of dc directly below, [sc in each of next 3 dc, fptr around post of dc directly below] rep around to last 2 dc, sc in each of next 2 dc, join in beg sc. (12 fptr; 36 sc)

Rnd 14: Rep Rnd 7.

Rnd 15: Ch 1, sc in each of next 3 sts, *[sc, ch 3, sc] in next sc **, sc in each of next 3 sc, rep from * around, ending last rep at **, join in beg sc, fasten off.

Basket No. 2
Rnds 1–9: Rep Rnds 1–9 of Basket No. 1. (48 sc)

Rnd 10: Beg pc in first st, *dc in each of next 3 sts **, pc in next st, rep from * around, ending last rep at **, join in top of beg pc.

Rnd 11: Ch 1, sc in joining of beg pc, *sk 1 dc, shell in next dc, sk 1 dc **, sc in joining of next pc, rep from * around, ending last rep at **, join in beg sc.

Rnd 12: [Ch 2, {sl st, ch 2, sl st} in center dc of next shell, ch 2, sl st in next sc] rep around, fasten off. ✄

Accessory Pockets

Continued from page 79

sc in next dc, sk next dc, 2 dc in next sc, sk next dc, sc in last dc, turn. (3 sc; 4 dc)

Row 30: Ch 1, sc in first sc, sk next 2 dc, [2 dc, ch 5, 2 dc] in next sc (button lp), sk next 2 dc, sc in last sc, fasten off.

Row 31 (RS): Attach cotton to side of strap at top of case, ch 1, sc evenly sp up side edge of strap working 2 sc in side edge of each dc row and 1 sc in side edge of each sc row to ch-5 sp, work 5 sc in ch-5 sp, sc in same manner down opposite side of strap, fasten off.

Sew button to center front of case over Rnd 14.

Eyewear Case
Rnd 1: Ch 5, join to form a ring, ch 3, 19 dc in ring, join in 3rd ch of beg ch-3. (20 dc)

Rnd 2: Ch 3, dc in same dc as beg ch-3, 2 dc in each rem dc around, join in 3rd ch of beg ch-3. (40 dc)

Rnd 3: Rep Rnd 2 of cell phone case. (10 sc; 10 shells)

Rnds 4–26: Rep Rnds 3 and 4 of cell phone case. At the end of Rnd 26, turn.

Rows 27–38: Rep Rows 20–31 of cell phone case.

Sew button to center front of case over Rnd 20. ✄

Dainty Scallops Lingerie Bag

Continued from page 84

[Rep Row 2] approximately 83 times or until back measures the same length as front, ending last rep with a RS row.

Rep Rows 10 and 11.

[Rep Row 2] 4 times.

Ch 1, hdc in each st across, working 2 buttonholes evenly sp across, ch 6, sk next 6 sts (buttonhole), turn.

[Rep Row 2] 4 times. At the end of last rep, turn.

Flap Scallop Trim
Ch 1, sc in first st, *sk next 2 sts, 7 dc in next st, sk next 2 sts, sc in next st, rep from * across making adjustments as needed to end with sc in last st, fasten off.

Sew buttons on button flap in line with buttonholes.

Border
Note: *Fold bag on fold lines at top and bottom on rem free lps and pin bag with straight pins.*

Rnd 1 (RS): Attach cotton in top right edge in rem free lps, ch 1, sc evenly sp across top edge, working through all 3 thicknesses of buttonhole flap, button flap and back, sc evenly sp across edge, working through both thicknesses down rem side, sc evenly sp, working across bottom edge, sc in rem free lps across bottom edge, sc across rem edge through both thicknesses and then through all 3 thicknesses at top edge, join in beg sc, remove straight pins.

Rnd 2: Ch 1, [sc in sc, sk next 2 sc, 7 dc in next sc, sk next 2 sc] rep around outer edge making adjustments as needed by skipping 1, 2 or 3 sts to have a sc st in each corner, join in beg sc, fasten off. ✄

Furry Friends

For many of us, one of life's most enriching experiences is the pleasure of being thoroughly owned and operated by loving and loyal pets. We love to spoil them with a variety of creature comforts, from snuggly blankets and cozy beds to stylish accessories and entertaining toys. With that in mind, we've created a delightful array of pet-pleasing projects for the endearing, furry friends who steal our hearts and ask no more of us than the simple comforts of good care and the pleasures of being loved.

Animals are such agreeable friends— they ask no questions, they pass no criticisms.

—George Eliot

Play Tunnel

Design by Bendy Carter

Cats will enjoy hours of entertainment in this irresistible tunnel of fun! Double-strand worsted weight yarn reinforced with metal rings gives it a sturdy construction, and fuzzy pompoms and jingle bells add extra intrigue for Kitty's delight!

Skill Level: Beginner

Size: 12 inches in diameter x 45 inches long

Materials

- Coats & Clark Red Heart Super Saver worsted weight yarn (8 oz per skein): 1 skein black #312
- Coats & Clark Kids worsted weight yarn (5 oz per skein): 2 skeins each red #2390, blue #2845, yellow #2230, orange #2252 and green #2677
- Sizes G/6 and J/10 crochet hooks or size needed to obtain gauge
- 6 (12-inch) craft rings
- 4 (18mm) jingle bells
- Yarn needle

Gauge

With J hook, 14 sts = 5 inches
Check gauge to save time.

Pattern Notes

Weave in loose ends as work progresses.

Join rnds with a sl st unless otherwise stated.

Roll black skein into 2 equal balls of yarn.

Work with 2 strands of yarn held tog unless otherwise stated.

Tunnel

First section

Ring rnd (RS): With 2 strands of black and hook size J, ch 108, join to form a ring, holding first craft ring with ch, ch 1, working over ring into ch, sc in each ch around, join in beg sc, fasten off. (108 sc)

Rnd 1: Attach 2 strands of red in opposite side of foundation ch, ch 1, [sc in next ch, hdc in next ch] 54 times, join in beg sc, turn. (108 sts)

Rnds 2–23: Ch 1, [sc in next hdc, hdc in next sc] rep around, join in beg sc, turn, at the end of Rnd 23, fasten off, attach 2 strands of black.

Second section

Ring rnd: Holding next ring in place and working over ring and into sts of previous rnd, ch 1, sc in each st around, join in beg sc, fasten off. (180 sc)

Rnd 1: Attach 2 strands of blue, ch 1, [sc in next st, hdc in next st] 54 times, join in beg sc, turn. (108 sts)

Rnds 2–23: Rep Rnds 2–23 of first section.

Third section

Ring rnd: Rep ring rnd of 2nd section.

Rnd 1: Attach 2 strands of yellow, ch 1, [sc in next st, hdc in next st] 54 times, join in beg sc, turn. (108 sts)

Rnd 2: Ch 1, [sc in next hdc, hdc in next sc] rep around, join in beg sc, turn.

Rnds 3–5: Rep Rnd 2.

Rnd 6: Ch 1, sc in first hdc, [hdc in next sc, sc in next hdc] 12 times, ch 5, sk next 5 sts, sc in next hdc, [hdc in next sc, sc in next hdc] 23 times, ch 5, sk next 5 sts, [sc in next hdc, hdc in next sc] 13 times, join in beg sc, turn.

Rnd 7: Ch 1, [sc in next st, hdc in next st] rep around, join in beg sc, turn. (108 sts)

Rnds 8–11: Rep Rnd 2.

Rnd 12: Ch 1, sc in first hdc, [hdc in next sc, sc in next hdc] 25 times, ch 5, sk next 5 sts, [sc in next hdc, hdc in next sc] 26 times, join in beg sc, turn.

Rnd 13: Rep Rnd 7.

Rnds 14–17: Rep Rnd 2.

Rnds 18–23: Rep Rnds 6–11, at the end of Rnd 23, fasten off, attach 2 strands of black.

Fourth section

Ring rnd: Rep ring rnd of 2nd section.

Rnds 1–23: With orange rep Rnds 1–23 of 2nd section.

Fifth section

Ring rnd: Rep ring rnd of 2nd section.

Rnds 1–23: With green, rep Rnds 1–23 of 2nd section.

Rnd 24: With 2 strands of black, working over last ring, ch 1, sc in each st around, join in beg sc, fasten off. (108 sc)

Jingle Bell Trim

Thread 4 jingle bells onto 1 strand black, with G hook, attach black in first sc of first ring rnd with a sl st, [ch 17, slide 1 bell up next to hook, ch 17, sk next 26 sc on ring, sl st in next st] 4 times, fasten off.

String Trim

With hook size G, attach 1 strand black to 13th sc of last ring with sl st, ch 39 sk next 28 sc, sl st in next sc, fasten off. Sk next 24 sc, attach 1 strand black in next sc with a sl st, ch 39, sk next 28 sc, sl st in next sc, fasten off.

Pompom

Make 2 pompoms each red, blue, yellow and orange. Using same color tog, tie 2 pompoms in 13th and 26th ch made on each string.

Trim

Rnd 1: With J hook, attach 1 strand black in any sc worked over first ring, ch 1, reverse sc in each sc around, join in beg sc, fasten off.

Rep Rnd 1 over sc sts of last ring attached to tunnel. ✄

One can choose a cat to fit almost any kind of decor, color scheme, income, personality or mood. But under the fur, whatever color it may be, there still lies, essentially unchanged, one of the world's truly free souls.

—Eric Gurney

Cozy Pet Bed & Blanket

Designs by Ruthie Marks

When it's time to relax, your pampered pet can sleep in comfort and style in this cushiony-soft and handsome pet bed. A textured stitch pattern around the sides adds interest to the design, and a removable blanket serves as a bed liner!

Skill Level: Beginner

Size

Small: 12 inches square

Medium: 15 inches square

Large: 18 inches square

Extra-large: 21 inches square

Materials

- Coats & Clark Red Heart Super Saver worsted weight yarn: 7½ (9, 11, 13) oz light sage #631, 3½ (4, 5, 6) oz dark sage #633, 2½ (3, 3½, 4) oz burgundy #376

- Sizes G/6 and J/10 crochet hooks or sizes needed to obtain gauge

- 1 (2, 2, 2) sheets 7-count 13½ x 22½ inches ultra stiff plastic canvas

- Yarn needle

Gauge

With G hook, 11 sc = 3 inches; 11 sc rnds = 3 inches; with J hook, 6 sc = 2 inches; 6 sc rnds = 2 inches

Check gauge to save time.

Pattern Notes

Weave in loose ends as work progresses.

Join rnds with a sl st unless otherwise stated.

Plastic Canvas Preparation

Cut 4 pieces of plastic canvas measuring 4⅛ x 11½ (4⅛ x 14½, 4⅛ x 17½, 4⅛ x 20½) inches.

Whipstitch the 4⅛-inch edges tog to form a 4-sided frame. Set aside.

Pattern Stitch

Extended sc: Insert hook in next st, yo, draw up a lp, [yo, draw through 1 lp on hook] 3 times, yo, draw through both lps on hook. Push ch to RS of work.

Bed

Bottom

Rnd 1: With G hook and light sage, ch 4, join to form a ring, ch 1, 8 sc in ring, join in beg sc. (8 sc)

Rnd 2: Ch 1, sc in first sc, 3 sc in next sc, [sc in next sc, 3 sc in next sc] rep around, join in beg sc. (16 sc)

Rnd 3: Ch 1, sc in each sc around, working 3 sc in center sc of each 3-sc group, join in beg sc. (24 sc)

Rnds 4–23 (4–28, 4–33, 4–39): Rep Rnd 3. (184, 224, 264, 304 sc)

Inner Side

Rnd 1: Working in back lps for this rnd only, ch 1, sc in each st around, join in beg sc.

Rnds 2–18: Ch 1, sc in each sc around, join in beg sc. At the end of Rnd 18, fasten off.

Outer Cuff

Rnd 1: Working in back lps for this rnd only, attach dark sage in

through sts of Rnd 13 and rem free lp of last rnd of bottom, sl st in each st around, fasten off.

Blanket

Note: *Fasten off color not in use as work progresses.*

Rnd 1: With hook size J and light sage, ch 2, 8 sc in 2nd ch from hook, join in beg sc.

Rnd 2: Ch 1, sc in first sc, 3 sc in next sc, [sc in next sc, 3 sc in next sc] rep around, join in beg sc. (16 sc)

Rnd 3: Ch 1, sc in each sc around, working 3 sc in each center sc of 3-sc group, join in beg sc. (24 sc)

Rnds 4 & 5: With dark sage, rep Rnd 3. (40 sc)

Rnd 6: With burgundy, rep Rnd 3. (48 sc)

Rnds 7–9: With light sage, rep Rnd 3. (72 sc)

Rep Rnds 4–9 until 17 (21, 25, 29) rnds are completed, maintaining color pattern. At the end of last rep, fasten off. (136, 168, 200, 232 sc)

Place blanket inside bed. ✂

Rnd 18, ch 1, sc in same st as beg ch-1, sc in each rem st around, join in beg sc. (184, 224, 264, 304 sc)

Rnd 2: Ch 1, sc in first st, extended as in next sc, [sc in next sc, extended sc in next sc] rep around, join in beg sc.

Rnd 3: Working in front lps for this rnd only, ch 4 (counts as first dc, ch 1), sk next extended sc, [dc in next sc, ch 1, sk next extended sc] rep around, join in 3rd ch of beg ch-4.

Rnd 4: Ch 1, sc in same st as beg ch-1, sc in next ch-1 sp, [sc in next dc, sc in next ch-1 sp] rep around, join in beg sc. (184, 224, 264, 304 sc)

Rnds 5–7: Rep Rnds 2–4.

Rnd 8: Working in front lps only, ch 1, sc in each st around, join in beg sc.

Rnds 9–13: Ch 1, sc in each sc around, join in beg sc. At the end of Rnd 13, draw up a lp, remove hook, do not fasten off.

Cuff Lining

Note: *Cuff lining is worked on WS of outer cuff.*

Rnd 1: Working in rem free lps of Rnd 2 of outer cuff, attach burgundy in any st, ch 1, sc in same st as beg ch-1, sc in each st around, join in beg sc.

Rnds 2–8: Ch 1, sc in each st around, join in beg sc.

Rnd 9: Working in sts of Rnd 8 and rem free lps of Rnd 7 of outer cuff at same time, ch 1, sc in each st around, join in beg sc, fasten off.

Finishing

Insert plastic canvas frame between sides and outer cuff.

Rnd 14: Pick up dropped lp from Rnd 13 of outer cuff, working

Adopting Spot

"Can't we take them all home?"
The little boy sadly said.
"Our house is too small,"
Said Mother, shaking her head.
"Choose one puppy to love,
and I'll crochet it a bed."
He chose a mixed-breed pup,
Brown with one white, spotted ear.
It rode home snuggled on his lap
And soon lost all its fear.
"This is your new home, Spot!
You're going to like it here!"
Mother kept her promise,
And chose soft yarn to crochet.
She finished the puppy's bed
By the middle of the day,
And then crocheted another
For a dog that had to stay.

Woven Jewel Blankie

Design by Bendy Carter

Your favorite dog or cat will appreciate the snuggly softness of his or her own blanket when settling down for a restful nap. Worsted weight yarn worked in a woven-look design creates the pretty pattern in this cozy pet comforter!

Skill Level: Beginner

Size: 24 inches square

Materials
- Coats & Clark Red Heart Super Saver worsted weight yarn: His: 12 oz fiesta jewel print #399 (MC), 8 oz black #312 (CC) Hers: 12 oz monet print #310 (MC), 8 oz soft white #316 (CC)
- Size G/6 crochet hook or size needed to obtain gauge
- Size F/5 crochet hook
- Yarn needle

Gauge
17 sts = 4 inches
Check gauge to save time.

Pattern Notes
Weave in loose ends as work progresses.

Join rnds with a sl st unless otherwise stated.

Wind CC into 3 separate balls before beg.

All crochet sts are worked with MC. Three strands of CC are held tog throughout unless otherwise stated.

Blankie
Row 1 (RS): With hook size G and MC, ch 101, holding 3 strands of CC on top of ch and working over 3 strands and into ch sts with MC, sc in 2nd ch from hook, [ch 2, sk next 2 chs, sc in next ch] rep across, turn. (34 sc; 33 ch-2 sps)

Row 2: Using MC, work ch 1 around CC, lay CC across row just made, working over CC with MC, sc in first sc, [ch 2, sk next ch-2 sp, working over CC, sc in next sc] rep across, turn.

Rep Row 2 until blankie measures 23½ inches from beg, ending with a WS row. At the end of last rep, fasten off CC, turn.

Edging
Rnd 1 (RS): With hook size F and MC, ch 1, work 100 sc evenly sp across each side, working ch 2 at each corner, join in beg sc.

Rnd 2 (RS): Ch 1, sc in each sc around, working [sc, ch 2, sc] in each corner ch-2 sp, join in beg sc, fasten off. ✄

Terry Pet Mat

Design by Bendy Carter

This scrumptiously soft and wonderfully warm mat is quick to stitch in an easy, one-piece pattern with luscious, light worsted terry yarn. Your pet will especially appreciate it when the weather is extra-frigid!

Skill Level: Beginner

Size: 21 inches square

Materials

- Coats & Clark Red Heart Baby Teri 3-ply worsted weight yarn
- (3 oz per skein): 2 skeins each white #9101 (MC) and lilac #9145 (CC)
- Size K/10½ crochet hook or size needed to obtain gauge
- Yarn needle

Gauge

11 sts = 4 inches

Check gauge to save time.

Pattern Notes

Weave in loose ends as work progresses.

Join rnds with a sl st unless otherwise stated.

Work with 2 strands held tog throughout.

Mat

Rnd 1: With 2 strands white held tog, ch 2, [2 sc, ch 2] 4 times in 2nd ch from hook, join in beg sc, turn. (8 sc; 4 ch-2 sps)

Rnd 2: Sl st into ch-2 sp, ch 1, sc in same ch-2 sp, *sc in each sc across to next ch-2 sp **, [sc, ch 2, sc] in corner ch-2 sp, rep from * around, ending last rep at **, sc in same ch-2 sp as beg sc, ch 2, join in beg sc, turn.

Rep Rnd 2 in the following color sequence. Fasten off color not in use.

Rnds 3 & 4: With 1 strand each white and lilac, rep Rnd 2.

Rnds 5 & 6: With 2 strands lilac, rep Rnd 2.

Rnds 7 & 8: With 1 strand each white and lilac, rep Rnd 2.

Rnds 9–12: With 2 strands white, rep Rnd 2.

Rnds 13–22: Rep Rnds 3–12.

Rnds 23–29: Rep Rnds 3–9. At the end of Rnd 29, fasten off. ✂

He is your friend and defender, your dog. He will be yours, faithful and true, to the last beat of his heart.

—Unknown

Feline Monitor Perch

Design by Bendy Carter

This cozy, easy-to-construct monitor perch is sure to make any high-tech feline happy while keeping kitty hair out of the computer. It makes a great floor perch for bird-watching, too!

Skill Level: Beginner

Size: 15 x 17 inches

Materials

- Coats & Clark Red Heart Super Saver worsted weight yarn: 8 oz black #312
- Coats & Clark Red Heart Baby Clouds yarn (6 oz per skein): 2 skeins aquamarine #9364
- Sizes H/8 and N/15 crochet hooks or sizes needed to obtain gauge
- 15 x 17 inches ¼-inch plywood
- 2 (1½ x 2⅛-inch) wooden spools*
- Tacky glue
- 4 size 3 snap fasteners
- 15 x 17 x 3-inch foam cushion
- 2 x 4 inches industrial strength hook-and-loop tape
- 48 inches elastic cord
- Sewing needle and black thread
- Yarn marker
- Yarn needle

Gauge

With N hook, 5 sts = 3 inches; 10 rows = 7 inches; with H hook, 6 sc = 2 inches; 6 sc rnds = 2 inches
Check gauge to save time.

Pattern Notes

Weave in loose ends as work progresses.

Join rnds with a sl st unless otherwise stated.

*All monitors are different. To find size spool needed, place plywood on top of monitor, measure to see what size legs are needed to make plywood level.

Board Casing

Rnd 1: With hook size H and black yarn, ch 46, 3 sc in 2nd ch from hook, sc in each of next 43 chs, 3 sc in last ch, working on opposite side of foundation ch, sc in each of next 43 chs, do not join. (92 sc)

Rnd 2: Sc in each sc around, do not join.

Rep Rnd 2 until casing is same size as board, do not stretch, sl st in next st, leaving a long length of yarn, fasten off.

Leg Pad

Make 2

Rnd 1: With hook size H and black, leaving an 8-inch length at beg, ch 2, 6 sc in 2nd ch from hook, do not join rnd. (6 sc)

Rnd 2: 2 sc in each sc around, do not join. (12 sc)

Rnd 3: Rep Rnd 2. (24 sc)

Rnd 4: Sc in each sc around, do not join.

Rnd 5: [Sc dec over next 2 sc] rep around, do not join. (12 sc)

Rnd 6: Rep Rnd 5, leaving a long length of yarn, fasten off. (6 sc)

Weave rem length through 6 sts; draw both beg and ending lengths through top opening, pull tight to close. Run both tails through center of spool. Place board in board casing and place board on monitor and mark where legs should go. Tie legs to bottom of board casing with beg and end tails. Apply tacky glue between leg pad and leg, leg and board casing, and board casing and board where legs are attached.

With rem length, sew board casing closed.

Using needle and black thread, sew snap fasteners on bottom of foam cushion and on top of board casing 1¼ inches from each corner. Snap cushion form onto board casing.

Place perch on top of monitor, mark bottom front of board casing and top of monitor where hook-and-loop tape should go. Stick gripper side to bottom front of board casing and stick pad side on top of monitor.

Perch Cover

Row 1: With hook size N and aquamarine, ch 26, sc in 2nd ch from hook, [hdc in next ch, sc in next ch] rep across, turn. (25 sts)

Row 2: Ch 1, sc in first st, [sc in next st, hdc in next st] rep across to last 2 sts, sc in each of next 2 sts, turn.

Row 3: Ch 1, sc in first st, [hdc in next st, sc in next st] rep across, turn.

Row 4: Rep Row 2, fasten off, turn.

Row 5: Ch 6, sc in first st, [hdc in next st, sc in next st] rep across, turn.

Row 6: Ch 7, sc in 2nd ch from hook, [sc in next st, hdc in next st] rep in each ch and each st across to last 2 chs, sc in each of next 2 chs, turn. (37 sts)

Row 7: Rep Row 3.

Rows 8–29: Rep Rows 2 and 3.

Row 30: Rep Row 2, fasten off.

Row 31: Sk first 6 sts, attach aquamarine in 7th st, ch 1, sc in same st as beg ch-1, [hdc in next st, sc in next st] rep across to last 6 sts, turn. (25 sts)

Rows 32–35: Rep Rows 2 and 3. At the end of Row 35, fasten off. Sew each of the 4 corner seams.

Edging

Rnd 1: With hook size N, attach aquamarine in any corner, ch 1, sc around entire bottom, working 25 sc on each short side and 28 sc on each long side, join in beg sc.

Rnd 2: Ch 1, holding elastic cord next to last rnd and working over elastic cord, sc in each st around, join in beg sc, fasten off.

Place perch cover over foam cushion, tuck last rnd between foam cushion and board casing, pull ends of elastic cord to adjust fit, tie ends in a knot, trim off excess elastic cord. ✂

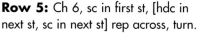

The smallest feline is a masterpiece.

—Leonardo Da Vinci

Doggy Barbells

Designs by Bendy Carter

Dogs and puppies will have hours of fun playing with these intriguing and versatile barbell toys! With the "weights" in place, you can enjoy a tug-of-war game with your favorite canine. For additional fun, remove the weights and toss them like Frisbees, and use the center bar like a stick for a fun game of fetch.

Skill Level: Beginner

Size:

Small barbell: 12 inches long
Large barbell: 18 inches long

Materials

- Coats & Clark Red Heart Kids worsted weight yarn (5 oz per skein): 2 skeins each red #2390, blue #2845, yellow #2230, 1 skein green #2677
- Size G/6 crochet hook or size needed to obtain gauge
- 12 inches ½-inch-diameter wooden dowel (small barbell)
- 18 inches 1-inch-diameter wooden dowel (large barbell)
- Fiberfill
- Yarn needle

Gauge

6 sc rnds = 1½ inches; 4 sc = 1 inch

Check gauge to save time.

Pattern Notes

Weave in loose ends as work progresses.

Join rnds with a sl st unless otherwise stated.

Small Doggy Barbell

Red Disk

Make 2

Rnd 1: With red, ch 12, join to form a ring, ch 1, sc in each sc around, join in beg sc. (12 sc)

Rnd 2: Ch 1, 2 sc in each sc around, join in beg sc. (24 sc)

Rnd 3: Ch 1, sc in each sc around, join in beg sc.

Rnd 4: Ch 1, [sc in each of next 2 sc, 2 sc in next sc] rep around, join in beg sc. (36 sc)

Rnd 5: Rep Rnd 3.

Rnd 6: Ch 1, [sc in each of next 3 sc, 2 sc in next sc] rep around, join in beg sc. (48 sc)

Rnds 7–10: Rep Rnd 3.

Rnd 11: Ch 1, [sc in each of next 3 sc, sc dec over next 2 sc] rep around, join in beg sc. (36 sc)

Rnd 12: Rep Rnd 3.

Rnd 13: Ch 1, [sc in each of next 2 sc, sc dec over next 2 sc] rep around, join in beg sc. (24 sc)

Rnd 14: Rep Rnd 3.

Rnd 15: Ch 1, [sc dec over next 2 sc] rep around, join in beg sc, leaving a length of yarn, fasten off. (12 sc)

Blue Disk

Make 2

Rnd 1: With blue, ch 12, join to form a ring, ch 1, sc in each ch around, join in beg sc. (12 sc)

Rnds 2–4: Rep Rnds 2–4 of red disk. (36 sc)

Rnds 5–8: Ch 1, sc in each sc around, join in beg sc.

Rnds 9–11: Rep Rnds 13–15 of red disk. (12 sc)

Yellow Disk

Make 2

Rnd 1: With yellow, ch 12, join to form a ring, ch 1, sc in each ch around, join in beg sc. (12 sc)

Rnd 2: Rep Rnd 2 of red disk. (24 sc)

Rnds 3–6: Ch 1, sc in each sc around, join in beg sc.

Rnd 7: Rep Rnd 11 of red disk, leaving a length of yarn, fasten off. (12 sc)

For each disk, sew last rnd to opposite side of foundation ch, stuffing with fiberfill as work progresses.

Bar

Rnd 1 (RS): With green, leaving a length at beg, ch 2, 6 sc in 2nd ch from hook, join in beg sc. (6 sc)

Rnd 2: Ch 1, 2 sc in each sc around, join in beg sc. (12 sc)

Rnd 3: Ch 1, [sc in next sc, 2 sc in next sc] rep around, join in beg sc. (18 sc)

Note: *Pull rem beg length from Rnd 1 and secure on WS of bar.*

Rnd 4: Ch 1, sc in each sc around, join in beg sc.

Rnd 5: Ch 1, [sc in next sc, sc dec over next 2 sc] rep around, join in beg sc. (12 sc)

There is no psychiatrist in the world like a puppy licking your face.

—Ben Williams

Rnds 6–28: Rep Rnd 4. At the end of last rep, draw up a lp, remove hook.

Insert 12-inch wooden dowel into opening, stuffing with fiberfill around dowel. Continue stuffing with fiberfill as work progresses. Pick up dropped lp.

Rnds 29–51: Rep Rnd 4.

Rnd 52: Rep Rnd 3. (18 sc)

Rnd 53: Rep Rnd 4.

Rnd 54: Rep Rnd 5. (12 sc)

Rnd 55: Ch 1, [sc dec over next 2 sc] rep around, join in beg sc, leaving a length of yarn, fasten off. (6 sc)

Weave rem length through sts of Rnd 55, draw opening closed, secure and fasten off.

Place 3 weight disks on each end of bar.

Large Doggy Barbell

Red Disk
Make 2

Rnd 1: With red, ch 24, join to form a ring, ch 1, sc in each ch around, join in beg sc. (24 sc)

Rnd 2: Ch 1, 2 sc in each sc around, join in beg sc. (48 sc)

Rnd 3: Ch 1, sc in each sc around, join in beg sc.

Rnd 4: Ch 1, [sc in each of next 2 sc, 2 sc in next sc] rep around, join in beg sc. (64 sc)

Rnd 5: Rep Rnd 3.

Rnd 6: Ch 1, [sc in each of next 3 sc, 2 sc in next sc] rep around, join in beg sc. (80 sc)

Rnd 7: Rep Rnd 3.

Rnd 8: Ch 1, [sc in each of next 4 sc, 2 sc in next sc] rep around, join in beg sc. (96 sc)

Rnds 9–14: Rep Rnd 3.

Rnd 15: Ch 1, [sc in each of next 4 sc, sc dec over next 2 sc] rep around, join in beg sc. (80 sc)

Rnd 16: Rep Rnd 3.

Rnd 17: Ch 1, [sc in each of next 3 sc, sc dec over next 2 sc] rep around, join in beg sc. (64 sc)

Rnd 18: Rep Rnd 3.

Rnd 19: Ch 1, [sc in each of next 2 sc, sc dec over next 2 sc] rep around, join in beg sc. (48 sc)

Rnd 20: Rep Rnd 3.

Rnd 21: Ch 1, [sc dec over next 2 sc] rep around, join in beg sc, leaving a length of yarn, fasten off. (24 sc)

Blue Disk
Make 2

Rnd 1: With blue, ch 24, join to form a ring, ch 1, sc in each ch around, join in beg sc. (24 sc)

Rnds 2–6: Rep Rnds 2–6 of red disk. (80 sc)

Rnds 7–12: Ch 1, sc in each sc around, join in beg sc.

Rnds 13–17: Rep Rnds 17–21 of red disk. (24 sc)

Continued on page 111

His & Her Dog Sweaters

Designs by Bendy Carter

The well-dressed canine will appreciate having a smartly styled coat for those cold-weather outings. The pattern is styled for either boy or girl, and can be made in three sizes with soft wool-blend worsted yarn.

Skill Level: Beginner

Size
Length: Back neck to beg of tail, 9 (13, 17) inches
Chest: 11 (15, 19) inches

Materials
- Lion Brand Wool-Ease worsted weight yarn (3 oz per skein solid, 2½ oz per skein multi): His: 2 (2, 3) skeins natural heather #98; Hers: 2 (3, 4) skeins white multi #301
- Size H/8 crochet hook or size needed to obtain gauge
- Size G/6 crochet hook
- 3 (4, 5) snap fasteners each sweater
- 3 (4, 5) 15mm bow tie buttons for him
- 3 (4, 5) 15mm bow buttons for her
- Yarn markers
- Sewing needle and thread
- Yarn needle

Gauge
With H hook, 4 sts = 1 inch; 3 rows = 1 inch
Check gauge to save time.

Pattern Notes
Weave in loose ends as work progresses.

Join rnds with a sl st unless otherwise stated.

Ch-2 counts as first hdc throughout.

Pattern Stitches
Front lp hdc: When looking at top of hdc there are 3 horizontal lps, work hdc in first lp only.

Back lp hdc: When looking at top of hdc there are 3 horizontal lps, work hdc in last lp only.

His Body
Row 1 (WS): Beg at tail end, with hook size H, ch 33 (45, 57), hdc in 3rd ch from hook, hdc in each rem ch across, turn. (32, 44, 56 hdc)

Row 2: Ch 2, [front lp hdc in next st, back lp hdc in next st] rep across to last st, hdc in last st, turn.

Rep Row 2 until body measures 1 (2¾, 4½) inches.

Row 3: Ch 2, [front lp hdc, back lp hdc, front lp hdc] in next st, [back lp hdc in next st, front lp hdc in next st] rep across to last 2 sts, [back lp hdc, front lp hdc, back lp hdc] in next st,

hdc in last st, turn. (36, 48, 60 sts)
[Rep Row 3] 1 (2, 3) times. (40, 56, 72 sts)

Place a yarn marker at beg and end of last row.

Rep Row 2 until body measures 3½ (5¾, 8¼) inches.

Her Body
Row 1 (WS): Beg at tail end, with hook size H, ch 41 (57, 73), hdc in 3rd ch from hook, hdc in each rem ch across, turn. (40, 56, 72 hdc)

Row 2: Ch 2, [front lp hdc in next st, back lp hdc in next st] rep across, turn.

Rep Row 2 until body measures 1¾ (3¾, 5¾) inches. Place a yarn marker at beg and end of last row.

Rep Row 2 until body measures 3¼ (5¾, 8¼) inches.

His & Her Armhole Shaping
First front
Row 1: Ch 2, [front lp hdc in next st, back lp hdc in next st] 2 (3, 4) times, hdc in next st, turn.

Rep Row 2 of body until armhole opening measures 2¾ (3¾, 4¾) inches, working an odd number of rows, fasten off.

Back
Row 1: Sk next 2 sts on last row of body, attach yarn in next st, ch 2, [front lp hdc in next st, back lp hdc in next st] 11 (17, 23) times, hdc in next st, turn.

Rep Row 2 of body until armhole opening measures 2¾ (3¾, 4¾) inches, working an odd number of rows, fasten off.

Second front
Row 1: Sk next 2 sts in last row of body, attach yarn in next st, ch 2, [front lp hdc in next st, back lp hdc in next st] 2 (3, 4) times, hdc in next st, turn.

Rep Row 2 of body until length measures the same as first front, do not fasten off, turn.

Neck Shaping
Row 1: Ch 2, [front lp hdc in next st, back lp hdc in next st] 2 (3, 4)

times, hdc in next st, hdc in first st on back, [front lp hdc in next st, back lp hdc in next st] 11 (17, 23) times, hdc in next st, hdc in first st on first front, [front lp hdc in next st, back lp hdc in next st] 2 (3, 4) times, turn. (36, 52, 68 sts)

Rep Row 2 of body until neck shaping measures 1 (1½, 2) inches, then fasten off.

His & Her Sleeve
Make 2

Rnd 1 (RS): With hook size G, attach yarn at opening, ch 2, working an even number of sts, hdc around opening, join in 2nd ch of beg ch-2.

Rnd 2: Ch 2, [fpdc around next st, bpdc around next st] rep around, join in 2nd ch of beg ch-2.

Rnd 3: Ch 2, [fpdc around next fpdc, bpdc around next bpdc] rep around, join in 2nd ch of beg ch-2.

Rep Rnd 3 until his sleeve measures 2 (2½, 3) inches, fasten off.

Rep Rnd 3 until her sleeve measures 1¾ (2¼, 2¾) inches, do not fasten off.

Her sleeve trim
Rnd 1: Ch 1, sc in same st as beg ch-1, ch 3, [sc in next st, ch 3] rep around, join in beg sc, fasten off.

His & Her Bottom Ribbing
Row 1 (RS): With hook size G, attach yarn at opening in beg ch, ch 2, working around post of hdc of Row 1, [fpdc around post of next st, bpdc around post of next st] rep across to last st, hdc in last st, turn.

Row 2: Ch 2, [fpdc around post of next st, bpdc around post of next st] rep across to last st, hdc in last st, turn.

Rep Row 2 for his until ribbing measures 2 inches, fasten off.

Rep Row 2 of ribbing for her until ribbing measures 1¾ inches, ending on a WS row, turn.

Her trim
Ch 1, sc in first st, [ch 3, sc in next st] rep across edge, fasten off.

His & Her Right
Front Edging
Row 1 (RS): With size G hook attach yarn at bottom opening, ch 1, sc evenly sp up front edge, turn.

Row 2: Ch 1, sc in each sc across to marker, turn, leaving rem sts unworked.

Rows 3–5: Ch 1, sc in each sc of previous row, turn. At the end of last rep, fasten off.

His & Her Left Front Edging
Row 1 (RS): With hook size G, attach yarn at top opening, ch 1, sc evenly sp down front edge, fasten off, turn.

Row 2 (WS): Attach yarn in line with marker, ch 1, sc in each sc across, turn.

Rows 3–5: Ch 1, sc in each sc of previous row, turn. At the end of last rep, fasten off.

Sew buttons evenly sp across left front band for his and right front band for her. Sew snap fasteners under buttons.

His & Her Neckline Ribbing
Row 1 (RS): With hook size G, attach yarn at right neck opening (not in front edging), ch 2, work an even number of hdc across neckline to left front edging, turn.

Row 2: Ch 2, [fpdc around post of next st, bpdc around post of next st] rep across to last st, hdc in last st, turn.

Rep Row 2 for his until ribbing measures 3 inches, leaving a length of yarn, fasten off.

Rep Row 2 for her until ribbing measures 3 inches from beg, ending with a WS row, turn.

Her trim
Ch 1, sc in first st, [ch 3, sc in next st] rep across, leaving a length of yarn, fasten off.

For both, fold neckline ribbing in half and sew first and last ribbing rows tog. ✀

Love My Pet Mat & Toys

Designs by Bendy Carter

This versatile, pet-pleasing mat can be customized for cats and dogs with interchangeable mouse and bone appliqués. It's cozy and chic in lustrous sport weight yarn, and even includes two fun stuffed toys!

Skill Level: Beginner

Size

Mat: 19 inches square

Materials

- J. & P. Coats Luster Sheen sport weight yarn (1¾ oz per ball): 4 balls white #1, 2 balls tea leaf #615, 1 ball crystal pink #206
- Size H/8 crochet hook or size needed to obtain gauge
- Size D/3 crochet hook
- Fiberfill
- Yarn needle

Gauge

With H hook, 5 sc = 1½ inches; 5 sc rows = 1½ inches

Check gauge to save time.

Pattern Notes

Weave in loose ends as work progresses.

Join rnds with a sl st unless otherwise stated.

Dog Bone Toy

Rnd 1: With hook size D and white, ch 6, sc in 2nd ch from hook, sc in each of next 4 chs, working on opposite side of foundation ch, sc in each of next 5 chs, do not join. (10 sc)

Rnd 2: Sc in each of next 10 sc, do not join.

Rep Rnd 2 until from beg tube it measures 14 inches, leaving a length of yarn, fasten off.

Using first 6 inches of tube, fold beg end down, around, then tuck under fold and sew in place. Stuff with fiberfill the next 2 inches of tube. Sew end of tube closed, using last 6 inches of tube, fold end down, around and then tuck under beg fold and sew in place.

Mouse Toy

With hook size D and white, ch 2, 4 sc in 2nd ch from hook, working in rnds without joining and working continuously around, sc in first st, [2 sc in next sc] twice, sc in each of next 3 sts, [2 sc in next sc] twice, sc in each of next 5 sts, [2 sc in next sc] twice, sc in each of next 7 sts, [2 sc in next sc] twice, sc in each of next 9 sts, [2 sc in next sc] twice, sc in each of next 38 sts, [sc dec over next 2 sts] twice, sc in each of next 8 sts, [sc dec over next 2 sts] 3 times, draw up a lp, remove hook, do not fasten off.

Eye

With crystal pink, embroider satin st eyes.

Ear

Make 2

With hook size D and crystal pink, ch 4, sl st in beg ch, fasten off. Sew ears to head. Stuff mouse with fiberfill.

Pick up dropped lp and continue on with mouse, sc in each of next 4 sts, [sc dec over next 2 sts] 3 times, sc in next 2 sts, sl st in next st, leaving a length of yarn, fasten off. Weave rem length through sts, pull to close opening and secure.

Tail

With hook size D and white, ch 13, sl st in 2nd ch from hook, sl st in each rem ch across, fasten off. Attach tail to back body of mouse.

Dog Bone Appliqué

Make 5

Row 1: With hook size D and white, ch 4, sc in 2nd ch from hook, sc in each rem ch across, turn. (3 sc)

Rows 2–12: Ch 1, sc in each of next 3 sc, turn.

Rnd 13: [Ch 4 (counts as first tr), dc, sc] in first sc, sl st in next sc, [sc, dc, tr] in next sc, *working down side edge of rows, 2 dtr in end of first row, [tr, dc, sc] in end of next row, sc in each of next 8 rows, [sc, dc, tr] in end of next row, 2 dtr in end of last row **, working across opposite side of foundation ch, [tr, dc, sc] in first ch, sl st in next ch, [sc, dc, tr] in next ch, rep from *, ending rep at **, join in 4th ch of beg ch-4, leaving a length of yarn, fasten off.

Mouse Appliqué

Make 5

Row 1 (RS): With hook size D and white, ch 31, sc in 2nd ch from hook, sc in each of next 11 chs, turn. (12 sc)

Row 2: Ch 1, sc in each sc across to last 2 sc, sc dec over next 2 sc, turn. (11 sc)

Row 3: Ch 1, sc dec over next 2 sc, sc in each sc across to last 2 sc, sc dec over next 2 sc, turn. (9 sc)

Row 4: Rep Row 2. (8 sc)

Row 5: Rep Row 3, fasten off. (6 sc)

Rnd 6 (RS): Attach yarn at bottom of mouse at tail, working across bottom of mouse, then around top of mouse, sl st evenly sp around mouse and sl st in each ch of beg foundation ch, leaving a length of yarn, fasten off.

Eye

With crystal pink work a cross-st on mouse for eye.

Ear

Make 1

Rep ear as for mouse toy and sew to head.

Heart Appliqué

Make 4

Row 1: With hook size D and crystal pink, ch 2, sc in 2nd ch from hook, turn. (1 sc)

Row 2: Ch 1, 3 sc in sc, turn. (3 sc)

Rows 3–6: Ch 1, 2 sc in first sc, sc in each sc across to last sc, 2 sc in last sc, turn. (11 sc)

Rows 7 & 8: Ch 1, sc in each st across, turn.

First lobe

Row 1: Ch 1, sc in each of next 5 sc, turn. (5 sc)

Row 2: Sl st in first 2 sts, ch 1, sc in same st as last sl st and in each rem sc across, turn. (4 sc)

Row 3: Sl st in first 2 sts, ch 1, sc in same st as last sl st, sc in next st, fasten off. (2 sc)

Second lobe

Row 1: Sk next sc of Row 8, attach yarn in next st, ch 1, sc in same st as beg ch-1, sc in each of next 4 sc, turn. (5 sc)

Row 2: Ch 1, sc in each of next 4 sc, turn. (4 sc)

Row 3: Rep Row 3 of first lobe, turn.

Rnd 4: Ch 1, working around outer edge of yarn, sc evenly sp around, join in beg sc, leaving a length of yarn, fasten off.

Blanket Square

Note: *Make 4 white and 5 tea leaf.*

Row 1: With hook size H and 2 strands held tog, ch 16, sc in 2nd ch from hook, sc in each rem ch across, turn. (15 sc)

Rows 2–16: Ch 1, sc in each sc across, turn.

Cat & Mouse

*A basketful of crocheted mice
Accompanies me to the vet's.
While my cat gets her booster shots,
I give toys to other folks' pets.
Each mouse is bulging with catnip
And each has a chain-crocheted tail.
They'll keep any feline happy
In the waiting room without fail!*

Row 17: Ch 1, sc in each sc across.

Rnd 18: Working around outer edge of square, ch 1, work 15 sc across edge, ch 2 in each corner, join in beg sc, fasten off.

Note: *Use 1 strand of each white and crystal pink held tog on white squares and 1 strand of each white and tea leaf held tog on tea leaf squares.*

Rnd 19: Ch 1, sc in each sc around, working [sc, ch 2, sc] in each corner ch-2 sp, join in beg sc, fasten off.

Continued on page 111

Braided-Look Pet Rug

Design by Darlene Polachic

Use as many or as few colors of worsted weight yarn as you like to create a cheerful and cozy rug for your favorite four-legged companion. This great scrap project can be made in almost any size to fit small and large pets.

Skill Level: Beginner

Size: 14½ x 19½ inches

Materials

- Worsted weight cotton yarn

- (1¾ oz per ball): 7 colors as desired
- Size C/2 crochet hook or size needed to obtain gauge
- Yarn needle

Gauge

5 dc = 1 inch; 4 dc rnds = 1½ inches

Check gauge to save time.

Pattern Notes

Weave in loose ends as work progresses.

Join rnds with a sl st unless otherwise stated.

Row 1 establishes RS of rug.

Ch-3 counts as first dc throughout.

With additional materials, rug can be enlarged to any size desired by maintaining inc of 6 dc on each rounded end of rug.

Rug

Row 1 (RS): With first color, ch 15, dc in 3rd ch from hook, dc in each rem ch across, fasten off. (14 dc)

Rnd 2: Attach next color in any dc, working around entire outer edge, ch 3, dc in each dc and each ch of opposite side of foundation ch, working 6 dc over each end dc of Row 1, join in 3rd ch of beg ch-3. (36 dc)

Rnd 3: Ch 3, dc in each dc around, working 2 dc in each of 6 dc sts on each rounded end of rug, join in 3rd ch of beg ch-3, fasten off. (48 dc)

Rnd 4: Attach next color in any dc, ch 3, dc in each dc around, working [2 dc in next dc, dc in next dc] 6 times on each rounded end of rug, join in 3rd ch of beg ch-3. (60 dc)

Rnd 5: Ch 3, dc in each dc around, working [2 dc in next dc, dc in next dc] 6 times on each rounded end of rug, join in 3rd ch of beg ch-3. (72 dc)

Rnd 6: Rep Rnd 5, fasten off. (84 dc)

Rnd 7: Attach next color in any dc, ch 3, dc in each dc around, working [2 dc in next dc, dc in each of next 2 dc] 6 times evenly

sp over 18 dc of each rounded end of rug, join in 3rd ch of beg ch-3. (96 dc)

Rnd 8: Ch 3, dc in each dc around, working [2 dc in next dc, dc in each of next 3 dc] 6 times evenly sp over 24 dc of each rounded end of rug, join in 3rd ch of beg ch-3. (108 dc)

Rnd 9: Ch 3, dc in each dc

around, working [2 dc in next dc, dc in each of next 4 dc] 6 times evenly sp over 30 dc of each rounded end of rug, join in 3rd ch of beg ch-3, fasten off. (120 dc)

Rnds 10–18: Continue in pattern of 3 rnds each color, ch 3, dc in each dc around, working [2 dc in next dc, dc in each of next 4 dc] 6 times evenly sp over 30 dc of each

rounded end of rug, join in 3rd ch of beg ch-3. (228 dc)

Rnd 19: Attach next color, ch 3, dc around, working [2 dc in next dc, dc in each of next 9 dc] 6 times evenly sp over 60 dc of each rounded end of rug, join in 3rd ch of beg ch-3. (240 dc)

Rnd 20: Rep Rnd 19, fasten off. (252 dc) ✂

Doggy Barbells

Continued from page 105

Yellow Disk
Make 2

Rnd 1: With yellow, ch 24, join to form a ring, ch 1, sc in each sc around, join in beg sc. (24 sc)

Rnds 2–4: Rep Rnds 2–4 of red disk. (64 sc)

Rnds 5–10: Ch 1, sc in each sc around, join in beg sc.

Rnds 11–13: Rep Rnds 19–21 of red disk. (24 sc)

For each disk, sew last rnd to opposite side of foundation ch, stuffing with fiberfill as work progresses.

Bar

Rnd 1 (RS): With green, leaving a length of yarn at beg, ch 2, 6 sc in 2nd ch from hook, join in beg sc. (6 sc)

Rnd 2: Ch 1, 2 sc in each sc around, join in beg sc. (12 sc)

Rnd 3: Ch 1, [sc in next sc, 2 sc in next sc] rep around, join in beg sc. (18 sc)

Note: *Pull rem beg length from Rnd 1 and secure on WS of bar.*

Rnd 4: Ch 1, [sc in each of next 2 sc, 2 sc in next sc] rep around, join in beg sc. (24 sc)

Rnd 5: Ch 1, [sc in each of next 3 sc, 2 sc in next sc] rep around, join in beg sc. (30 sc)

Rnd 6: Ch 1, [sc in each of next 4 sc, 2 sc in next sc] rep around, join in beg sc. (36 sc)

Rnd 7: Ch 1, sc in each sc around, join in beg sc.

Rnd 8: Rep Rnd 7.

Rnd 9: Ch 1, [sc in each of next 4 sc, sc dec over next 2 sc] rep around, join in beg sc. (30 sc)

Rnd 10: Ch 1, [sc in each of next 3 sc, sc dec over next 2 sc] rep

around, join in beg sc. (24 sc)

Rnds 11–40: Rep Rnd 7. At the end of Rnd 40, draw up a lp, remove hook.

Insert 18-inch dowel into opening, stuffing with fiberfill around dowel. Continue stuffing with fiberfill as work progresses. Pick up dropped lp.

Rnds 41–71: Rep Rnd 7.

Rnds 72–77: Rep Rnds 5–10. (24 sc)

Rnd 78: Ch 1, [sc in each of next 2 sc, sc dec over next 2 sc] rep around, join in beg sc. (18 sc)

Rnd 79: Ch 1, [sc in next sc, sc dec over next 2 sc] rep around, join in beg sc. (12 sc)

Rnd 80: Ch 1, [sc dec over next 2 sc] rep around, join in beg sc, leaving a length of yarn, fasten off. (6 sc)

Weave rem length through sts of Rnd 80, pull to close opening and secure. Place 3 weight disks on each end of bar. ✂

Love My Pet Mat & Toys

Continued from page 109

Rnd 20: Using 2 strands of white held tog for each square, attach white in back lp of any st, ch 1, sc in back lp of each st around, working [dc, ch 1, dc] into ch-2 sp of Rnd 18 and working sts behind ch-2 sp

of Rnd 19, join in beg sc, fasten off.

Assembly
Sew a heart appliqué to center of each white square; sew a bone or mouse appliqué to center of each tea leaf square.

Sew 3 squares tog for first row: tea leaf, white and tea leaf. Sew 3 squares tog for 2nd row: white, tea leaf and white. Third row of squares is the same as the first. Sew rows tog.

Edging
Rnd 1: With hook size H attach 2

strands of white in corner ch-1 sp, ch 1, sc in same corner sp, *work 57 sc across edge to next corner ch-1 sp **, [sc, ch 2, sc] in corner ch-1 sp, rep from * around, ending last rep at **, sc in same ch-1 sp as beg sc, ch 2, join in beg sc.

Rnd 2: Ch 1, sc in same st as beg ch-1, *[ch 3, sl st in first ch of ch-3, sk next st, sc in next st] 29 times, ch 3, sl st in first ch, sc in corner ch-2 sp, ch 3, sl st in first ch **, sc in next st, rep from * around, ending last rep at **, join in beg sc, fasten off. ✂

Sensational Seniors

Today's seniors are more young at heart than ever! They enjoy a variety of fun hobbies, give countless hours volunteering in their communities, and many are even beginning second careers. Style as well as comfort plays an important part in their everyday lives, and for this chapter, we've selected a special assortment of projects to answer both needs. From fashions and accessories to a variety of cozy comforts, you're sure to find the perfect gifts to delight the sensational seniors in your life!

Whether 17 or 70, there is in every being's heart the love of wonder, the unfailing childlike appetite for what is next, and joy in the game of life.

—S. Hall Young

Shawl-Collar Cardigan

Design by Melissa Leapman

This beautiful jacket-style sweater makes a stunning gift for any special lady in your life. Simple, classic styling and gorgeous hand-painted yarn combine to create a true work of fashion art!

Skill Level: Beginner

Size: Lady's small (medium, large, extra-large)

Garment chest: 37¾ (40, 43½, 46¾) inches

Back length: 23½ (24, 24½, 25) inches

Materials
- Wool-blend jewel tone variegated worsted weight yarn: 28 (32, 36, 40) oz sapphire
- Size H/8 crochet hook or size needed to obtain gauge
- 7 matching ¾-inch shank buttons
- Yarn markers
- Sewing needle and thread
- Tapestry needle

Gauge

14 sts = 4 inches; 12 rows = 4 inches

Check gauge to save time.

Pattern Notes

Weave in loose ends as work progresses.

Ch-3 counts as first dc throughout.

To avoid color blotches when working with variegated yarns, use 2 balls of yarn alternately, working 2 rows with first ball, then 2 rows with the 2nd ball throughout.

Pattern st of cardigan is established in Rows 2 and 3 of back unless otherwise stated, working sc in each dc, dc in each sc.

Back

Row 1 (RS): Beg at bottom, ch 66 (70, 76, 82), sc in 2nd ch from hook, [dc in next ch, sc in next ch] rep across, turn. (65, 69, 75, 81 sts)

Row 2: Ch 3, [sc in next dc, dc in next sc] rep across, turn.

Row 3: Ch 1, [sc in next dc, dc in next sc] rep across, turn.

Rows 4–47: Rep Rows 2 and 3.

Armhole shaping

Row 48: Sl st in each of next 4 (6, 6, 8) sts, [sl st, ch 3] in next st, [sc in next dc, dc in next sc] rep across leaving last 4 (6, 6, 8) sts unworked, turn. (57, 57, 63, 65 sts)

Row 49: Rep Row 3.

Rows 50–72 (50–76, 50–76, 50–78): Rep Rows 2 and 3. At the end of last rep, fasten off.

Pocket Lining

Make 2

Row 1: Ch 18, sc in 2nd ch from hook, [dc in next ch, sc in next ch] rep across, turn. (17 sts)

Rows 2–17: Rep Rows 2 and 3 of back, at the end of last rep, fasten off.

Left Front

Row 1 (RS): Ch 36 (38, 42, 44), sc in 2nd ch from hook, [dc in next ch, sc in next ch] rep across, turn. (35, 37, 41, 43 sts)

Rows 2–19: Rep Rows 2 and 3 of back.

Row 20 (WS): Ch 3, work in pattern across 7 (9, 11, 11) sts, pick up pocket lining and holding in place, work in pattern across 17 sts of pocket lining, sk next 17 sts of front, work in pattern across rem 10 (10, 12, 14) sts, turn.

Row 21: Rep Row 3 of back.

Rows 22–47: Rep Rows 2 and 3 of back.

Armhole shaping

Row 48 (WS): Ch 3, work in pattern across leaving last 4 (6, 6, 8) sts unworked, turn. (31, 31, 35, 35 sts)

Rows 49–50 (49–52, 49–52, 49–54): Rep Rows 3 and 2 of back.

Note: *Place a marker at neckline edge, this will be the ending point of collar.*

You can take no credit for beauty at 16; it was given to you. But if you are beautiful at 60, it will be your own doing. Then you may be proud of it, and be loved for it.

—Marie Stopes

Neck shaping

Row 1 (RS): Ch 1, work in pattern across to last 2 sts, dc dec over last 2 sts, turn. (30, 30, 34, 34 sts)

Row 2: Ch 1, sk first st, work in pattern across, turn. (29, 29, 33, 33 sts)

Rows 3–8: Rep Rows 1 and 2 of neck shaping. (23, 23, 27, 27 sts)

Row 9: Ch 1, work in pattern across, turn.

Row 10: Ch 1, sk first st, work in pattern across row, turn. (22, 22, 26, 26 sts)

Rows 11–18 (11–18, 11–22, 11–22): Rep Rows 9 and 10. (18, 18, 20, 20 sts)

Rows 19–22 (19–24, 23 & 24, 23 & 24): Work in pattern across each row, turn. At the end of last rep, fasten off.

Right Front

Rows 1 & 2: Rep Rows 1 and 2 of left front.

Row 3: Ch 1, work first 2 sts in

pattern, ch 2, sk next 2 sts (button-hole), work in pattern across rem sts, turn.

Row 4: Ch 3, work in pattern in each st across, turn.

Row 5: Ch 1, work in pattern across, turn.

Rows 6–10: Rep Rows 4 and 5, ending with a Row 4.

Rows 11–18: Rep Rows 3–10.

Row 19: Rep Row 3.

Row 20 (WS): Ch 3, work in pattern across 9 (9, 11, 13) sts, pick up pocket lining and holding in place, working in pattern across 17 sts of pocket lining, sk next 17 sts of right front, work in pattern across rem 8 (10, 12, 12) sts, turn.

Rows 21–26: Rep Rows 5 and 4.

Rows 27–47: Rep Rows 3–10, ending with pattern Row 7.

Armhole shaping

Row 48: Sl st in first 4 (6, 6, 8) sts, [sl st, ch 3] in next st, work in pattern across row, turn. (31, 31, 35, 35 sts)

Rows (49 & 50, 49 & 50, 49 & 50) (for medium, large and extra-large sizes only): Rep Rows 5 and 4.

Row 49 (51, 51, 51) (all sizes): Rep Row 3.

Row 50 (52, 52, 52): Rep Row 4.

Rows 53 & 54 (extra-large size only): Rep Rows 5 and 4.

Note: Place a marker at neckline edge, this will be the starting point of collar.

Neck shaping

Row 1: Ch 1, sk first st, work in pattern across, turn. (30, 30, 34, 34 sts)

Row 2: Ch 1, work in pattern across to last 2 sts, dc dec over last 2 sts, turn. (29, 29, 33, 33 sts)

Rows 3–8: Rep Rows 1 and 2 of

neck shaping, ending with Row 2. (23, 23, 27, 27 sts)

Row 9: Ch 1, work in pattern across, turn.

Row 10: Ch 1, work in pattern across to last 2 sts, dc dec over last 2 sts, turn. (22, 22, 26, 26 sts)

Rows 11–18 (11–18, 11–22, 11–22): Rep Rows 9 and 10. (18, 18, 20, 20 sts)

Rows 19–22 (19–24, 23 & 24, 23 & 24): Ch 1, work in pattern across row, turn. At the end of last rep, fasten off.

Sleeve

Make 2

Row 1 (RS): Ch 32 (32, 34, 36), rep Row 1 of back. (31, 31, 33, 35 sts)

Row 2: Ch 3, work in pattern across, turn.

Row 3: Ch 1, work in pattern across, turn.

Notes: *Inc at beg of a row (beg inc): work [ch 1, sc, dc] into sc st or work [ch 3, sc] into dc st.*

Inc at end of a row (end inc): work [sc, dc] into sc st or work [dc, sc] into dc sts.

Row 4 (WS): Beg inc, work in pattern across row to last st, end inc in last st, turn. (33, 33, 35, 37 sts)

Row 5: Ch 1, work in pattern across row, turn.

Rows 6 & 7 (6–9, 6–15, 6–19): Rep Rows 4 and 5. (35, 37, 45, 51 sts)

Rows 8–10 (10–12, 16–18, 20–22): Rep Rows 2, 3 and 2.

Row 11 (13, 19, 23): Beg inc, work in pattern across row to last st, end inc in last st, turn. (37, 39, 47, 53 sts)

Rep Rows 8–11 (10–13, 16–19, 20–23] until there are 57 (63, 63, 69) sts.

Rep Rows 2 and 3 until sleeve

measures 20 inches or desired sleeve length, fasten off.

Assembly

With tapestry needle, sew each pocket lining to WS of sweater.

Matching ends of rows of back and fronts tog, leaving center 21 (21, 23, 25) sts of back free, sew each front to back tog across 18 (18, 20, 20) sts at each edge.

Matching center of last row of sleeve to shoulder seam, sew last row of sleeve to ends of rows on front and back to underarm; sew ends of rows at top of sleeve to underarm on front and back.

Sew sleeve and side seams.

With sewing needle and thread, sew buttons on left front opposite button-holes on right front.

Collar

Row 1: With RS facing, working around neckline edge, attach yarn with sl st at marker on right front, ch 1, sc in same st, work 30 (30, 32, 43) sc evenly sp across to shoulder seam, sc in next 21 (21, 23, 25) sts across back to next shoulder seam, work 31 (31, 33, 35) sc evenly sp across to marked row on left front, turn. (83, 83, 89, 95 sts)

Row 2: Ch 1, sc dec over next 2 sts, dc in next st, [sc in next st, dc in next st] rep across to last 2 sts, sc dec over last 2 sts, turn. (81, 81, 87, 93 sts)

Rows 3–16: Ch 1, sc dec over next 2 sts, work in pattern across to last 2 sts, sc dec over last 2 sts, turn. (53, 53, 59, 65 sts)

Rows 17–24: Ch 1, draw up a lp in each of next 3 sts, yo, draw through all 4 lps on hook, work in pattern across to last 3 sts, draw up a lp in each of next 3 sts, yo, draw through all 4 lps on hook, turn. (21, 21, 27, 33)

At the end of Row 24, fasten off. ✄

Beddy-Bye Booties

Design by Sharon Phillips

Sleep in cozy comfort on cold winter nights when you treat your feet with these soft, snuggly booties that work up quickly in easy-care wool-blend yarn. You'll want to make several pairs for yourself and for gifts!

Skill Level: Beginner

Size: One size fits most

Materials
- Lion Brand Wool-Ease worsted weight yarn: 3 oz rose heather #140
- Size I/9 crochet hook or size needed to obtain gauge
- 2 white ribbon bows
- Sewing needle and thread
- Yarn needle

Gauge
4 dc = 1 inch; 2 dc rnds = 1 inch
Check gauge to save time.

Pattern Notes
Weave in loose ends as work progresses.

Join rnds with a sl st unless otherwise stated.

Bootie
Make 2

Rnd 1: Ch 4, 11 dc in 4th ch from hook, join in 4th ch of beg ch-4. (12 dc)

Rnd 2: Ch 3, dc in same st as beg ch-3, 2 dc in each rem dc around, join in 3rd ch of beg ch-3. (24 dc)

Rnd 3: Ch 3, dc in same st as beg ch-3, dc in each of next 3 dc, [2 dc in next dc, dc in each of next 3 dc] rep around, join in 3rd ch of beg ch-3. (30 dc)

Rnd 4: Ch 3, dc in each dc around, join in 3rd ch of beg ch-3.

Rnds 5–12: Rep Rnd 4.

Note: *Rep Rnd 4 to desired length from toe to heel.*

Rnd 13: Ch 3, dc in same dc as beg ch-3, dc in next dc, [2 dc in next dc, dc in next dc] 3 times, hdc in each of next 5 dc, sc in each of next 5 dc, hdc in each of next 5 dc, [2 dc in next dc, dc in next dc] 3 times, 2 dc in next dc, join in 3rd ch of beg ch-3. (38 sts)

Rnds 14–19: Ch 3, dc in each of next 11 sts, hdc in each of next 5 sts, sc in each of next 5 sts, hdc in each of next 5 sts, dc in each of next 11 sts, join in 3rd ch of beg ch-3.

Rnd 20: Ch 3, dc dec over next 2 sts tog, [dc in next st, dc dec over next 2 sts] 3 times, hdc in each of next 5 sts, sc in each of next 5 sts, hdc in each of next 5 sts, dc dec over next 2 sts, [dc in next st, dc dec over next 2 sts] 3 times, join in 3rd ch of beg ch-3. (30 sts)

Rnd 21: Ch 3, dc in each st around, join in 3rd ch of beg ch-3.

Rnd 22: Ch 3, [fpdc around next st, bpdc around next st] rep around, join in 3rd ch of beg ch-3.

Rnds 23–28: Ch 3, [fpdc around fpdc, bpdc around bpdc] rep around, join in 3rd ch of beg ch-3.

At the end of Rnd 28, fasten off. Sew white ribbon bow to center front of bootie over Rnd 20. ✂

Summer Roses Lap Robe

Design by Rena Stevens

Even warm-weather seasons can have chilly days or evenings when a soft, cozy lap robe is just the thing to keep the chill at bay. Sport weight yarn worked on a large hook creates a light, airy design that's bordered by big, beautiful roses!

Skill Level: Intermediate

Size: 33 x 43 inches

Materials
- Sport weight yarn: 12½ oz peach, 10 oz white, 3½ oz green
- Sizes G/6 and I/9 crochet hooks or sizes needed to obtain gauge
- Tapestry needle

Gauge

With G hook, rose motif = 3½ inches square; with I hook, in pattern, 2 shells = 3 inches

Check gauge to save time.

Pattern Notes

Weave in loose ends as work progresses.

Join rnds with a sl st unless otherwise stated.

Pattern Stitches

Shell: 5 tr in indicated st.

3-tr cl: [Yo hook twice, insert hook in indicated st, yo, draw up a lp, {yo, draw through 2 lps on hook} twice] 3 times, yo, draw through all 4 lps on hook.

Beg 3-tr cl: Ch 4, [yo hook twice, insert hook in indicated st, yo, draw up a lp, {yo, draw through 2 lps on hook} twice] twice, yo, draw through all 3 lps on hook.

Rose Border

Make 2

Note: *Make 2 rose border strips each containing 6 motifs joined tog.*

First rose motif

Rnd 1 (RS): With hook size G and peach, ch 8, join to form a ring, ch 1, [sc in ring, ch 3] 8 times, join in beg sc. (8 sc; 8 ch-3 sps)

Rnd 2: Ch 1, working behind and between sc sts of Rnd 1, [sc in ch-8 ring of Rnd 1 between sc sts, ch 3] 8 times, join in beg sc. (8 sc; 8 ch-3 sps)

Rnd 3: Sl st into ch-3 sp of Rnd 2, ch 1, [{sc, ch 2, 2 dc, ch 2, sc} in ch-3 sp] rep in each ch-3 sp of Rnd 2 around, join in beg sc.

Rnd 4: Ch 1, sc in last sc of previous rnd, ch 3, sk next sc and next 2 dc, [sc in next sc, ch 3, sk next sc and next 2 dc] rep around, join in beg sc. (8 ch-3 sps)

Rnd 5: Sl st into ch-3 sp, ch 1, [{sc, ch 1, 4 dc, ch 1, sc} in ch-3 sp] rep in each ch-3 sp around, join in beg sc, change to green, fasten off peach. (8 petals)

Rnd 6: Ch 1, sc in last sc of previous rnd, ch 5, sk next sc and next 4 dc, [sc in next sc, ch 5, sk next sc and next 4 dc] rep around, join in beg sc. (8 ch-5 sps)

Rnd 7: Sl st in next ch-5 sp, beg 3-tr cl, [ch 3, 3-tr cl] twice in same ch-5 sp, *ch 5, sc in next ch-5 sp, ch 5 **, 3-tr cl in next ch-3 sp, [ch 3, 3-tr cl] twice in same ch-5 sp, rep from * around, ending last rep at **, join in top of beg cl, fasten off.

Rnd 8: Attach white in ch-3 sp after beg 3-tr cl of previous rnd, ch 1, *4 sc in ch-3 sp, ch 7 (corner sp), 4 sc in next ch-3 sp, ch 1, 5 sc in next ch-5 sp, sl st in next sc, 5 sc in next ch-5 sp, ch 1, rep from * around, join in beg sc, fasten off.

Second–sixth rose motifs

Rnds 1–7: Rep Rnds 1–7 of first rose motif.

Rnd 8: Using Rnd 8 from first rose motif as a guide, rep Rnd 8 to 2nd corner ch-7 sp, ch 4, sl st in 5th ch of corner ch-7 sp of previous motif, ch 2, 4 sc in ch-3 sp, sl st in 1 lp of corresponding ch-1 sp of previous motif, 5 sc in next ch-5 sp, sl st in next sc, 5 sc in next ch-5 sp, sl st in 1 lp of corresponding ch-1 sp of

Take your needle, my child, and work at your pattern; it will come out a rose by and by. Life is like that—one stitch at a time taken patiently and the pattern will come out all right.

—Oliver Wendell Holmes

sc, shell in next sc, sk next 2 sc, sc in next sc] rep across, ch 7, drop lp from hook, do not fasten off, do not turn.

Row 6: Working in back lps only, pick up dropped lp of white, sc in first sc, sc in each sc across, turn.

Rep Rows 3–6 until width of afghan is within ¼ inch of length of rose border, fasten off both colors.

Edging

Row 1: Working along foundation ch with RS facing, attach white with sl st in first ch sp, ch 1, sc in same sp, *sc in the free lp of same ch as next shell, [sc, sl st] in next ch sp, [sl st, ch 1, sc] next ch sp, rep from * across, ending with 2 sc, sl st] in last ch sp, fasten off.

Finishing

Sew rose border to each end of lap robe as follows. With RS of lap robe facing, overlap rose border slightly along end, with white, whipstitch rose border to lap robe. ✄

Someone Else's Grandma

*Grandma's room is happier
Because her family is here.
They bring her little things from home
To fill her world with cheer.
An aloe plant, some photographs,
Some peaches from her tree,
An afghan that a child crocheted
For her grandmother's knees.
But Grandma motions down the hall
To where a neighbor lives.
"No one visits her with gifts
Like these my family gives."
The granddaughter won't forget next time.
She knows just what to do.
She'll get an afghan ready
For someone else's grandma, too.*

previous motif, 4 sc in next ch-3 sp, ch 2, sl st in 1 lp of 3rd ch of next ch-7 corner sp of previous motif, ch 4, 4 sc in next ch-3 sp, continue to rep in pattern around rem of motif, join in beg sc, fasten off.

Lap Robe

Row 1 (RS): With hook size I and peach, ch 170, sc in 2nd ch from hook, [sk next 3 chs, shell in next ch, sk next 3 chs, sc in next ch] rep across, ch 7, drop peach lp, do not fasten off, do not turn.

Row 2 (RS): Working in back lps only, attach white with sl st in first sc, ch 1, sc in each st across, turn.

Row 3: Ch 6 (counts as first tr, ch 2 throughout), sk next 3 sc, [sl st in next sc, ch 5, sk next 5 sc] rep across through sl st in last shell, ch 2, sk next 2 sc, tr in ch-1, turn.

Row 4: Ch 1, sc in first tr, 2 sc in next ch sp, [sc in next sl st, 5 sc in next ch sp] rep across, ending with sc in last sl st, 3 sc in last ch sp, ch 2, drop white, do not fasten off, turn.

Row 5: Insert hook in dropped peach lp, sc in first sc, [sk next 2

Victorian Collar Pins

The elegant appeal of Victorian-style fashion accessories is timeless, and vintage accents can add a touch of sophisticated charm to today's stylish wardrobes. Dress up a pretty blouse with these delightful collar pins stitched in size 10 thread and accented with glittering jewels and ribbon roses.

Skill Level: Beginner

Size

Jeweled Collar Pin: 2½ x 4 inches

Rose Collar Pin: 2½ x 5 inches, excluding crocheted pompoms

Materials

- Crochet cotton size 10: Small amount cream and ecru
- Size 7 steel crochet hook or size needed to obtain gauge
- 5 (¾-inch) plastic rings
- 2 (2-inch) safety pins
- 2 (⅞-inch) jeweled antique gold button
- 3 (¾-inch) green star flower beads
- 3 (⅜-inch) pink ribbon roses
- 12 inches 1-inch-wide pre-gathered ecru cotton lace
- Scrap of fiberfill
- Craft glue
- Tapestry needle

Gauge

10 sc = 1 inch

Check gauge to save time.

Pattern Notes

Weave in loose ends as work progresses.

Join rnds with a sl st unless otherwise stated.

Pattern Stitches

Small rolled st: Yo hook 6 times, insert hook in indicated st, yo, draw this yo through all lps on hook, ch 1 to lock.

Large rolled st: Yo hook 20 times, insert hook in a thread of a hdc st of Rnd 1 of ring, yo, draw this yo through all lps on hook, ch 1 to lock.

Jeweled Collar Pin

Pin Back

Row 1: Attach cream in ring end of pin, ch 1, work 5 sc in ring, working on edge of safety pin that does not open, work 20 sc over long edge of pin, 5 sc in head of pin. (30 sc)

Rnd 2: Ch 1, working in front lps of sts of Row 1, 3 sc in first st, sc in each st across to last st, 3 sc in last st, working in rem free lps of sts of Row 1, 3 sc in first st, sc in each st across, ending with 3 sc in last st, join in beg sc.

Rnds 3–5: Ch 1, sc in each sc around, inc sts as needed on each end to keep piece flat, join in beg sc. At the end of Rnd 5, fasten off.

Pin Front

Rnd 1 (RS): Attach cream to plastic ring, ch 1 loosely, fill ring with hdc sts, join in beg hdc, pick up another ring, [work 3 hdc on 2nd ring, sl st in adjacent hdc on first ring, ch 3, small rolled st in hdc on first ring] 3 times, fill rem of 2nd ring with hdc sts, join in beg hdc.

Rnd 2: Ch 1, sc in each hdc around both rings, inc as needed and sk sts at joining of rings to keep work flat, join in beg sc.

Rnd 3: Ch 1, sc around, inc as needed and sk sc at joining of rings to keep piece flat and at same time work 2 large rolled sts at center top and bottom of each ring and at center outer edge of each ring, join in beg sc.

Rnd 4: [Ch 5, sk 2 sts, sl st in next st] rep around entire outer edge, join in beg st.

Rnd 5: Sl st into 3rd ch of ch-5, [ch 7, sl st in 5th ch from hook, sl st in next ch-5 sp] rep around, join in beg st, fasten off.

Finishing

Glue pin back centered over back of pin front. Glue an antique button to center of each ring.

Rose Collar Pin

Pin Back

Row 1: With ecru cotton, rep Row 1 of pin back as for jeweled collar pin. (30 sc)

Rnd 2: Working in front lps only of Row 1, ch 1 loosely, work 3 hdc in first st, hdc in each st across to last st, 3 hdc in last st, working in rem lps of Row 1, 3 hdc in first st, hdc in

each st across, ending with 3 hdc in last st, join in beg hdc.

Rnd 3: Ch 1 loosely, hdc in each st around, inc hdc sts as needed on each end to keep work flat, join in beg hdc.

Rnd 4: Ch 1, sc in each st around, inc sc sts as needed on each end to keep work flat, join in beg sc, fasten off.

Three-Ring Pin Front

Rnd 1: Attach ecru cotton on a ring, ch 1 loosely, fill ring with hdc, join in beg hdc, pick up next ring, [3 hdc on 2nd ring, draw up a lp, remove hook, insert hook in adjacent hdc in first ring, pick up dropped lp and draw through st on hook] twice, work 19 more hdc in 2nd ring, pick up 3rd ring, [3 hdc on 3rd ring, draw up a lp, remove hook, insert hook in adjacent hdc on 2nd ring, pick up dropped lp, draw through st on hook] twice, continue to fill 3rd ring with hdc sts, join in beg hdc of 3rd ring, working on rem of 2nd ring, fill rem half of 2nd ring with hdc sts, join in beg hdc of 2nd ring, fasten off.

Pompom
Make 3

Rnd 1: Ch 3, join to form a ring,

ch 1, work 8 sc in ring, do not join. (8 sc)

Rnd 2: Working in a continuous rnd, work 2 sc in each of next 12 sc, do not join. (20 sc)

Rnds 3 & 4: Sc in each of next 20 sc, do not join.

Rnd 5: Working around opening, stuffing with fiberfill before opening is too small, [sk next sc, sc in next sc] rep until opening is closed, sl st in next sc.

Hanging lp
On 2 pompoms at the end of Rnd 5, ch 10, leaving a length of cotton, fasten off. On 3rd pompom at the end of Rnd 5, ch 13, leaving a length of cotton, fasten off.

Finishing
With WS of three-ring pin front facing, glue pre-gathered lace around entire outer edge. Glue pin back centered over back of pin front. With rem length of cotton, secure pompom chs to center bottom of center ring. Glue a green star flower bead over center of each ring. Glue a ribbon rose to the center of each bead. ✂

To be 70 years young is sometimes far more cheerful than to be 40 years old.

—Oliver Wendell Holmes

Cozy Shrug

Design by Shirley Zebrowski

Fluffy bulky weight yarn that's soft as a cloud creates the sumptuous texture and cozy comfort in this pretty, sky blue shrug that will wrap you in heavenly warmth!

Skill Level: Beginner

Size: 31½ X 60 inches

Materials

- Coats & Clark Red Heart Baby Clouds bulky yarn (6 oz per skein): 6 skeins blue sky #9025
- Coats & Clark Red Heart Super Saver worsted weight yarn: 4 oz light blue #381
- Sizes I/9 and J/10 crochet hooks or sizes needed to obtain gauge
- Yarn needle

Gauge

With J hook, 2 shells = 2 inches; with I hook, 7 sc = 2 inches; 7 sc rows = 2 inches

Check gauge to save time.

Pattern Notes

Weave in loose ends as work progresses.

Ch-3 counts as first dc throughout.

Pattern Stitch

Shell: 5 dc in indicated st.

Shrug

Row 1: With hook size J and blue sky, ch 122, sc in 2nd ch from hook, [sk next 2 chs, shell in next ch, sk next 2 chs, sc in next ch] rep across, turn. (21 sc; 20 shells)

Row 2: Ch 3, 2 dc in same sc as beg ch-3, sk 2 dc, sc in next dc, sk 2 dc, [shell in next sc, sk next 2 dc, sc in next dc, sk next 2 dc] rep across, ending with 3 dc in last sc, turn.

Row 3: Ch 1, sc in first dc, [sk next 2 dc, shell in next sc, sk next 2 dc, sc in next dc] rep across, turn.

Rows 4–38: Rep Rows 2 and 3, at the end of last rep, fasten off.

Cuff

Make 2

Row 1 (RS): Working across ends of rows with I hook, attach light blue, ch 1, gathering edge slightly, work 49 sc evenly sp across edge, turn. (49 sc)

Row 2: Ch 1, sc in first sc, [draw up a lp in each of next 3 sc, yo, draw through all 4 lps on hook, sc in next sc] rep across, turn. (25 sc)

Rows 3–16: Ch 1, working in back lps only, sc in each st across, turn.

Row 17 (RS): Ch 1, working in back lps only, sc in each st across, do not turn.

Row 18 (RS): Ch 1, sc evenly sp across long edge of shrug to opposite end, do not turn.

Row 19 (RS): Ch 1, working across ends of row, ch 1, gathering edge slightly, work 49 sc evenly sp across edge, turn. (49 sc)

Rep Rows 2–18, fasten off.

Finishing

With length of light blue, beg at end of cuff, sew seam tog from beg of cuff and along shrug for a total of 10 inches. Sew opposite cuff and shrug in same manner. ✄

Warm & Soothing Heat Pack

Design by Ruthie Marks

Treat aching muscles and joints with this cleverly designed pack that can either be microwaved or frozen for hot or cold applications. It's filled with uncooked rice kernels to drape comfortably on body areas, and the cover is removable for hand-washing.

Skill Level: Beginner

Size: 10 X 15 inches

Materials

- Brown Sheep Lambs Pride Superwash wool worsted weight yarn: 2 skeins sea foam #SW16, 1 skein emerald city #SW52
- Size E/4 crochet hook or size needed to obtain gauge
- 9 x 24½ inches untreated cotton fabric
- Sewing needle and thread
- Uncooked rice kernels
- Yarn needle

Gauge

[Sc, hdc] 4 times = 1½ inches; 4 rows = 1½ inches

Check gauge to save time.

Pattern Notes

Weave in loose ends as work progresses.

Join rnds with a sl st unless otherwise stated.

Body

Make 2

Row 1: With sea foam, ch 43, sc in 2nd ch from hook, [sc, hdc] in next ch sk next ch, [{sc, hdc} in next ch, sk next ch] rep across, ending with sc in last ch, turn. (20 groups hdc, sc)

Row 2: Working in front lps only, ch 1, sc in first sc, [{sc, hdc} in next hdc] rep across, ending with sc in last sc, turn.

Rows 3–34: Rep Row 2. At the end of Row 34 fasten off.

Neck

Row 1: Sk next 13 sts of Row 34, attach sea foam in next sc, ch 1, sc in same sc, sk next hdc and next sc, [{sc, hdc} in next hdc] 6 times, sc in next sc, turn. (6 groups of hdc, sc)

Rows 2–5: Rep Row 2 of body.

Edging

Rnd 1: Ch 1, 3 sc in corner st, sc in each st across Row 5 of neck, 3 sc in corner st, 4 sc evenly sp down side edge of neck, sc dec over inner corner, sc in each rem st across Row 34, 3 sc in corner, work 47 sc evenly sp down side edge, 3 sc in corner, sc in each st across bottom edge, 3 sc in corner st, work 47 sc evenly sp up opposite side edge, 3 sc in corner, sc in each rem st across Row 34, sc dec over inner corner, work 4 sc evenly sp up side edge of neck, join in beg sc, fasten off.

Bottom Trim

Note: *Work bottom trim on both body sections.*

Row 1 (RS): Working across bottom edge, attach emerald city in first st after 3 corner sc, ch 1, sc in same st, sc in each st across, ending with last sc in st before 3 corner sc sts, turn.

Row 2: Ch 4 (counts as first dc, ch 1), sk next sc, dc in next sc, [ch 1, sk next sc, dc in next sc] rep across, fasten off.

Joining

Row 1: Holding body sections with WS tog, attach emerald city in first sc of 3 corner sc sts and working through both thicknesses, ch 1, sc in same sc as beg ch-1, 3 sc in next sc, sc in each sc around, working 3 sc in each corner sc and sc dec in each inner corner of neck, ending with 3 sc in corner sc before bottom edge, sc in next sc, turn.

Row 2: Ch 3, sl st in side edge of bottom trim, ch 2, [dc in next sc, ch 2] twice, sk next st, dc in next st across corner *ch 1, sk next st, dc in next st, rep from * around, adjust sts if necessary to work at each of the 7 sc sts at each corner, dc in next st, ch 2, sk next sc, [dc in next sc, ch 2] 3 times, sk next sc, dc in next sc, rep around to opposite edge of bottom trim, sl st to join last dc in bottom trim, fasten off.

Weaving Chain

Holding 2 strands of emerald city tog, ch 250 to measure approximately 55 inches, fasten off.

Cotton Inner Bag

Fold material with RS tog in half 9 x 12¼ inches; sew ¼-inch seam along one short and one long edge, turn bag RS out. Reinforce edge by sewing around sewn edge again. Place uncooked rice kernels in bag, turn edges under ¼ inch and sew rem edge closed. Fold bag in half so that each is half full of the rice kernels; working across center fold of bag, sew across to make 2 rice pockets.

Finishing

Insert rice bag into crocheted body. With weaving ch, beg at center bottom edge, weave ch under and over the dc around outer edge of crocheted piece, and tie ends in a bow.

For warm therapy, place pack in microwave and heat on high for 30-second increments until desired temperature.

For cool therapy, place pack in a plastic bag in the freezer and chill until desired temperature. ✂

The greatest comfort of my old age, and that which gives me the highest satisfaction, is the pleasing remembrance of the many benefits I have done to others.

—Cato the Elder

Anniversary Sachets

Designs by Cora Rattle

Celebrate important wedding milestones with these beautiful gift sachets to commemorate silver and gold anniversaries. Stitched in glittering metallic thread, they're sure to add an extra touch of sparkle to a special couple's happy celebration!

Skill Level: Beginner

Size: 3½ inches

Materials

- J. & P. Coats Metallic Knit-Cro-Sheen crochet cotton size 10: 50 yds each white/silver #1S and ecru/gold #61G
- Size 7 steel crochet hook or size needed to obtain gauge
- 4 (4-inch) squares netting
- 6 tbsp dry sachet granules
- Fiberfill
- 10 inches ⅛-inch-wide ribbon or cording
- 2 (½-inch) pin backs
- 4 (4mm) pearl beads
- Red heart-shape stone
- Hot-glue gun
- ¾-inch numbers 25 and 50
- Sewing needle and thread
- Yarn needle

Gauge

3 rows = 1 inch; 4 V-sts = 1 inch
Check gauge to save time.

Pattern Notes

Weave in loose ends as work progresses.

Join rnds with a sl st unless otherwise stated.

Materials listed will make 2 anniversary sachets.

Pattern Stitches

V-st: [Dc, ch 1, dc] in indicated st.

Beg V-st: Ch 4 (counts as first dc, ch 1), dc in same st as beg ch-4.

Heart Sachet

Make 2

Row 1: Starting at top edge, ch 26, dc in 5th ch from hook, dc in each of next 7 chs, ch 3, sk next 3 chs, [dc, ch 5, dc] in next ch, ch 3, sk next 3 chs, dc in each of next 8 chs, turn.

Row 2: Sl st in sp between first and 2nd dc, beg V-st in same sp, [sk 2 dc, V-st in sp between dc] 3 times, sk next ch-3 sp 10 dc in ch-5 sp, sk next ch-3 sp V-st between first and 2nd dc, [sk next 2 dc, V-st in sp between dc] 3 times, turn. (8 V-sts; 10 dc)

Row 3: Sl st into ch-1 sp of V-st, beg V-st in same ch-1 sp, [V-st in next ch-1 sp] 3 times, V-st between first and 2nd dc of 10-dc group, [sk next 2 dc, V-st in sp between dc] 4 times, [V-st in next ch-1 sp] 4 times, turn. (13 V-sts)

Row 4: Sl st into ch-1 sp of V-st, beg V-st in same ch-1 sp, [V-st in next ch-1 sp] 12 times, turn. (13 V-sts)

Continued on page 131

Peaceful Waters Afghan

Design courtesy of Caron International

Pretty scallops and soothing shades of blue bring to mind the gentle ripples of a peaceful lake at twilight. Easy motifs worked in panels for later joining make this a great take-along project.

Skill Level: Beginner

Size: 45 x 65 inches

Materials

- Caron Simply Soft worsted weight yarn: 12 oz each white #2601 (A), soft blue #2615 (B), light country blue #2624 (C), country blue #2626 (D) and dark country blue #2628 (E)
- Size F/5 crochet hook or size needed to obtain gauge
- Yarn needle

Gauge

5 ch sts = 1 inch; 1 motif = 3¼ x 5½ inches

Check gauge to save time.

Pattern Notes

Weave in loose ends as work progresses.

Join rnds with a sl st unless otherwise stated.

Ch-3 counts as first dc throughout.

When ending last row of each motif, leave approximately a 7-inch length of yarn. This will be used later for sewing panels tog.

Panel

Make 8

First Motif

Row 1 (WS): With A, ch 13, dc in 9th ch from hook, ch 5, sl st in last ch, turn.

Row 2 (RS): Ch 3, 9 dc in next ch sp, dc in next dc, 9 dc in next ch sp, turn. (20 dc)

Row 3 (WS): Ch 5 (counts as first dc, ch 2 throughout), dc in 2nd dc, [ch 2, sk next dc, dc in next dc] 9 times, turn. (11 dc; 10 ch-2 sps)

Row 4 (RS): Ch 3, [3 dc in next ch-2 sp, dc in next dc] 9 times, 2 dc in next ch-2 sp, dc in 3rd ch of ch-5, turn. (40 dc)

Row 5 (WS): Ch 5, dc in 2nd dc, [ch 2, sk next dc, dc in next dc] 19 times, leaving a length of yarn, fasten off. (21 dc; 20 ch-2 sps)

Second Motif

Row 1: With WS of previous motif facing, attach B with a sl st in 10 dc of previous motif (next dc after 9th ch-2 sp), ch 5, sk next ch-2 sp, dc in next dc (this is the center top dc of previous motif), ch 5, sk next ch-2 sp, sl st in next dc (this is the next dc to the left of center dc), ch 2 (this ch-2 counts as first dc of following row throughout), sl st in next dc of Row 5 of previous motif, turn.

Row 2 (RS): 8 dc in next ch-5 sp, 1 dc in next dc, 9 dc in next ch-5 sp, sk next ch-2 sp, sl st in next dc of Row 5 of previous motif, ch 2, sl st in next dc of Row 5 of previous motif, turn.

Row 3 (WS): Ch 2, [sk next dc, dc in next dc, ch 2] 9 times, sl st in next dc of Row 5 of previous motif, ch 2, sl st in next dc of Row 5 of previous motif, turn. (10 ch-2 sps)

Row 4 (RS): 2 dc in next ch-2 sp, [dc in next dc, 3 dc in next ch-2 sp] 9 times, sl st in next dc of Row 5 of previous motif, ch 2, sl st in next dc of Row 5 of previous motif, turn.

Row 5 (WS): [Ch 2, sk next dc, dc in next dc] 19 times, ch 2, sl st in next dc of Row 5 of previous motif, leaving a length of yarn, fasten off.

Third Motif

Rows 1–5: With C, rep Rows 1–5 of 2nd motif.

Fourth Motif

Rows 1–5: With D, rep Rows 1–5 of 2nd motif.

Fifth Motif

Rows 1–5: With E, rep Rows 1–5 of 2nd motif.

Father Time, though he tarries for none of his children, often lays his hand lightly upon those who have used him well, leaving their hearts and spirits young and in full vigour. The gray head is but the impression of the old fellow's hand in giving them his blessing, and every wrinkle but a notch in the quiet calendar of a well-spent life.

—Charles Dickens

[Rep Rows 1–5 of 2nd motif with A, B, C, D and E] 3 times. (20 motifs per panel)

Joining
Place 2 panels on a flat surface with RS facing, matching sts, sew panels tog using rem lengths from each motif picking up the back of sts only. Rep joining until all 8 panels are joined.

Border
Rnd 1 (RS): Attach A in any ch-2 sp, ch 1, working around outer edge, work 2 sc in each ch sp and 1 sc in each dc, join in beg sc, fasten off.

Rnd 2 (RS): Working in back lps only, attach B, ch 1, sc in each st around, working 3 sc in each center corner st, join in beg sc, fasten off.

Rnd 3 (RS): With C, rep Rnd 2.

Rnd 4 (RS): With D, rep Rnd 2.

Rnd 5 (RS): With E, rep Rnd 2. ✀

Chevron Strips

Design by Margaret Dick

A classic ripple design worked in simple strips of variegated yarn creates the striking pattern in this handsomely styled lap robe that makes a great take-along project for busy, on-the-go crocheters!

Skill Level: Intermediate

Size: 32 x 47 inches

Materials
- Coats & Clark Red Heart Super Saver worsted weight yarn: 18 oz plumberry #982 and 6 oz dark plum #533
- Size H/8 crochet hook or size needed to obtain gauge
- Yarn needle

Gauge
5 dc = 1½ inches; 3 dc rows = 1¾ inches

Check gauge to save time.

Pattern Notes
Weave in loose ends as work progresses.

Join rnds with a sl st unless otherwise stated.

Pattern Stitches
To change yarn color: Work indicated number of sts, working last dc until 2 lps rem on hook, pick up next color, yo, draw through rem 2 lps on hook.

Shell: [Sc, hdc, 2 dc, hdc, sc] in indicated ch-2 sp.

Wide Strip
Make 3

Row 1: With plumberry, ch 24, dc in 3rd ch from hook (beg dc dec), dc in each of next 9 chs, changing to dark plum in last step of 9th dc, working over plumberry, 3 dc in next ch, changing to plumberry in last step of 3rd dc, drop dark plum, dc in each of next 9 chs, dc dec over next 2 chs, turn. (23 sts)

Row 2: Ch 2, dc in next dc (beg dc dec), dc in each of next 9 dc, changing to dark plum in last step of 9th dc, working over plumberry, 3 dc in next dc, changing to plumberry in last step of 3rd dc, dc in each of next 9 dc, dc dec over next 2 dc, turn. (23 sts)

Rows 3–70: Rep Row 2, at the end of Row 70, fasten off.

Narrow Strip
Make 2

Row 1: With plumberry, ch 18, dc in 3rd ch from hook (beg dc dec), dc in each of next 6 chs, changing to dark plum in last step of 6th dc, working over plumberry, 3 dc in next ch, changing to plumberry in last step of 3rd dc, drop dark plum, dc in each of next 6 chs, dc dec over next 2 chs, turn. (17 sts)

Row 2: Ch 2, dc in next dc (beg dc dec), dc in each of next 6 dc, changing to dark plum in last step of 6th dc, working over plumberry, 3 dc in next dc, changing to plumberry in last step of 3rd dc, dc in each of next 6 dc, dc dec over next 2 dc, turn. (17 sts)

Rows 3–70: Rep Row 2, at the end of Row 70, fasten off.

Strip Trim & Joining
Wide strip
Rnd 1: Attach dark plum to top right corner of Row 70, ch 1, sc in same st, ch 2, sc in next st, ch 2, sk 1 st, sc in next st, ch 2, sk next 2 sts, sc in next st, [ch 2, sk next st, sc in next st] twice, ch 2, sk next st (center dc of 3-dc point), sc in next st, [ch 2, sk next st, sc in next st] twice, ch 2, sk next 2 sts, sc in next st, ch 2, sk next st, sc in next st, ch 2, sc in last st (11 ch-2 sps), working down left side edge of strip, ch 2, sc in top of Row 69, [ch 2, sc in top of next row] rep across, ending with ch 2, sc in first ch on opposite side of foundation ch (70 ch-2 sps), working across foundation ch, ch 2, sk 2 sts, sc in next st, [ch 2, sk next st, sc in next st] twice, ch 2, sk next 2 sts, sc in next st, ch 2, sk next st (center bottom ch that has 3-dc group), sc in next ch, ch 2, sk next 2 sts, sc in next st, [ch 2, sk next st, sc in next st] twice, ch 2, sk next 2 sts, sc in end st (9 ch-2 sps), working up right side edge, ch 2, sc in top edge of Row 1, [ch 2, sc in top edge of next row] rep across, ending with last sc in top edge of Row 69, ch 2, join in beg sc, fasten off.

Narrow strip
Rnd 1: Attach dark plum to top right corner of Row 70, ch 1, sc in same st, ch 2, sc in next st, [ch 2, sk next st, sc in next st] 3 times, ch 2, sk next st (center dc of 3-dc point), sc in next st, [ch 2, sk next st, sc in next st] 3 times, ch 2, sc in last st (9 ch-2 sps), working down left edge of strip, ch 2, sc in top of Row 69, [ch 2, sc in top of next row] rep across, ending with ch 2, sc in first ch on opposite side of foundation ch (70 ch-2 sps), working across foundation ch, [ch 2, sk 1 st, sc in next st] twice, ch 2, sk next 2 sts, sc in next st, ch 2, sk next st (center bottom ch that has 3-dc group), sc in next st, ch 2, sk next 2 sts, sc in next st, ch 2, sk

next st, sc in next st, ch 2, sk next st, sc in last st (7 ch-2 sps), working up right side edge, ch 1, sc in adjacent ch-2 sp of previous strip, ch 1, sc in top edge of Row 1 on working strip, [ch 1, sc in next ch-2 sp on previous panel, ch 1, sc in top of next row of working strip] rep to top of panel, ending with join in beg sc.

Alternating strips, continue to rep trim on each wide and narrow strip, joining right edge of working strip to left edge of previous strip until all strips are joined.

Border

Rnd 1: Attach dark plum in first ch-2 sp of first strip at top right corner, ch 1, beg in same ch-2 sp, *sc in first ch-2 sp of wide strip, [shell in next ch-2 sp, sc in next ch-2 sp] 5 times **, sk joining of strips, shell in first ch-2 sp of narrow strip, [sc in next ch-2 sp, shell in next ch-2 sp] 4 times, sk joining of strips, rep from * across, ending last rep at **, working down left edge, [shell in next ch-2 sp, sc in next ch-2 sp] 35 times, working across bottom, [working across wide strip, shell in next ch-2 sp, {sc in next ch-2 sp, shell in next ch-2 sp} 4 times, sk joining of strips, working across narrow strip, sc in next ch-2 sp, {shell in next ch-2 sp, sc in next ch-2 sp} twice, sk joining of strips] twice, working across wide strip, shell in next ch-2 sp, [sc in next ch-2 sp, shell in next ch-2 sp] 4 times, working up right edge, [sc in next ch-2 sp, shell in next ch-2 sp] 35 times, join in beg sc, fasten off. ✂

The Pattern Library

My old hands are tired now,
My eyesight has gone downhill.
I'm not so steady on my feet
But I can help others still.
I may not be able to crochet
(I'm clumsy now with a hook),
But I can offer to lend my patterns,
Would you like to borrow a book?
When folks browse through my library
I know what they hope to find.
Projects to meet the special needs
Of friends they bear always in mind.
It's all right that I can't read a pattern
Or wrestle a skein of yarn.
I know that I am helping my friends
Who are helping theirs in turn.

Pocket Shawl

Design by Karen Rigsby

Eye-catching fringe and pretty button accents add sophisticated charm to this chic and cozy wrap that will chase away the chill in style. Decorative pockets make snuggly places to tuck cold hands, or to carry small essentials.

Skill Level: Beginner

Size: 18 x 60 inches, excluding fringe

Materials

- Bernat denim style 70 percent acrylic, 30 percent cotton yarn (3½ oz per skein): 5 skeins sweatshirt #3044, 1 skein canvas #3006
- Size F/5 crochet hook or size needed to obtain gauge
- 2 (⅞-inch) decorative buttons
- Yarn needle

Gauge

21 sts = 6 inches; 14 rows = 6 inches

Check gauge to save time.

Pattern Note

Weave in loose ends as work progresses.

Pattern Stitch

Extended sc (esc): Insert hook below horizontal sts and between the 2 vertical threads that form the V-shape of st, yo, draw up a lp, yo, draw through 2 lps on hook.

If wrinkles must be written on our brows, let them not be written upon the heart. The spirit should never grow old.

—James A. Garfield

Shawl

Row 1 (RS): With sweatshirt, ch 66, [sc, ch 1, dc] in 3rd ch from hook, sk next 2 chs, [{sc, ch 1, dc} in next ch, sk next 2 chs] rep across, ending with sc in last ch, turn. (21 pattern groups)

Row 2: Ch 1, sk first sc and next dc, [{sc, ch 1, dc} in next ch-1 sp] rep across, ending with sk last sc, sc in turning ch, turn.

Rep Row 2 until shawl measures 60 inches, fasten off.

Pocket

Make 2

Row 1 (RS): With canvas, ch 24, [sc, ch 1, dc] in 3rd ch from hook, sk next 2 chs, [{sc, ch 1, dc} in next ch, sk next 2 chs] rep across, ending with sc in last ch, turn. (7 pattern groups)

Rep Row 2 of shawl until pocket measures 6 inches, ending on a WS row.

Cuff

Row 1 (RS): With RS facing, working in front lps for this row only, ch 1, sc in each st across, turn.

Rows 2–4: Ch 1, esc in each st across, turn. At the end of Row 4, fasten off.

Row 5: Fold cuff to front of pocket and working in rem free lp of last row of pocket (rem back lp from working cuff in front lp), attach canvas with sl st in first st, sl st in each rem st across, fasten off.

Finishing

Sew pocket to front of shawl 4 inches from bottom edge and 5 inches from edge 2 inches off center, or place as desired for individual comfort.

Shawl fringe

Cut strands of canvas 16 inches long. Fold 2 strands of canvas in half, insert hook in end of shawl, draw strands through at fold to form a lp on hook, draw cut ends through lp on hook, pull gently to secure. Rep fringe in every other st across both ends of shawl.

Pocket fringe

With 6-inch strands of canvas, attach fringe in same manner as for shawl fringe.

Sew decorative button to the center of pocket cuff. ✂

Anniversary Sachets

Continued from page 125

Row 5: Sl st into ch-1 sp of V-st, ch 3, [V-st in ch-1 sp of next V-st] 11 times, dc in last ch-1 sp of V-st, turn. (11 V-sts)

Row 6: Sl st into ch-1 sp of V-st, ch 3, [V-st in ch-1 sp of next V-st] 9 times, dc in ch-1 sp of last V-st, turn. (9 V-sts)

Row 7: Sl st into ch-1 sp of V-st, ch 3, [V-st in next ch-1 sp of V-st] 7 times, dc in ch-1 sp of last V-st, turn. (7 V-sts)

Row 8: Sl st into ch-1 sp of V-st, ch 3, [V-st in ch-1 sp of next V-st] 5 times, dc in last ch-1 sp of last V-st, turn. (5 V-sts)

Rnd 9: Sl st into ch-1 sp of V-st, ch 3, [V-st in ch-1 sp of next V-st] 3 times, dc in ch-1 sp of last V-st, turn. (3 V-sts)

Row 10: Sl st into ch-1 sp of V-st, ch 3, V-st in next ch-1 sp of next V-st, dc in ch-1 sp of last V-st, fasten off. (1 V-st)

Sachet Insert

Using heart as a pattern, cut 2 from netting ¾-inch larger than heart sachet. Sew around outer edge leaving an opening, stuff with fiberfill and 3 tbsp of dry sachet granules, sew rem opening closed.

Edging

Rnd 1: Holding front and back tog, matching sts and working through both thicknesses, attach cotton in right top corner of heart, ch 1, sc in same st, [ch 5, sl st] 3 times in top of last sc, [sc in each of next 3 sts, {ch 5, sl st} 3 times in last sc] 3 times, sc in next sc, sc in next st, ch 40, sl st in first ch of ch-40, sc in each of next 2 sts, [ch 5, sl st] 3 times in top of last sc, [sc in each of next 3 sts, {ch 5, sl st} 3 times in top of last sc] 3 times, *[3 sc in side edge of next row, {ch 5, sl st} 3 times in last sc] rep across side edge of rows *, sc in ch-1 sp of Row 10, [ch 5, sl st in last sc] 3 times, rep from * to *, join in beg sc, fasten off.

Mini Heart

Make 2

Row 1: Ch 2, 3 sc in 2nd ch from hook, turn. (3 sc)

Row 2: Ch 1, 2 sc in first sc, sc in next sc, 2 sc in next sc, turn. (5 sc)

Row 3: Ch 1, 2 sc in first sc, sc in each of next 3 sc, 2 sc in next sc, turn. (7 sc)

Row 4: Ch 1, sc in each of next 7 sc, turn.

Row 5: Ch 1, sc in first sc, 3 dc in next sc, hdc in next sc, sc in next sc, hdc in next sc, 3 dc in next sc, sc in last sc, fasten off.

Row 6: Attach cotton to center sc of Row 5, ch 18, sl st in same sc, fasten off.

Finishing

Adorn pin front as desired, with 3 pearl beads or pearl beads and red stone heart. Glue a number to each mini heart. Attach pin to front of heart sachet, passing ch-18 lps through pin before securing.

Attach ribbon or cording to center top of heart and tie ends in a bow. ✂

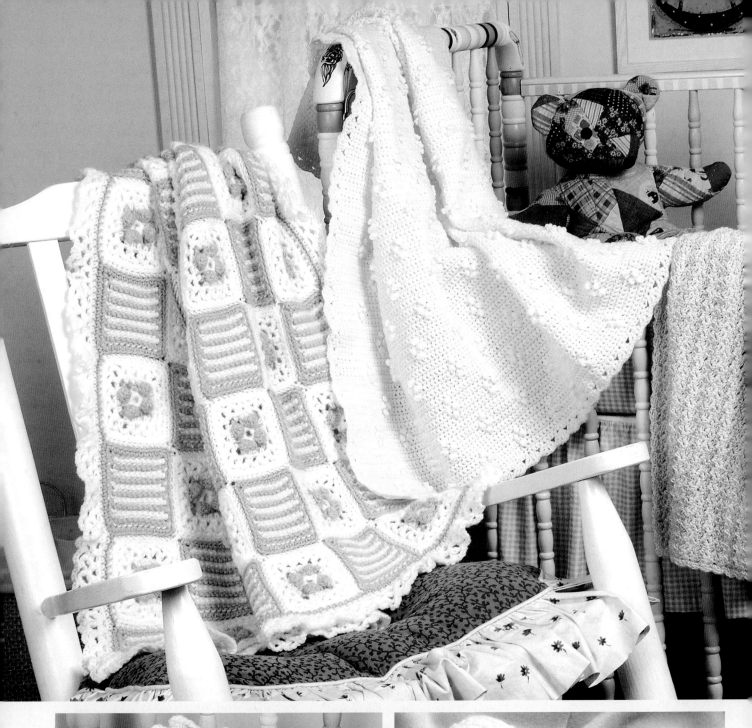

Tiny Treasures

I t was said by the renowned poet Carl Sandburg that "a baby is God's opinion that the world should go on." Every newborn is a gift from Heaven—a divine offering of humanity at its best. Celebrating the arrival of a new baby is one of life's happiest occasions, and crocheting a special gift for a precious little one is especially joyous. In this chapter, you'll find an enchanting collection of baby designs to lovingly stitch for all of the priceless, tiny treasures in your life!

Every child born into the world is a new thought of God, an ever-fresh and radiant possibility.

—Kate Douglas Wiggin

Strawberry Parfait Ensemble

Designs by Rosanne Kropp

A dainty cluster-stitch design perfectly paired with a textured ribbed pattern creates the striking style of this precious sweater, bonnet and booties set. Your newborn is sure to be the best-dressed baby on trips out and about!

Skill Level: Intermediate

Size: Newborn–3 months

Materials
- Sport weight yarn: 6 oz pink, 2 oz pompadour white
- Sizes F/5 and G/6 crochet hooks or sizes needed to obtain gauge
- 5 (10mm) shank buttons
- Sewing needle and thread
- Stitch markers
- Yarn needle

Gauge

With hook size F, 9 sc = 2 inches; 5 sc rows = 1 inch; with hook size G, 4 sts = 1 inch; 5 lace pattern rows = 3 inches

Check gauge to save time.

Pattern Notes

Weave in loose ends as work progresses.

Join rnds with a sl st unless otherwise stated.

Sweater is crocheted beg at neckline.

Sweater

Yoke

Row 1: With hook size F and pink, ch 50, sc in 2nd ch from hook, sc in each of next 6 chs (right front), 3 sc in next ch, sc in each of next 7 chs (right sleeve), 3 sc in next ch, sc in each of next 17 chs (back), 3 sc in next ch, sc in each of next 7 chs (left sleeve), 3 sc in next ch, sc in each of next 7 chs (left front), turn. (57 sc)

Notes: Mark the center sc of each 3-sc group with a st marker for next 11 rows.

Work the following color sequence, Rows 2–8 with pink, Rows 9 and 10 with white and Rows 11 and 12 with pink.

Rows 2–11: Working in back lps only, ch 1, sc in each st across, working 3 sc in center marked sc of each of 4 groups, turn. (137 sc)

Row 12: Working in back lps only, ch 1, sc in each st to 2nd marked sc on Row 11, work 1 sc in marked sc, drop lp from hook, insert hook from back through both lps in first marked sc on Row 12 and draw dropped lp through forming left sleeve opening, work 2 sc in same st as last sc, continue in pattern to 4th marked sc of Row 11, work 1 sc in marked sc, drop lp from hook, insert hook from front to back in 3rd marked sc on Row 12 and draw dropped lp through forming right sleeve opening, work 2 sc in same st as last sc, continue in pattern to end of row, turn.

Note: There are 19 sc on each front section (do not count the 4 marked sts that are joined at underarm), and 41 sts on back section. Lace pattern will be worked over these 79 sts.

Body

Row 1: Change to hook size G, ch 2, sk first sc, 2-dc cl over next 2 sc, *5 dc in next sc, [yo hook, insert hook in next sc, yo, draw up a lp, yo, draw through 2 lps on hook] twice, sk next sc, [yo hook, insert hook in next sc, yo, draw up a lp, yo, draw through 2 lps on hook] twice, yo, draw through all 5 lps on hook, ch 1 to lock, rep from * 11 times, 5 dc in next sc, [yo, insert hook in next sc, yo, draw up a lp, yo, draw through 2 lps on hook] 3 times, yo, draw through all 4 lps on hook, turn. (13 groups of 5-dc)

Note: Work Rows 2–4 with pink, Row 5 with white, Row 6 with pink, Row 7 with white and Row 8 with pink.

Rows 2–8: Ch 2, sk next cl, [yo,

It is the morning of your life and all of your dreams are just beginning. May you grow up knowing how very much you are loved, and may you forever be surrounded by gracious hearts and people who care. Welcome to the world, sweet baby, it's been waiting for you.

—Flavia Weed

insert hook in next dc, yo, draw up a lp, yo, draw through 2 lps on hook] twice, yo, draw through all 3 lps on hook, ch 1 to lock (beg 2-dc cl), *5 dc in next dc, [yo hook, insert hook in next dc, yo, draw up a lp, yo, draw through 2 lps on hook] twice, sk cl st, [yo hook, insert hook in next dc, yo, draw up a lp, yo, draw through 2 lps on hook] twice, yo, draw through all 5 lps on hook, ch 1 to lock, rep from * 11 times, 5 dc in next dc, yo hook, insert hook in next dc, yo, draw up a lp, yo, draw through 2 lps on hook, sk next ch-1 sp, yo hook, insert hook in next cl st, yo, draw up a lp, yo, draw through 2 lps on hook, yo, draw through all 4 lps on hook, turn. At the end of Row 8, fasten off.

Sleeve
Make 2

Note: *There are 31 sts on each sleeve, do not include marked sts.*

Row 1: With WS of Row 12 facing, attach pink to first sc after marked st on Row 12, ch 2, work a 2-dc cl over next 2 sc and continue in lace pattern around sleeve opening as established for Row 1 on main body of sweater, ending with a 3-dc cl over last 3 sc, turn. (5 groups of 5-dc)

Note: *Work Rows 2–4 with pink, Row 5 with white and Row 6 with pink.*

Rows 2–6: Work in lace pattern as established for main body of sweater. At the end of Row 6, fasten off.

Sew sleeve seam.

Collar

Row 1 (RS): Working in opposite side of foundation ch, attach pink in first ch-3, dc in same ch, dc in each of next 47 chs, 2 dc in last ch, turn. (51 dc)

Row 2: Ch 2, dc in first dc (beg cl), *ch 1, [yo hook, insert hook in next dc, yo, draw up a lp, yo, draw through 2 lps on hook] twice in same dc, yo, draw through all 3 lps on hook (2-dc cl), rep from * across, fasten off, turn.

Row 3: Attach white in top of first cl, ch 2, dc in same st, [ch 1, 2-dc cl in top of next cl] rep across, fasten off.

Collar edging

Row 4: With RS facing and working up left side of collar, attach white to beg ch at base of collar, ch 1, 2 sc evenly sp in ends of each row of collar, 2 sc in cl on Row 3, [2 sc in next ch-1 sp, sl st in next cl] rep across, working 2 sc in last cl, working in ends of rows, work 2 sc evenly sp in each of next 3 rows, sl st in beg ch at base of collar, fasten off.

Right Front Opening

Row 1 (RS): Attach pink to bottom corner of right front edge, ch 1, sc in cl st at end of last lace pattern row, working in ends of rows, work 2 sc evenly sp in each lace pattern row and 1 sc in each sc row, turn. (29 sc)

Row 2: Ch 1, sc in first sc, [ch 1, sk next sc, sc in each of next 4 sc] 4 times, ch 1, sk next sc, sc in each of next 3 sc, turn. (5 buttonholes)

Row 3: Ch 1, sc in each sc and each ch-1 sp across, fasten off.

Left Front Opening

Row 1 (RS): Attach pink to top left front edge, ch 1, working in ends of rows, sc in each of next 12 rows, work 2 sc evenly sp in each lace pattern row, sc in cl st at end of last row, turn. (29 sc)

Rows 2 & 3: Ch 1, sc in each sc across, turn. At the end of Row 3, fasten off.

Edging

With RS facing, attach pink to top left front at beg ch at base of collar, ch 1, sc in ends of next 3 sc rows of left front opening, 2 sc in corner st, sc in each sc to bottom corner, 2 sc

in corner sc in ends of next 3 rows of left front opening, sc in each st along lower edge of sweater, 3 sc across bottom right front opening, 2 sc in corner, sc across right front opening, 2 sc in corner 3 sc across edge of rows of right front opening, sl st in beg ch at base of collar, fasten off.

Sew buttons opposite buttonholes.

Bonnet
Back

Row 1: Starting at back of neck with hook size F and pink, ch 5, sc in 2nd ch from hook, sc in each of next 4 chs, turn. (4 sc)

Note: Work back of bonnet in back lps only.

Row 2: Ch 1, 2 sc in first sc, sc in each sc across to last sc, 2 sc in last sc, turn. (6 sc)

Rows 3–6: Rep Row 2. (14 sc)

Row 7: Ch 1, sc in each st across, turn.

Row 8: Rep Row 2. (16 sc)

Rows 9–18: Rep Row 7.

Row 19: Ch 1, sk first st, sc in each st across to last 2 sts, sc dec over next 2 sts, turn. (14 sc)

Row 20: Rep Row 19, fasten off. (12 sc)

Row 21: Working in ends of rows, attach pink in end of Row 1, ch 1, sc in same st, sc in each of next 19 rows, working in back lps only of Row 20, sc in each of next 12 sts, work 1 sc in each of next 20 rows, turn, do not fasten off. (52 sc)

Sides

Note: Sides of bonnet are worked in same cl and lace pattern as sweater.

Row 1: Change to hook size G, ch 2, sk first sc, 2-dc cl over next 2 sc, ch 1, [5 dc in next sc, 4-dc cl over next 4 sc, ch 1] 9 times, 5 dc in next sc, work 3-dc cl over last 3 sc, turn. (10 groups of 5-dc)

Note: Work Rows 2–4 with pink, Row 5 with white and Row 6 with pink.

Rows 2–6: Work in lace pattern established for body of sweater. At the end of last row, fasten off, turn.

Row 7: Attach white in first cl on Row 6, ch 1, sc in same st, *[sc in next dc, ch 1, sk next dc] twice, ch 1, sc in next dc, sk cl, rep from * across, ending with sc in last dc, sc in last cl, turn. (32 sc)

Row 8: Ch 1, sc in each sc and each ch-1 sp across, turn. (61 sc)

Row 9: Ch 2, dc in first sc, [ch 1, 2-dc cl in next sc] rep across, turn.

Row 10: Ch 1, [2 sc in next ch-1 sp, sl st in next cl] rep across, ending with sl st in last cl st, fasten off.

Neck edging & ties

With WS facing and hook size F, attach pink to end of Row 7, ch 1, sc in same st, 2 sc evenly sp in each of next 6 rows, sc in next row, sc in each of next 4 chs, sc in next row, 2 sc evenly sp in each of next 6 rows, sc in next row, ch 45, working in back of ch, sl st in 2nd ch from hook, sl st in each rem ch across, sc in each of next 32 sc, ch 45, working in back of ch, sl st in 2nd ch from hook, sl st in each rem ch across, sl st in corner of bonnet, fasten off.

To finish ruffle, sew ends of Row 9 to adjacent end of neck edging rows.

Bootie
Make 2

Rnd 1: With hook size F and pink, ch 10, 2 sc in 2nd ch from hook (heel), sc in each of next 7 chs, 6 sc in last ch (toe), working on opposite side of foundation ch, sc in each of next 7 chs, 2 sc in last ch, join in beg sc, turn. (24 sc)

Rnd 2: Ch 1, 2 sc in each of next 2 sc, sc in each of next 7 sc, 2 sc in each of next 6 sc, sc in each of next 7 sc, 2 sc in each of next 2 sc, join in beg sc, turn. (34 sc)

Rnd 3: Ch 1, [2 sc in next sc, sc in next sc] twice, sc in each of next 7 sc, [2 sc in next sc, sc in next sc] 6

Continued on page 154

Broomstick Lace Cradle Blanket

Design by Bendy Carter

The traditional technique of broomstick lace creates the delicate design in this beautiful blanket. The light, airy pattern, worked in sport weight yarn, makes it the perfect addition to Baby's warm-weather accessories.

Skill Level: Beginner

Size: 26½ x 30 inches

Materials

- J. & P. Coats Luster Sheen 3-ply sport weight yarn (1¾ oz per ball): 5 balls vanilla #7, 4 balls serenity #30
- Size H/8 crochet hook or size needed to obtain gauge
- Size 15 knitting needle
- Yarn needle

Gauge

4 sc or 2 lp groups = 1 inch;
6 rows = 2 inches

Check gauge to save time.

Pattern Notes

Weave in loose ends as work progresses.

Join rnds with a sl st unless otherwise stated.

Body of blanket is worked with 1 strand each vanilla and serenity held tog as one. When pattern indicates to slip next 2 lps from knitting needle onto crochet hook, remember you are working with 2 strands held tog as one so you will be passing 4 lps from needle to hook.

If you crochet left-handed, remember to work in reverse of what pattern indicates. When pattern says working left to right, remember to work right to left.

Blanket

Row 1 (RS): With 1 strand each color held tog, ch 100, place last lp on knitting needle, hold knitting needle in left hand, using crochet hook and working from left to right across ch, [insert hook in next ch, yo, draw up a lp, place lp on knitting needle] rep across ch. (100 lps on knitting needle), working from right to left, sl first 2 lps onto crochet hook, holding these lps tog as a group, yo, draw up a lp, ch 1, work 2 sc in center of same group, [sl next 2 lps onto crochet hook, yo, draw up a lp, yo, draw through 2 lps on hook, insert hook in same sp, yo, draw up a lp, yo, draw through 2 lps on hook] rep across, do not turn. (50 groups of 2 sc)

Row 2: Place last lp on knitting needle, holding knitting needle in left hand and working from left to right across row, [insert crochet hook in back lp only of next sc, yo, draw up a lp and place on knitting needle] rep across (100 lps on hook), working from right to left, sl first 2 lps onto crochet hook, holding these lps

Continued on page 155

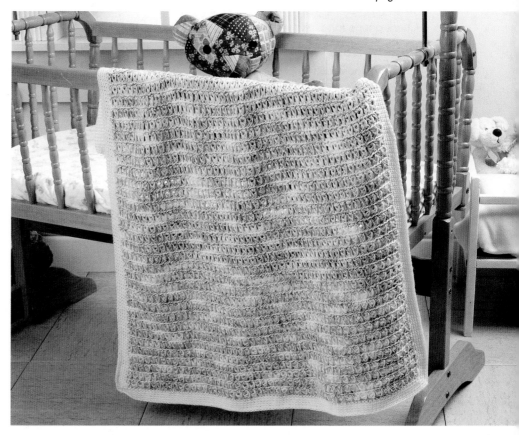

Baby Mittens

Design by Shirley Patterson

These adorable little hand warmers work up so quickly and easily they make a great last-minute gift for a baby shower. Or, add them as a package decoration for a purchased baby gift for a two-in-one present!

Skill Level: Beginner

Size: 0–3 months

Materials
- Coats & Clark Red Heart Baby fingering 3-ply yarn: ¾ oz white #1
- Size E/4 crochet hook or size needed to obtain gauge
- 28 inches ⅛-inch-wide blue satin ribbon
- 2 blue satin ribbon rosebuds
- Sewing needle and thread
- Tapestry needle

Gauge
5 hdc = 1 inch
Check gauge to save time.

Pattern Note
Weave in loose ends as work progresses.

Mitten
Make 4

Row 1: Ch 27, sl st in 2nd ch from hook, sl st in each of next 2 chs, sc in each of next 4 chs, hdc in each of next 12 chs, sc in each of next 4 chs, sl st in each of next 3 chs, turn. (26 sts)

Rows 2–10: Ch 1, working in back lps only, sl st in each of next 3 sts, working in both lps of sts, sc in each of next 4 sc, hdc in each of next 12 hdc, sc in each of next 4 sc, working in back lps only, sl st in each of next 3 sts, turn. (26 sts)

At the end of Row 10, fasten off.

Row 11: Holding 2 mitten pieces tog, matching sts and working through both thicknesses, attach white in opposite side of foundation ch of Row 1, sl st in each of next 26 sts, sl st evenly sp across ends of rows, sl st in each of next 23 sts across Row 10, leaving rem 3 sl sts unworked, fasten off.

Finishing
Weave a 12-inch double length of yarn through sl sts of Row 11 at fingertips, pull gently to gather slightly, secure end, fasten off rem lengths.

Cut ribbon in half, starting at center front, weave ribbon through sc sts just below 3 sl sts of cuff, tie ends in a bow at center front. Sew a rosebud directly below bow.

Rep in same manner for 2nd mitten.

Attach white at center back of mitten in cuff, ch 100, sl st at center back of 2nd mitten, sl st in each ch across, fasten off. ✂

There are no unwanted children, just unfound families.

—The National Adoption Center

Sunshine Dots Blanket

Design by Carol Carlile

Textured stitches created with simple chains "dot" the surface of this easy one-piece blanket to create a perfect pattern of dimensional diamonds. Stitched in sunny sport weight yarn, this cheery design will brighten any baby's nursery!

Skill Level: Beginner

Size: 38 x 39 inches

Materials

- Coats & Clark Red Heart Baby
- Sport weight yarn: 24 oz baby yellow #224
- Size G/6 crochet hook or size needed to obtain gauge
- Yarn needle

Gauge

4 sc = 1 inch; 5 sc rows = 1 inch
Check gauge to save time.

Pattern Notes

Weave in loose ends as work progresses.

Work in only sc sts of each row, sk ch-4 lps and keep all on RS of blanket.

Blanket

Row 1 (WS): Ch 151, sc in 2nd ch from hook, sc in each rem ch across, turn. (150 sc)

Rows 2 & 3: Ch 1, sc in each sc across, turn.

Row 4: Ch 1, sc in each of next 10 sc, [ch 4, sc in each of next 10 sc] 14 times, turn.

Row 5: Ch 1, sc in each sc across, turn.

Row 6: Ch 1, sc in each of next 9 sc, ch 4, sc in each of next 2 sc, ch 4, [sc in each of next 8 sc, ch 4, sc in each of next 2 sc, ch 4] 13 times, sc in each of next 9 sc, turn.

Row 7: Rep Row 5.

Row 8: Rep Row 4.

Rows 9–11: Rep Row 5.

Row 12: Ch 1, sc in each of next 15 sc, ch 4, [sc in each of next 10 sc, ch 4] 12 times, sc in each of next 15 sc, turn.

Row 13: Rep Row 5.

Row 14: Ch 1, sc in each of next 14 sc, ch 4, sc in each of next 2 sc, ch 4, [sc in each of next 8 sc, ch 4, sc in each of next 2 sc, ch 4] 12 times, sc in each of next 14 sc, turn.

Row 15: Rep Row 5.

Row 16: Rep Row 12.

Rows 17–19: Rep Row 5.

Rows 20–171: Rep Rows 4–19, ending last rep with Row 11, fasten off.

Edging

Rnd 1: Attach yarn in any corner, [ch 3, dc {ch 1, 2 dc} twice] in same st as joining, sk next 3 sts or 3 rows, *[{2 dc, ch 1, 2 dc} in next st, sk next 3 sts or 3 rows] rep across to next corner st **, [2 dc {ch 1, 2 dc} twice] in corner st, sk next 3 sts of 3 rows, rep from * around, ending last rep at **, join in 3rd ch of beg ch-3, fasten off. ✄

Preemie Wardrobe

Designs by Bendy Carter

This versatile wardrobe features one pant pattern to coordinate with three differently styled tops. These precious outfits feature a variety of interesting stitches and can be made in three sizes to fit preemies and newborns from 4 to 8 pounds.

Skill Level: Intermediate

Size

Preemie: 4 (6, 8) pounds

Finished chest: 14 (16, 18) inches

Hips: 14 (16, 18) inches

Materials

- J. & P. Coats Luster Sheen sport weight yarn (1¾ oz per ball): Sweaters: 1 ball bluette #425, 2 balls aqua #673, 1 (2, 2) balls white #001, 2 (3, 3) balls ocean #995, 2 (2, 3) balls vanilla #7; Pants: 2 balls each bluette #425, vanilla #7, aqua #673

- Size D/3 crochet hook or size needed to obtain gauge

- Size B/1 crochet hook

- 12 (14, 16) inches ½-inch-wide elastic

- Sewing needle and thread

- Yarn needle

Gauge

With hook size D, 14 hdc = 3 inches; 10 hdc rows = 3 inches

Check gauge to save time.

Pattern Notes

Weave in loose ends as work progresses.

Join rnds with a sl st unless otherwise stated.

Pattern Stitch

Spring st: Yo hook 4 times, insert hook in indicated st, yo, draw up a lp, yo, draw through 5 lps on hook (**Note:** *Draw yarn through first 2 lps, then remove next 3 lps tog with fingers*), yo, draw through last 2 lps on hook.

Cream Sweater

Back Ribbing

Row 1: With hook size B and vanilla, ch 5, sc in 2nd ch from hook, sc in each rem ch across, turn. (4 sc)

Row 2: Ch 1, working in back lps only, sc in each st across, turn. (4 sc)

Rep Row 2 until a total of 30 (34, 38) ribbing rows are completed.

Back

Row 1 (RS): Change to hook size D and working across long edge of ribbing rows, ch 1, sc in each ribbing row across, turn. (30, 34, 38 sc)

Row 2: Ch 1, sc in each sc across, turn.

Rep Row 2 until back measures from beg 7¼ (7¾, 8¼) inches, ending at right shoulder, turn.

Working across right shoulder, ch 1, sc in each of next 8 (9, 11) sc, fasten off.

Note: *Left shoulder will be finished later.*

Front

Work back ribbing and front the same as back until from beg piece measures 4 (5, 5) rows less than back.

First neck shaping

Row 1: Ch 1, sc in each of next 11 (12, 14) sc, turn.

Row 2: Rep Row 2 of back and at the same time, dec 3 sts at neck edge. (8, 9, 11 sc)

If working right side shaping, rep Row 2 of back 2 (3, 3) times, fasten off.

If working left side shaping, rep Row 2 of back 0 (1, 1) times, fasten off.

Second neck shaping

Sk next 8 (10, 10) sc, attach vanilla in next st, rep as for first neck shaping.

Using hook size D and vanilla, surface ch st design on front according to diagram.

Sew right shoulder seam.

Back left shoulder

Row 1: With hook size B, attach vanilla at corner of left shoulder, ch 5, sc in 2nd ch from hook, sc in each rem ch across, sl st in same st as beg ch, sl st in next st on shoulder, turn. (4 sc)

Row 2: Sk sl sts, working in back lps only, sc in each of next 4 sts, turn.

Row 3: Ch 1, working in back lps only, sc in each of next 4 sts, sl st in next 2 sts on shoulder, turn.

Rep Rows 2 and 3 across the 8 (9, 11) sts of shoulder.

Front left shoulder

Rep the same as back left shoulder, working 2 buttonholes evenly sp across edge. To work a buttonhole on any row, sc in back lp of first st, ch 2, sk next 2 sts, sc in back lp of next st.

Neckline Ribbing

Row 1 (RS): With hook size B, attach vanilla at left front neck opening at shoulder, ch 1, work an even number of sc sts around neckline opening, turn.

Row 2: Ch 5, sc in 2nd ch from hook, sc in each of next 3 chs, sl st in same sc as beg ch-5, sl st in next sc, turn. (4 sc)

Row 3: Working in back lps only, sk sl sts, sc in each of next 4 sc, turn.

Row 4: Ch 1, working in back lps only, sc in each of next 4 sts, sl st in next 2 sts of Row 1, turn.

Rep Rows 3 and 4 around neckline, working another buttonhole at left shoulder in line with buttonholes of left shoulder. Work buttonhole in same manner.

Button

Make 3

With hook size B, leaving a length at beg, ch 2, 6 sc in 2nd ch from hook, join in beg sc, leaving a length of yarn, fasten off.

Using beg and ending lengths, secure sts, sew buttons opposite buttonholes.

With left shoulder buttoned, sew ribbing rows at left shoulder tog across the end.

Sleeve

Make 2

Ribbing

Rep the same as back ribbing until 22 (24, 26) rows are completed.

Sleeve body

Row 1: With hook size D, working across long edge of ribbing, ch 1, work 22 (24, 26) sc across, turn.

Row 2: Ch 1, sc in each sc across, turn.

Rep Row 2 until from beg sleeve measures 3½ (4¼, 5) inches, and at

the same time, inc 1 sc at beg and end of every 5th (6th, 7th) rows until a total of 28 (30, 32) sc sts. At the end of last rep, fasten off.

Using hook size D and vanilla, surface ch st design on sleeve according to diagram on page 143.

Fold sleeve in half lengthwise, position center fold at shoulder seam and sew sleeve to body of sweater, sew sleeve and side seams.

Variegated Blue Sweater

Body Ribbing

Row 1: With hook size B and bluette, ch 5, sc in 2nd ch from hook,

sc in each rem ch across, turn. (4 sc)

Row 2: Ch 1, working in back lps only, sc in each st across, turn. (4 sc)

Rep Row 2 until 61 (71, 81) rows are completed, fasten off.

Body

Foundation row: With hook size D, working across long edge of ribbing, attach ocean in end of ribbing, ch 1, work 61 (71, 81) sc across, turn.

Row 1 (RS): Ch 3 (counts as first dc throughout), spring st each st across to last st, dc in last st, turn.

Row 2: Ch 1, sc in each st across, turn.

Before you were conceived
I wanted you.
Before you were born
I loved you.
Before you were here an hour
I would die for you.
This is the miracle of life.

—Maureen Hawkins

Rep Rows 1 and 2 until from beg piece measures 4¼ (4½, 4¾) inches.

First Front

Work in pattern across 14 (17, 19) sts, turn.

Continue in pattern rows until from armhole piece measures 2½ inches, ending with a Row 1 pattern.

Neck shaping

Work in pattern Row 2, at the same time dec 3 (4, 4) sts at neck edge.

Work in pattern Row 1, at the same time, dec 2 (3, 3) sts at neckline edge.

Continue in established pattern until from beg of front piece measures 3¼ (3½, 3¾) inches, fasten off.

Back

Sk 1 st on body, attach ocean in next st, work in established pattern across 31 (35, 41) sts, turn.

Continue in pattern rows until back is 1 row less than front.

First shoulder shaping

Ch 1, work across 9 (10, 12) sts, fasten off.

Second shoulder shaping

Sk next 13 (15, 17) sts on back, attach ocean in next st, ch 1, work across 9 (10, 12) sts, fasten off.

Second Front

Sk next st on body, attach ocean in next st, rep as for first front.

Sew shoulder seams.

Sleeve

Make 2

Ribbing

Rep the same as for body ribbing until 23 (26, 29) rows are completed, fasten off.

Sleeve body

Foundation row: With hook size D and working across long edge of ribbing, attach ocean, ch 1, work 23 (26, 29) sc across ribbing, turn.

Row 1 (RS): Rep Row 1 of pattern.

Row 2: Rep Row 2 of pattern, at the same time inc 1 st at each end of row.

Row 3: Rep Row 1 of pattern.

Row 4: Rep Row 2 of pattern.

Row 5: Rep Row 1 of pattern.

Rep Rows 2–5 until a total of 31 (34, 35) sts across row.

Continue in pattern until sleeve measures from beg 3½ (4¼, 5) inches, fasten off.

Sew sleeve in armhole opening.

Neckline Ribbing

Row 1: With hook size B, attach bluette at right front neckline, ch 1, sc evenly sp around neckline, ending with an even number of sts, turn.

Row 2: Ch 3, sc in 2nd ch from hook, sc in next ch, sl st in same st as beg ch-3, sl st in next st, turn. (2 sc)

Row 3: Working in back lps only, sc in each of next 2 sts, turn.

Row 4: Ch 1, working in back lps only, sc in each of next 2 sts, sl st in next 2 sts of Row 1, turn.

Rep Rows 3 and 4 around neckline opening, fasten off.

Button Edge

Row 1 (RS): With hook size B, attach bluette at neckline edge, ch 1, sc evenly sp down front, turn.

Rows 2 & 3: Ch 1, sc in each sc across, turn. At the end of Row 3, fasten off.

Buttonhole Edge

Row 1 (RS): With hook size B, attach bluette at right bottom edge, ch 1, sc evenly sp up right front, turn.

Note: *With a scrap of CC yarn, mark position of 4 (5, 5) buttonholes evenly sp on edge of Row 1.*

Row 2: Ch 1, sc in each sc to marker, [ch 2, sk 2 sts] for buttonhole, rep across edge until all buttonholes are completed, turn.

Row 3: Ch 1, sc in each sc and each ch sp across, fasten off.

Button

Make 4 (5, 5)

With bluette, rep button pattern the same as cream sweater.

Sew buttons opposite buttonholes on left front edge.

Aqua Sweater

Back Ribbing

Row 1: With hook size B and aqua, ch 5, sc in 2nd ch from hook, sc in each rem ch across, turn. (4 sc)

Row 2: Ch 1, working in back lps only, sc in each st across, turn.

Rep Row 2 until 34 (38, 42) rows are completed.

Back body

Row 1: With hook size D, working across long edge of ribbing, ch 1, work 34 (38, 42) sc sts across, turn.

Row 2: Ch 1, sc in each st across, changing to white in last st, turn.

Note: *Throughout sweater: If a row begins with an fpdc because of inc sts or dec sts, ch 1 to beg row.*

Row 3: Ch 1, sc in each of next 2 sts, [fpdc around each of next 2 sc of Row 1, sk sts directly behind fpdc sts, sc in each of next 2 sts] rep across, turn.

Row 4: Ch 1, sc in each st across, changing to aqua in last st of row, turn.

Row 5: Ch 1, sc in each of next 2 sc, [fpdc around each of next 2 fpdc directly below, sk 2 sts directly behind fpdc sts, sc in each of next 2 sts] rep across, turn.

Row 6: Ch 1, sc in each st across, changing to white in last st, turn.

Row 7: Ch 1, sc in each of next 2 sc, [fpdc around each of next 2 fpdc directly below, sk 2 sts directly behind fpdc sts, sc in each of next 2 sts] rep across, turn.

Note: *Rows 4–7 establish sweater pattern and color changes to be worked throughout sweater.*

Rep pattern Rows 4–7 until from beg back measures 7¼ (7¾, 8¼) inches from beg, ending with a pattern Row 5 or 7.

First neck shaping

Work in pattern across 11 (12, 14) sts, turn.

Work in pattern across row, fasten off.

Second neck shaping
Sk next 12 (14, 14) sts for neckline opening, attach yarn in next st, ch 1, work in established pattern rows for 2 rows, fasten off.

Front
Work the same as for back ribbing and back body until from beg front measures 4¼ (4½, 4¾) inches, ending with a pattern Row 5 or 7.

First front
Work in pattern across 15 (17, 19) sts, turn.

Continue in pattern rows until front measures 2½ inches, ending with a pattern Row 5 or 7.

Neck shaping
Row 1: Work in pattern row across, dec 2 sts at neck edge, turn.

Row 2: Work in pattern row across, turn.

Rows 3 & 4: Rep Rows 1 and 2.

Row 5: Work in pattern row across, dec 0 (1, 1) st at neck edge, turn.

Continue in established pattern until front measures the same as back, fasten off.

Second front
Sk next 4 sts on front, attach yarn in next st, work 15 (17, 19) sts in established pattern the same as first front. Work neckline shaping the same as first front.

Sew shoulder seams.

First front neck ribbing
Row 1: With hook size B and RS facing, attach aqua at neck edge, ch 1, sc evenly sp down neck opening in side edge of row of first front, turn.

Row 2: Ch 3, sc in 2nd ch from hook, sc in next ch, sl st in same st as beg ch-3, sl st in next st of Row 1, turn. (2 sc)

Row 3: Working in back lps only, sk sl sts, sc in each of next 2 sc, turn.

Row 4: Ch 1, working in back lps only, sc in each of next 2 sts, sl st in

each of next 2 sts of Row 1, turn.

Rep Rows 3 and 4 across sts of Row 1 of first front neck ribbing, fasten off.

Second front neck ribbing
Row 1: With hook size B and RS facing, attach aqua at bottom edge in 2nd front, ch 1, sc evenly sp up neck opening in side edge of rows of 2nd front, turn.

Row 2: Rep Row 2 of first front neck ribbing.

Rep Rows 3 and 4 of first front neck ribbing across sts of Row 1 of ribbing, fasten off.

Sew the 2 sts of Row 2 of the bottom edges of both front neck ribbings to the 4 sk center front sts of sweater and sew up center of ribbing rows ¾ inch.

Collar
Row 1 (RS): With hook size B, attach aqua in top right front of ribbing rows, ch 1, work 2 sc across ribbing rows, sc evenly sp around neckline opening, working 2 sc across ribbing rows of left front, turn.

Row 2: Ch 1, sc in each sc across, turn.

Rep Row 2 until collar from beg measures 1½ inches, fasten off.

Sleeve
Make 2

Ribbing
Work the same as back ribbing for 22 (26, 30) rows.

Sleeve body
Working across long edge of ribbing, ch 1, work 22 (26, 30) sc evenly sp across, turn.

Rep Rows 2 and 3 of back body.

Rep pattern Rows 4–7, at the same time inc 1 st at each end of next row and every 6 (6, 8) rows, keeping with established pattern rows until a total of 28 (32, 35) sts.

Continue in established pattern rows until sleeve from beg measures 3½ (4¼, 5) inches, fasten off.

Fold sleeve in half lengthwise, center fold at shoulder seam and sew sleeve to body of sweater. Sew sleeve and side seams.

Pants

Pant Leg
Make 2

Ribbing
Row 1: With hook size B and matching pant color for sweater, ch 5, sc in 2nd ch from hook, sc in each rem ch across, turn. (4 sc)

Row 2: Ch 1, working in back lps only, sc in each st across, turn.

Rep Row 2 until ribbing is 29 (31, 33) rows.

Leg body
Row 1: With hook size D, working across long edge of ribbing, ch 1, work 29 (31, 33) sc across edge, turn.

Continued on page 153

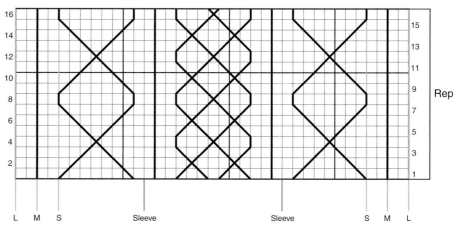

Cream Sweater

Carnival Colors Layette

Designs by Sandy Rideout

Baby will be a standout in this vibrant, striped ensemble stitched in bright primary colors. Using only simple, basic stitches, this fun set makes an easy project even for beginners!

Skill Level: Beginner

Size
Sweater & hat: Newborn
Afghan: 39 x 42 inches

Materials
- Coats & Clark Red Heart sport weight yarn: 12 oz cherry red #912, 10½ oz each yellow #230, skipper blue #846 and paddy green #687
- Sizes G/6 and K/10½ crochet hooks or sizes needed to obtain gauge
- Size F/5 crochet hook
- 6 yellow 13mm star-shape shank buttons
- Stitch markers
- Tapestry needle

Gauge
With hook size G, 4 sts = 1 inch; 4 rows = 1 inch; with K hook, 6 sts = 2 inches; 6 pattern rows = 2 inches
Check gauge to save time.

Pattern Notes
Weave in loose ends as work progresses.

Join rnds with a sl st unless otherwise stated.

Change color in last step of last st of row.

Sweater & Hat
Note: Color sequence to be repeated throughout sweater and hat is cherry red, skipper blue, paddy green and yellow.

Back
Row 1 (RS): With hook size G and cherry red, ch 37, sc in 2nd ch from hook, sc in each rem ch across, changing to skipper blue in last st, turn. (36 sts)

Row 2: Ch 1, sc in first st, hdc in next st, [sc in next st, hdc in next st] rep across, changing to paddy green in last st, turn.

Row 3: Ch 1, sc in each st across, changing to yellow in last st, turn.

Row 4: Ch 1, sc in first st, hdc in next st, [sc in next st, hdc in next st] rep across, changing to cherry red in last st, turn.

Row 5: Ch 1, sc in each st across, changing to skipper blue in last st, turn.

Rows 6–36: Rep Rows 2–5 for pattern and color sequence, ending last rep with pattern Row 4.

Note: Place a st marker at each edge of Row 24 for sleeve underarm.

First shoulder shaping
Row 37: With cherry red, ch 1, sc in each of next 12 sts, fasten off.

Second shoulder shaping
Row 37: Sk center 12 sts, attach cherry red in next st, ch 1, sc in each of next 12 sts, fasten off.

Right Front
Row 1 (RS): With hook size G and cherry red, ch 18, sc in 2nd ch from hook, sc in each rem ch across, turn. (17 sc)

Rows 2–31: Rep the same as for back in pattern st and color sequence on 17 sts.

Neck shaping
Row 32: Work in pattern across 16 sts, turn.

Row 33: Sk first st, work in pattern across rem sts, turn. (15 sts)

Row 34: Work in pattern across to last st, sk last st, turn. (14 sts)

Rows 35 & 36: Rep Rows 33 and 34. (12 sts)

Row 37: Work in pattern across, fasten off.

Left Front
Rows 1–31: Rep Rows 1–31 of right front. (17 sts)

Shoulder shaping
Row 32: Sk first st, work in pattern across rem sts, turn. (16 sts)

Row 33: Work in pattern across to last st, sk last st, turn. (15 sts)

Row 34: Sk first st, work in pattern across rem sts, turn. (14 sts)

Rows 35 & 36: Rep Rows 33 and 34. (12 sts)

Row 37: Work in pattern across, fasten off.

Holding back to front, sew shoulder seams.

Sleeve
Make 2

Row 1 (RS): With hook size G and cherry red, ch 25, sc in 2nd ch from hook, sc in each rem ch across, turn. (24 sc)

Rows 2–21: Work in pattern as

for back, inc 1 st at each end on Rows 5 and 9. (28 sts)

At the end of last rep, leaving a length of yarn, fasten off.

Cuff

Row 1 (RS): With hook size F, attach cherry red in opposite side of foundation ch, ch 3 (counts as first dc), dc in each ch across, turn. (24 dc)

Row 2: Ch 2, [fpdc around next dc, bpdc around next dc] rep across, turn.

Row 3: Ch 2, [fpdc around each fpdc and bpdc around each bpdc] rep across, leaving a length of yarn, fasten off.

Sew sleeve into armhole opening between marker. Sew sleeve and side seam of sweater.

Bottom Ribbing

Row 1 (RS): With hook size F, attach cherry red in opposite side of foundation ch, ch 3, dc in each ch across bottom edge of sweater, turn. (70 dc)

Rows 2 & 3: Rep Rows 2 and 3 of cuff for sleeve.

Neckline Ribbing

Row 1: With hook size F, attach cherry red at neckline edge, ch 3, work 30 dc evenly sp around neckline, turn. (31 dc)

Row 2: Ch 2, [fpdc around next dc, bpdc around next dc] rep around neckline, fasten off.

Right Button Edge

Row 1 (RS): With hook size F, attach cherry red at bottom edge of sweater, ch 1, work 38 sc evenly sp up front opening of sweater, turn. (38 sc)

Rows 2–4: Ch 1, sc in each sc across, turn. At the end of Row 4, fasten off.

Right Buttonhole Edge

Row 1 (RS): With hook size F, attach cherry red at neckline edge, ch 1, work 38 sc evenly sp down front opening of sweater, turn.

Row 2: Ch 1, sc in each sc across, turn.

Row 3: Ch 1, sc in first sc, [ch 1, sk next sc, sc in each of next 6 sc] 5 times, ch 1, sk next sc, sc in next sc, turn. (6 buttonholes)

Row 4: Ch 1, sc in first sc, [sc in next ch-1 sp, sc in each of next 6 sc] 5 times, sc in next ch-1 sp, sc in next sc, fasten off. (38 sc)

Sew buttons opposite buttonholes.

Hat

Note: *Work same color sequence and pattern as sweater.*

Rnd 1 (RS): With hook size G and cherry red, ch 60, join to form a ring, ch 1, sc in each sc around, join in beg sc, turn. (60 sc)

Rnd 2: Ch 1, sc in first st, hdc in next st, [sc in next st, hdc in next st] rep around, join in beg sc, turn.

Rnd 3: Ch 1, sc in each st around, join in beg sc, turn.

Rnds 4–10: Working established color sequence, rep Rnds 2 and 3.

Rnd 11: Ch 1, working in pattern around, dec 6 sts evenly sp around, join in beg st, turn. (54 sts)

Rnds 12–14: Work in established pattern.

Rnd 15: Rep Rnd 11. (48 sts)

Rnds 16–18: Work in established pattern.

Rnds 19–24: Rep Rnd 11. (12 sts)

Rnd 25: Ch 1, [sc dec over next 2 sts] 6 times, join in beg sc, leaving a length of yarn, fasten off.

Continued on page 155

You come with a birthright, written in love, which promises that no matter where you're at, you are home; that no matter who you're with, you are welcome; that no matter who you are, you are loved.

—Rita Ramsey

Sweetie Pie Baby

Design by Kathleen Stuart

In her nightcap and sleeper, this precious little doll is ready to share Baby's sweet angel dreams. She's cuddly and soft, and just the right size for little arms to hug and tiny hands to hold!

Skill Level: Beginner

Size: 11 inches tall

Materials

- Sport weight yarn: 2 oz pink, 1 oz off-white, scrap of each pale yellow, red and light brown
- Size G/6 crochet hook or size needed to obtain gauge
- Stitch marker
- Fiberfill
- Tapestry needle

First leg

Rnd 1: Dc in each of next 9 dc, sk next 18 dc, dc in each of next 9 dc. (18 dc)

Rnds 2–8: Dc in each dc around.

Rnd 9: [Dc in next dc, dc dec over next 2 sts] rep around. (12 dc)

Rnd 10: [Dc dec over next 2 dc] 6 times, sl st in next st, leaving a length of yarn, fasten off.

Stuff leg with fiberfill and sew leg opening closed.

Continued on page 154

Gauge

5 sc = 1 inch

Check gauge to save time.

Pattern Notes

Weave in loose ends as work progresses.

Do not join rnds unless otherwise stated; use a st marker to mark rnds.

Head & Body

Rnd 1: Starting at top of head, with off-white, ch 2, 6 sc in 2nd ch from hook. (6 sc)

Rnd 2: 2 sc in each sc around. (12 sc)

Rnd 3: [Sc in next sc, 2 sc in next sc] rep around. (18 sc)

Rnd 4: [Sc in each of next 2 sc, 2 sc in next sc] rep around. (24 sc)

Rnd 5: [Sc in each of next 3 sc, 2 sc in next sc] rep around. (30 sc)

Rnd 6: [Sc in each of next 4 sc, 2 sc in next sc] rep around. (36 sc)

Rnds 7–12: Sc in each sc around.

Rnd 13: [Sc in each of next 4 sc, sc dec over next 2 sc] rep around. (30 sc)

Rnd 14: [Sc in each of next 3 sc, sc dec over next 2 sc] rep around. (24 sc)

Rnd 15: [Sc in each of next 2 sc, sc dec over next 2 sc] rep around. (18 sc)

Stuff head with fiberfill.

Rnd 16: [Sc in next st, sc dec over next 2 sc] rep around, changing to pink in last sc. (12 sc)

Rnds 17 & 18: Working with pink, rep Rnds 3 and 4. (24 sc)

Rnd 19: [Dc in each of next 3 sc, 2 dc in next sc] rep around. (30 dc)

Rnd 20: [Dc in each of next 4 dc, 2 dc in next dc] rep around. (36 dc)

Rnds 21–29: Dc in each dc around.

Stuff body with fiberfill.

Mint Twinkle Blanket

Design by Aline Suplinskas

Shimmering stripes of watercolor pastels create the lustrous look of this sweet and simple blanket that's the perfect size for bringing Baby home from the hospital. Baby pompadour yarn worked on a large hook makes it extra-soft and light!

Skill Level: Beginner

Size: 26 x 32 inches

Materials

- Caron Cuddlesoft pompadour baby yarn (1¾ oz per skein):
- 2 skeins each baby blue #2814, rainbow print #2830, baby green #2811
- Size H/8 crochet hook or size needed to obtain gauge
- Yarn needle

Gauge

[Sc, ch 2, dc] twice = 1½ inches; 3 rows = 1 inch

Check gauge to save time.

Pattern Notes

Weave in loose ends as work progresses.

Do not fasten off yarns at end of rows, drop old color and complete last step of last sc with new color.

Blanket

Row 1: With baby blue, ch 155, dc in 3rd ch from hook, sk each of next 3 chs, [{sc, ch 2, dc} in next ch, sk each of next 3 chs] 37 times, sc in last ch, changing to rainbow print in last step of sc, turn.

Row 2: Ch 3, dc in same st as beg ch-3, [{sc, ch 2, dc} in next ch-2 sp] rep across, ending with sc in last ch sp, changing to baby green in last step of sc, turn.

Row 3: Rep Row 2, changing to baby blue in last step of sc, turn.

Row 4: Rep Row 2, changing to rainbow print in last step of sc, turn.

Rows 5–92: Rep Row 2, maintaining the established color sequence.

At the end of Row 92, fasten off baby blue and rainbow print yarns, leaving baby green, turn.

Trim

Rnd 1: Ch 1, [sc, ch 2, dc] twice in end st for corner, working down side edge of rows, sk next row, [{sc, ch 2, dc} in side edge of next row, sk next row] rep to bottom corner, [sc, ch 2, dc] twice in first ch of opposite side of foundation ch, [sk next 3 chs, {sc, ch 2, dc} in next ch] rep across to last 4 chs, sk next ch, [sc, ch 2, dc] twice in end ch, working across side edge of rows, sk next row, [{sc, ch 2, dc} in side of next row, sk next row] rep across to first st of last row of blanket, [sc, ch 2, dc] twice in end st for corner, [sc, ch 2, dc] in each ch-2 sp across, fasten off. ✂

Garden Baby Headbands

Designs by Lori Zeller

A dainty butterfly and delicate flower adorn these fashionable little headbands that make cute accessories for Baby's wardrobe. The pattern for these easy-to-stitch thread bands can be easily adjusted to fit any length of elastic for a perfect, comfortable fit!

Skill Level: Beginner

Size: Head circumference 13–15 inches

Materials

- Crochet cotton size 10: 50 yds each white and pink, 5 yds pastels, 2 yds mint
- Size 5 steel crochet hook or size needed to obtain gauge
- 26 inches ¼-inch-wide elastic
- 4mm white pearl bead
- Sewing needle and thread
- Tapestry needle

Gauge

4 sts = ½ inch; 3 pattern rows = ½ inch

Check gauge to save time.

Pattern Notes

Weave in loose ends as work progresses.

Join rnds with a sl st unless otherwise stated.

Inc or dec number of rows of headband to fit infant head comfortably and adjust elastic as needed.

Elastic Preparation

Cut a 13-inch length of elastic, overlapping ends ¼ inch; sew ends tog to form a circle.

Butterfly Headband

Band

Make 2

Row 1: With white, ch 5, sc in 2nd ch from hook, dc in next ch, sc in next ch, dc in next ch, turn. (4 sts)

Rows 2–108: Ch 1, sc in first dc, dc in next sc, sc in next dc, dc in next sc, turn. At the end of Row 108, fasten off.

Joining

Row 1: Holding bands tog and working through both thicknesses along long edge of band, attach white in side edge of Row 1, ch 1, [sc, ch 3, sc] in same st as beg ch-1, ch 1, [sk next st, {sc, ch 3, sc} in next st, ch 1] rep across edge, ending with sl st in last st, fasten off.

Row 2: Holding elastic circle sandwiched between bands and working through both thicknesses along long edge, attach white, ch 1, [sc, ch 3, sc] in same st, ch 1, [sk next st, {sc, ch 3, sc} in next st, ch 1] rep across, ending with sl st in last st, leaving a length of cotton, fasten off.

With rem length, sew beg and ending of rows tog.

Butterfly

Wings

Rnd 1: With pastels, ch 2, [sc, ch

Continued on page 155

Sweet Dreams Poncho & Blanket

Designs by Glenda Winkleman

Snuggle Baby soft and warm in this cozy, fluffy-as-a-cloud set stitched in heavenly, light worsted terry yarn. The poncho can be made in sizes to fit newborn to toddler!

Skill Level: Intermediate

Size

Blanket: 30 x 36 inches

Poncho: 0–6 months, 1 year and 18 months–2 years

Materials

- Coats & Clark Red Heart Baby Terri light worsted weight 3-ply yarn (3 oz per skein): 6 skeins yellow #9121, 3 skeins pink #9137, 2 skeins each blue #9181 and mint #9180, 1 skein lilac #9145
- Size I/9 afghan crochet hook or size needed to obtain gauge
- Sizes H/8 and I/9 crochet hooks
- Yarn needle

Gauge

8 sts = 2 inches; 6 rows = 2 inches
Check gauge to save time.

Pattern Notes

Weave in loose ends as work progresses.

Join rnds with a sl st unless otherwise stated.

Pattern Stitch

Afghan st: [Insert hook under next vertical bar, yo, draw up a lp] rep across retaining all lps on hook, yo, draw through first lp on hook, [yo, draw through 2 lps on hook] rep across until 1 lp rem on hook.

Blanket

Row 1: With afghan crochet hook and pink, ch 101, insert hook in 2nd ch from hook, yo, draw up a lp, [insert hook in next ch, yo, draw up a lp] rep across retaining all lps on hook (101 lps on hook), yo, draw through 1 lp on hook, [yo, draw through 2 lps on hook] rep across until 1 lp rem on hook and counts as first lp of next row, changing color before last lp is pulled through, fasten off pink.

Row 2: With yellow, first lp counts as first st, [with yarn to front of work on right-hand side of next vertical st, insert hook in next vertical st, yarn underneath and to the back of hook, yo, draw yarn through st, with yarn to back of work, insert hook in next vertical st, yo, draw yarn through st] rep across, yo, draw through 1 lp on hook, [yo, draw through 2 lps on hook] rep across until 1 lp rem on hook and counts as first lp of next row, drop yellow before pulling last lp through when changing color, carry yellow behind work throughout pattern.

Row 3: With mint, first lp counts as regular afghan st, [with yarn to the back of work, insert hook in next vertical st, draw yarn through st, with yarn to the front of work on right-hand side of next vertical st, insert hook in next vertical st, place yarn underneath and to the back of hook, yo, draw yarn through st] rep across to within last 2 sts, with yarn to the back, work last 2 sts as regular afghan st, yo, draw through 1 lp on hook, [yo, draw through 2 lps on hook] rep across until 1 lp rem on hook and counts as first lp of next row, changing color before last lp is pulled through, fasten off mint.

Row 4: With yellow, rep Row 2.

Row 5: With blue, rep Row 3.

Row 6: With yellow, rep Row 2.

Row 7: With lilac, rep Row 3.

Row 8: With yellow, rep Row 2.

Row 9: With pink, rep Row 3.

Rows 10–17: Rep Rows 2–9.

Row 18: With yellow, rep Row 2.

Rows 19–29: Work even in regular afghan st.

Row 30: With pink, rep Row 2.

Row 31: With yellow, rep Row 3.

Row 32: With mint, rep Row 2.

Row 33: With yellow, rep Row 3.

Row 34: With blue, rep Row 2.

Row 35: With yellow, rep Row 3.

Row 36: With lilac, rep Row 2.

Row 37: With yellow, rep Row 3.

Row 38: With pink, rep Row 2.

Row 39: With yellow, rep Row 3.

Rows 40–72: Rep Rows 32–39.

The angels light another star every time a baby is born to celebrate a precious new child God sends to Earth.

—Unknown

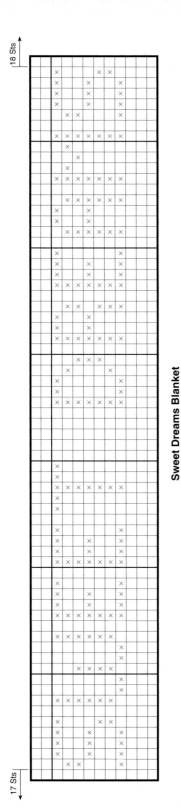

Sweet Dreams Blanket

18 Sts

17 Sts

Rows 73–83: Work even in regular afghan st.

Rows 84–99: Rep Rows 30–37.

Row 100: Rep Row 30.

Row 101: With pink, [yarn to the back, sl st in next vertical st, with

STITCH KEY
☒ Mint

Sew together

**Sweet Dreams Poncho
Assembly Chart**

yarn to the front, sl st in next vertical st] rep across to last 2 sts, yarn to the back, sl st in each of last 2 sts, fasten off.

Side Border

Row 1(RS): With hook size I, attach pink in lower right corner, ch 1, sc in each row across edge, fasten off.

Row 2 (RS): With hook size I, attach pink in top left corner, ch 1, sc in each row across edge, fasten off.

Border

Rnd 1 (RS): With I hook, attach yellow in upper right corner, ch 1, sc in each of next 5 sts, *[sk next st, sc in each of next 5 sts] rep across to last 5 sts, sk next st, sc in each of next 4 sts, ch 2, sc in each sc across length, ch 2 **, sc in each of next 5 sts, rep from * around, ending last rep at **, join in beg sc, fasten off.

Rnd 2 (RS): Attach mint in beg sc, ch 1, sc in each sc around, working [sc, ch 2, sc] in each corner ch-2 sp, join in beg sc, fasten off.

Rnd 3: With blue, rep Rnd 2.

Rnd 4: With lilac, rep Rnd 2.

Rnd 5: With pink, rep Rnd 2.

Rnd 6: With yellow, rep Rnd 2, do not fasten off.

Rnd 7: With yellow, ch 3 (counts as first dc), dc in each sc around, working 5 dc in each corner ch-2 sp, join in 3rd ch of beg ch-3.

Rnd 8: Ch 1, sc in each of next 2 dc, ch 3, sl st in top of last sc, [sc in each of next 2 dc, ch 3, sl st in top of last sc] rep around, join in beg sc, fasten off.

Embroidery

With mint, following diagram,

cross-stitch "Sweet Dreams" over Rows 19–29 and Rows 73–83.

Poncho

Notes: For each size poncho work a total of 36 squares.

Squares measure 2½ inches for 6 months, 2¾ inches for 1 year and 3 inches for 18 months–2 years.

Rows 1–6 (1–7, 1–8): With afghan hook size I and pink, ch 9 (11, 13), rep Rows 1–6 (1–7, 1–8) of blanket.

Row 7 (8, 9): Sl st in each vertical st across, fasten off.

Assembly

Using diagram as a guide, sew squares tog.

Bottom Border

Rnd 1 (RS): With hook size H, attach lilac in center bottom point of front of poncho, ch 1, 3 sc in point st, sc in each st around bottom edge of poncho working 3 sc in center back point, join in beg sc, fasten off.

Rnd 2: Attach yellow in first sc of previous rnd, ch 1, sc in same sc, ch 1, sk next sc, [sc in next sc, ch 1, sk next sc] rep around, join in beg sc, fasten off.

Rnd 3: Attach pink in first sc of previous rnd, ch 1, sc in same sc, *sc in next ch-1 sp, ch 3, sl st in top of last sc **, sc in next sc, rep from * around, ending last rep at **, join in beg sc, fasten off.

Neckline Trim

Rnd 1 (RS): With hook size H, attach lilac in front center st of neck opening, ch 1, sc in evenly sp around neckline, join in beg sc, fasten off.

Rnd 2: Rep Rnd 2 of bottom border.

Tie

Row 1: With hook size H and pink, ch 100, sc in 2nd ch from hook, sc in each rem ch across, fasten off.

Starting and ending at front center neckline opening, weave tie through ch-1 sps of Rnd 2, adjust tie ends even. ✂

Pistachio Stripes

Design courtesy of Caron International

Alternating squares of puffy flowers and Tunisian-stitch stripes create the eye-catching pattern in this precious afghan confection. It works up quickly in fluffy worsted yarn, and portability makes it a great take-along project!

Skill Level: Beginner

Size: 36 x 49 inches

Materials

- Caron Dazzleaire worsted weight yarn (3 oz per skein): 7 skeins white #2601, 4 skeins sage #2641
- Size K/10½ afghan crochet hook
- Size K/10½ crochet hook or size needed to obtain gauge
- Yarn needle

Gauge

Each square measures approximately 4 inches

Check gauge to save time.

Lullaby

Though despairing be our home,
You are not alone.
Sleep, Baby.
Your mother's arms enfold you
And she loves you true.
Sleep, Baby, sleep.
A pillow for your head
And a soft, warm bed
Are yours, little one.
The gifts that we receive
Help me to believe,
Help me to hope.
Crocheted shoes for your feet
So lacy and sweet;
Sleep, Baby.
Snuggly blanket cozy and warm,
You'll not come to any harm.
Sleep, Baby, sleep.

Pattern Notes

Weave in loose ends as work progresses.

Join rnds with a sl st unless otherwise stated.

Drop yarn not in use to WS, do not fasten off.

Pattern Stitch

Bobble: Yo hook, insert hook in next sc, yo, draw up a lp, yo, draw through 2 lps on hook, [yo hook, insert hook in same sc, yo, draw up a lp, yo, draw through 2 lps on hook] 3 times, yo, draw through all 5 lps on hook.

Floral Square

Make 40

Rnd 1 (RS): With hook size K and white, ch 4, join to form a ring, ch 1, 8 sc in ring, drop white, draw up a lp of sage, join in beg sc, turn. (8 sc)

Rnd 2 (WS): Ch 1, sc in same sc as beg ch-1, *[bobble, sc] in next sc, ch 3 **, sc in next sc, rep from * 3 times, ending last rep at **, drop sage, draw up a lp of white, turn. (4 bobbles; 8 sc)

Rnd 3 (RS): Ch 1, sc in same sc as beg ch-1, *sc in next ch-3 sp, ch 3 **, sc in each of next 3 sts, rep from * 3 times, ending last rep at **, sc in each of next 2 sts, join in beg sc.

Rnd 4 (RS): Sl st in next sc, ch 1, sc in same sc as joining, *ch 3, [sc, ch 3, sc] for corner in next ch-3 sp **, [ch 3, sk next sc, sc in next sc] twice, rep from * 3 times, ending last rep at **, ch 3, sk next sc, sc in next sc, ch 3, sk next sc, join in beg sc. (16 ch-3 sps)

Rnd 5 (RS): Ch 1, [sc in next ch-3 sp, ch 1] rep around, working [sc, ch 1, sc] in each corner ch-3 sp, join in beg sc. (20 ch-1 sps)

Rnd 6 (RS): Ch 1, sc in each sc and each ch-1 sp around, working 3 sc in each corner ch-1 sp, join in beg sc, fasten off. (48 sc)

Tunisian Square

Make 40

Row 1 (WS): With afghan hook size K and sage, ch 11, insert hook in 2nd ch from hook and draw up a lp, retaining all lps on hook, draw up a lp in each rem ch across (11 lps on hook), with white, make a sl knot on hook, draw through first lp on hook, [yo, draw through 2 lps on hook] rep across.

Row 2 (WS): With white, sk first vertical bar, [insert hook under next vertical bar, yo, draw up a lp] rep across (11 lps on hook), drop white, pick up sage, yo, draw through first lp on hook, [yo, draw through 2 lps on hook] rep across.

Row 3 (WS): With sage, sk first vertical bar, [insert hook under next vertical bar, yo, draw up a lp] rep across (11 lps on hook), drop sage, pick up white, yo, draw through first lp on hook, [yo, draw through 2 lps on hook] rep across.

Rows 4–10 (WS): Rep Rows 2 and 3 until piece is square.

Row 11 (WS): Continuing with

sage bind off, sk first vertical bar, [insert hook under next vertical bar, yo, draw up a lp and draw through st on hook] rep across until 1 lp rem on hook, turn.

Rnd 12 (RS): Working around outer edge of square, work 9 sc across each side edge and 3 sc in each corner st, join in beg sc, fasten off. (48 sc)

Assembly

Alternating squares, working in back lps only, whipstitch squares tog 8 x 10.

Border

Rnd 1 (RS): With hook size K, attach sage in any center corner st, ch 1, work 3 sc in each center corner sc, sc evenly sp around outer edge, join in beg sc, fasten off.

Rnd 2: Attach white in any center corner st, ch 1, work 3 sc in each center corner sc, sc in each sc around, join in beg sc.

Rnd 3: Sl st into center corner sc, ch 1, *[sc, ch 3, sc] in center corner sc, ch 3, sk next sc, [sc in next sc,

ch 3, sk next sc] rep across to next center corner sc, rep from * around, join in beg sc.

Rnd 4: Sl st into corner ch-3 sp, ch 1, *[sc, ch 4, sc] in corner ch-3 sp, ch 4, [sc in next ch-3 sp, ch 4] rep across to next corner ch-3 sp, rep

from * around, join in beg sc.

Rnd 5: Sl st into corner ch-4 sp, ch 1, *[sc, ch 4, sc] in corner ch-4 sp, ch 4, [sc in next ch-4 sp, ch 4] rep across to next corner ch-4 sp, rep from * around, join in beg sc, fasten off. ✂

Babies are such a nice way to start people.

—Don Herold

Preemie Wardrobe

Continued from page 143

Row 2 (RS): Ch 2 (counts as first hdc throughout), hdc in each rem st across, turn.

Row 3: Ch 2, hdc in same st as beg ch-2, hdc in each st across to last st, 2 hdc in last st, turn. (31, 33, 35 hdc)

Row 4: Rep Row 2.

Rep Rows 2–4 until a total of 37 (41, 45) sts across, ending with a Row 3 pattern.

Crotch shaping

Sl st across first 3 sts, ch 2, hdc in each st across to last 2 sts, turn. (33, 37, 41 hdc)

Rep Row 2 until from beg of crotch shaping body measures 4½ (5, 5½) inches, fasten off.

Sew front and back seams. Sew leg seams.

Waistband

Rnd 1 (RS): With hook size B, attach yarn at center back seam, ch 1, sc evenly sp around, join in beg sc, turn.

Rnd 2: Ch 1, sc in each sc around, join in beg sc, turn.

Rep Row 2 until waistband measures 1¼ inches, fasten off.

Fold 12- (14-, 16-) inch length of elastic into a circle, overlapping ends ½ inch, sew ends of elastic to secure.

Holding elastic circle on WS of pants, fold waistband inward over elastic to cover, on inner edge, sew last row of waistband to first row. ✂

Strawberry Parfait Ensemble

Continued from page 136

times, sc in each of next 7 sc, [2 sc in next sc, sc in next sc] twice, join in beg sc, turn. (44 sc)

Rnds 4–8: Ch 1, working in back lps only, sc in each st around, join in beg sc, turn. At the end of Rnd 8, fasten off.

Note: *WS of Rnd 8 is RS of bootie.*

Instep

Row 1: With WS of bootie facing, working in back lps only of each sc, sk first 10 sc on Rnd 7, attach pink in next sc, ch 1, sc in next sc, [sc dec over next 2 sc] 11 times, ch 3, do not turn.

Rnd 2: Work a dc in first sc worked on Row 1 (this forms a rnd), [sk next st, dc in next st] 5 times, sk ch-3, sl st in top of first dc to join, do not fasten off.

Cuff

Rnd 1: Working in top edge of instep and in both lps of each rem sc on Rnd 7, ch 2 (for beg sc and ch-1), sc in end of Rnd 2, ch 1, sc in end of Row 1 of instep, ch 1, sk first free sc on Rnd 7, sc in next sc, [ch 1, sk next sc, sc in next sc] 9 times, ch 1, sc in end of Row 1 of instep, ch 1, sc in next row, ch 1, sl st in beg sc.

Rnd 2: With hook size G, ch 1, [2 sc in next ch-1 sp] rep around, join in beg sc. (30 sc)

Rnd 3: Ch 3, 2 dc in same st, *[yo hook, insert hook in next sc, yo, draw up a lp, yo, draw through 2 lps on hook] twice, sk next sc, [yo hook, insert hook in next sc, yo, draw up a lp, yo, draw through 2 lps on hook] twice, yo, draw through all 5 lps on hook, ch 1, 5 dc in next sc, rep from * around, working 2 dc in same st as beg ch-3, join in 3rd ch of beg ch-3. (5 groups of 5-dc)

Rnd 4: Ch 3, 2 dc in same st, work in lace pattern around, working 2 dc in same st as beg ch-3, join in 3rd ch of beg ch-3, fasten off.

Rnd 5: Attach white in top of beg ch-3 of Rnd 4, ch 1, sc in same st, sc in each st around, join in beg sc, fasten off.

Tie
Make 2

With hook size F and white, ch 85, sl st in 2nd ch from hook, sl st in each rem ch across, fasten off. Beg at center front of bootie, weave through Rnd 1 of cuff and tie ends in a bow. ✄

Sweetie Pie Baby

Continued from page 146

Second leg

Rnd 1: Attach pink in next un-worked st of Rnd 29 of body, ch 3 (counts as first dc), dc in each of next 17 dc. (18 dc)

Rnds 2–10: Rep Rnds 2–10 of first leg.

With a length of pink, sew crotch opening closed.

Arm
Make 2

Rnd 1: With pink, ch 2, 6 sc in 2nd ch from hook.

Rnd 2: 2 dc in each sc around. (12 dc)

Rnds 3–9: Dc in each dc around, changing to off-white in last st of Rnd 9.

Stuff arm with fiberfill as work progresses.

Rnds 10 & 11: Dc in each dc around.

Rnd 12: [Dc dec over next 2 dc] rep around, sl st in next st, leaving a length of yarn, fasten off.

Sew arm to side of body over Rnds 17–19.

Bonnet

Rnds 1–6: With pink, rep Rnds 1–6 of head and body. (36 sc)

Rnd 7: [Sc in each of next 5 sc, 2 sc in next sc] rep around. (42 sc)

Rnd 8: [Sc in each of next 6 sc, 2 sc in next sc] rep around. (48 sc)

Rnd 9: [Sc in each of next 7 sc, 2 sc in next sc] rep around. (54 sc)

Rnd 10: [Sc in each of next 8 sc, 2 sc in next sc] rep around. (60 sc)

Row 11: Working in back lps only, work 2 dc in each of next 49 sts, [dc, ch 3, sl st] in next st, leaving rem 10 sts unworked, fasten off.

Finishing

Using photo as a guide, work eyes over Rnd 8 of head, leaving 2 sc free between eyes; with light brown, embroider V-shape for each eye.

With red, embroider smiley mouth centered below eyes over Rnds 11 and 12 of head.

For hair, wrap pale yellow around 2 fingers several times, remove lps from fingers and sew at center front of head over Rnd 2.

Weave a 10-inch length of pink yarn through base of dc sts of Row 11, leaving beg and ending lengths equal; place bonnet on head, pull ends gently and double-knot under chin, tie ends in a bow and trim ends even. Thread tapestry needle with a length of pink and sew bonnet to head. ✄

Broomstick Lace Cradle Blanket

Continued from page 137

tog as a group, yo, draw lp through, ch 1, work 2 sc in center of same group, [sl next 2 lps onto crochet hook, yo, draw lp through, yo, draw through 2 lps on hook, work 1 more sc in same group] rep across, do not turn. (50 groups of 2 sc)

Rep Row 2 until blanket from beg measures 28 inches, fasten off.

Edging

Rnd 1 (RS): With crochet hook, attach 1 strand of vanilla in top right corner, ch 1, work 100 sc across top edge, ch 1, working down left edge of blanket, work 119 sc evenly sp, ch 1, working across opposite side of foundation ch, work 100 sc across, ch 1, working up right edge of blanket, work 119 sc evenly sp across, ch 1, join in beg sc.

Rnds 2–5: Ch 1, sc in each sc around, working [sc, ch 1, sc] in each corner ch-1 sp, join in beg sc. At the end of Rnd 5, fasten off. ✄

Carnival Colors Layette

Continued from page 145

Weave rem length through sts of Rnd 25, draw opening closed and secure.

Hat ribbing

Rnd 1 (RS): With hook size F, attach cherry red in opposite side of foundation ch, ch 3, dc in each ch around, join in 3rd ch of beg ch-3, turn. (60 dc)

Rnd 2: Ch 2, [fpdc around next dc, bpdc around next dc] rep around, join in 2nd ch of beg ch-2, turn.

Rnd 3: Ch 2, [fpdc around each fpdc, bpdc around each bpdc] rep around, join in 2nd ch of beg ch-2, fasten off.

Afghan

Note: *Color sequence to be repeated throughout afghan is paddy green, yellow, cherry red and skipper blue. Change to next color at the end of each row.*

Row 1 (RS): With hook size K and paddy green, ch 117 loosely, sc in 2nd ch from hook, sc in each rem ch across, turn. (116 sc)

Row 2: Ch 1, sc in first st, hdc in next st, [sc in next st, hdc in next st] rep across, turn.

Row 3: Ch 1, sc in each st across, turn.

Rep Rows 2 and 3 for pattern, continue to rep established color sequence until afghan from beg measures 40 inches, fasten off.

Border

Rnd 1 (RS): With hook size K, attach cherry red in any st on outer edge, ch 3, dc evenly sp around outer edge, working 3 dc in each corner st, join in 3rd ch of beg ch-3.

Rnd 2 (RS): Ch 2, [fpdc around next dc, bpdc around next dc] rep around, join in 2nd ch of beg ch-2, fasten off. ✄

Garden Baby Headbands

Continued from page 148

3] 8 times in 2nd ch from hook, join in beg sc. (8 ch-3 sps)

Rnd 2: Sl st into ch-3 sp, [ch 3, dc, ch 2, 2 dc] in same ch-3 sp, [2 tr, ch 2, 2 tr] in each of next 2 ch-3 sps, [2 dc, ch 2, 2 dc] in next ch-3 sp, ch 1, [2 dc, ch 2, 2 dc] in next ch-3 sp, [2 tr, ch 2, 2 tr] in each of next 2 ch-3 sps, [2 dc, ch 2, 2 dc] in next ch-3 sp, with WS tog, fold Rnd 2 in half, sl st in ch-1 sp, join in 3rd ch of beg ch-3, fasten off.

Body & Antennae

With white, ch 12, wrap around center of wing pieces (tr end is front of butterfly), sl st in 4th ch from hook, ch 4, fasten off.

Sew butterfly centered over sewn seam of headband.

Flower Headband

With pink cotton, rep band as for butterfly headband.

Flower

Rnd 1: With white, ch 4, join to form a ring, ch 1, [sc in ring, ch 5] 6 times, join in beg sc.

Rnd 2: Sl st into ch-5 sp, ch 1, 6 sc in same ch-5 sp, sl st in next sc, [6 sc in next ch-5 sp, sl st in next sc] rep around, join in beg sc, leaving a length of cotton, fasten off.

Leaf

Make 2

Rnd 1: With mint, ch 5, sl st in 2nd ch from hook, sc in next ch, hdc in next ch, 5 hdc in next ch, working on opposite side of foundation ch, hdc in next ch, sc in next ch, sl st in last ch, leaving a length of cotton, fasten off.

Sew flower centered over sewn seam. Sew a leaf under flower petals on each side. Sew pearl bead to center of flower. ✄

Domestic Delights

For all of us, home can be many different things in many different places. Whether sprucing up our current dwelling or starting fresh in a new place, it's always meaningful to add our own personal touches to our surroundings. Whether simple or sophisticated, this enticing collection of home accents is sure to make any domestic setting more decorative and delightful!

Stay, stay at home, my heart, and rest; home-keeping hearts are happiest.

—Henry Wadsworth Longfellow

Hearts & Gingham Afghan

Design by Brenda Stratton

Classic country and contemporary styles go hand in hand with the charming combination of traditional gingham and elegant hearts in this stunning design. It will add a warm, friendly touch to any decor, from simple to sophisticated!

Skill Level: Intermediate

Size: 46 x 63 inches

Materials

- Patons Canadiana worsted weight yarn (3½ oz per skein): 7 skeins white #001, 6 skeins light jade #046, 3 skeins jade #047, 2 skeins light rosewood #133
- Size H/8 crochet hook or size needed to obtain gauge
- Sizes C/2 and G/6 crochet hooks
- Straight pins
- Tapestry needle

Gauge

Motif = 8½ inches square; 4 sc = 1 inch; 4 sc rows = 1 inch
Check gauge to save time.

Pattern Notes

Weave in loose ends as work progresses.

Join rnds with a sl st unless otherwise stated.

Every house where love abides and Friendship is a guest, is surely home—home, sweet home—for there the heart can rest.

—Henry Jackson van Dyke

Graphs for motifs are worked from bottom to top, odd-numbered rows are worked from right to left and even-numbered rows are worked from left to right.

Alternate working gingham motifs and heart motifs, join motifs as work progresses 5 x 7.

Pattern Stitches

Scallop: Sc in indicated st, ch 3, dc in side edge of last sc made, sk next 2 sts.

Corner scallop: Sc in indicated st, ch 3, dc in side edge of last sc, do not sk 2 sc. Work beg sc of next scallop in same st as last sc.

Joining scallop: Sc in indicated st, ch 1, sl st in ch-3 lp on corresponding scallop on opposing motif, ch 1, dc in last sc made, sk next 2 sts.

Surface sl st: Holding yarn in back of work, insert hook in st indicated, yo, draw lp through to front side (leaving a 6-inch tail on the back to weave in later), insert hook in next sp, yo, draw lp through to front, draw this lp through lp on hook (as if you were working a normal sl st). When finished, leaving a 6-inch length, cut yarn in back, draw the tail through to the front, then insert tail in tapestry needle and draw through work to draw the tail to the WS; weave in ends.

Gingham Motif

Make 18

Row 1: With hook size H and jade, following graph for gingham motif, ch 29, beg in 2nd ch from hook, sc in each st across, changing color as color changes on graph, turn. (28 sc)

Rows 2–28: Ch 1, sc in each sc across, changing color as colors change according to graph, turn. At the end of Row 28, fasten off.

Edging

Rnd 1: With hook size H, attach white in any corner, ch 1, 3 sc in same st, work 26 sc evenly sp across to next corner, *3 sc in next corner, work 26 sc evenly sp across to next corner, rep from * around, join in beg sc. (116 sc)

Rnd 2: Sl st in next st, work corner scallop in same st, work 10 scallops evenly sp across side, [corner scallop in next corner, work 10 scallops evenly sp across to next corner] rep around, join, fasten off.

Note: *Rnd 2 of edging will be repeated on each motif, with the exception of the edge joined to a previous motif, work joining scallops along edge that is being joined to a previous motif.*

Heart Motif

Make 17

Row 1: With hook size H and light jade, ch 29, sc in 2nd ch from hook, sc in each rem ch across, turn. (28 sc)

Rows 2–28: Following graph for heart motif, ch 1, sc in each st across, changing color as color changes, turn. At the end of Row 28, fasten off.

Edging
Rnd 1: Rep Rnd 1 of edging as for gingham motif.

Rnd 2: Rep Rnd 2 of edging as for gingham motif, substituting joining scallops for scallops on edge to be joined to previous motif.

Scalloped heart frame
Rnd 1: With hook size G and white, ch 67, join to form a ring, working in bump in back of ch, 3 sc in first ch (bottom point of heart trim), sc in each of next 31 chs, draw up a lp in each of next 3 chs, yo, draw through all 4 lps on hook (forms center top point of heart trim), sc in each rem ch to end, join in beg sc.

Rnd 2: Sl st in next sc, work corner scallop in same st, [sc in next st, ch 3, dc in side edge of last sc made, sk next 2 sts] rep around, join in beg sc, fasten off. (23 scallops)

Attaching frame to heart motif
Pin frame in place around the outside edge of the heart, covering the uneven edges.

With hook size G and jade, working through both the frame and the heart motif, attach frame to heart with surface sl st following the outline of the heart, working through the tops of the sc of Rnd 1 of scalloped frame for heart. Stay slightly inside the heart outline with the inner edge of the heart frame so the frame will fully cover the heart edges.

Heart Motif Flower
Make 17

Note: *Cut 1 strand of light rosewood 18 inches long. Separate strand of yarn into 2 plies (this will make 2 flowers).*

Cut 1 strand of white 60 inches

long. Separate strand of yarn into 2 plies (this will make 2 flowers).

Rnd 1: With hook size C and a strand of 2 plies of light rosewood, ch 2, 6 sc in 2nd ch from hook, join in beg sc, fasten off. (6 sc)

Rnd 2: Attach a strand of 2 plies of white in any sc, [ch 2, {yo, insert hook in same sc, yo, draw up a lp, yo, draw through 2 lps on hook} twice in same st, yo, draw through all 3 lps on hook, ch 2, sl st in same st, sl st in next st] rep around, fasten off. (6 petals)

Leaf Cluster
Make 17

Note: *Cut 1 strand of jade 75 inches long. Separate strand of yarn into 2 plies (this will make 2 leaf clusters).*

Rnd 1: With hook size C and 2 plies of jade, ch 4, join to form a ring, ch 1, [sc in ring, ch 3] 3 times, join in beg sc. (3 ch-3 sps)

Rnd 2: [Sl st into ch-3 sp, ch 3, {yo, insert hook in ch sp, yo, draw up a lp, yo, draw through 2 lps on hook} twice, yo, draw through all 3 lps on hook, ch 1, sl st in top of cl, ch 3, sl st in same ch-3 sp] 3 times, fasten off. (3-leaf cluster)

With matching split yarn, invisibly sew leaf cluster to center of heart on heart motif. Center a flower over leaf cluster and invisibly sew in place.

Afghan Border

Rnd 1: With hook size H, attach white in ch-3 sp at any corner of afghan, ch 1, [sc, ch 4, sc] in same corner, ch 3, [sc in next ch-3 sp, ch 3] rep across to next corner, *[sc, ch 4, sc] in corner ch-3 sp, ch 3, [sc in next ch-3 sp, ch 3] rep across to next corner, rep from * around, join in beg sc.

Rnd 2: Sl st into next ch-4 corner sp, [ch 3, 2 dc, ch 2, 3 dc] in same ch sp, [3 dc in next ch-3 sp] rep across to next corner ch sp, *[3 dc, ch 2, 3 dc] in corner ch-4 sp, [3 dc in next ch-3 sp] rep across to next corner ch sp, rep from * around, join in 3rd ch of beg ch-3.

Rnd 3: Sl st into corner ch-2 sp, ch 5 (counts as first dc, ch 2), dc in same ch-2 sp, dc in each dc across to next corner ch-2 sp, *[dc, ch 2, dc] in next corner ch-2 sp, dc in each dc across to next corner ch-2 sp, rep from * around, join in 3rd ch of beg ch-5, fasten off.

Rnd 4: Attach jade in any corner ch-2 sp, ch 3, 6 dc in same ch-2 sp, *sk next 2 dc, sc in next dc, sk next 2 dc, [5 dc in next dc, sk next 2 dc, sc in next dc, sk next 2 dc] rep across to corner ch-2 sp **, 7 dc in next corner ch-2 sp, rep from * around adjusting as necessary to allow 7 dc to fall at corner, ending last rep at **, join in 3rd ch of beg ch-3. ✂

Happy is the house that shelters a friend.

—Ralph Waldo Emerson

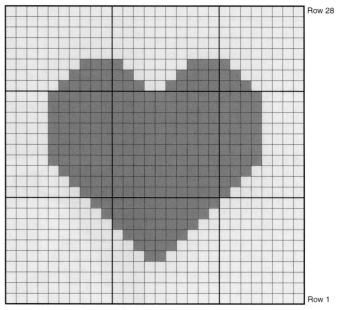

Row 28

Row 1

Heart Motif

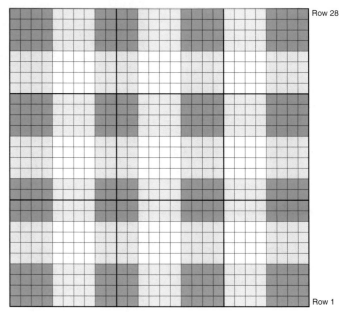

Row 28

Row 1

Gingham Motif

Rose Bath Pouf

Design by Nancy Nehring

A bit of wide lace and nylon thread will quickly create this beautiful rose pouf that's ideal for a last-minute birthday or hostess gift. Add a few purchased or handmade rose soaps to complete the package!

Skill Level: Beginner

Size: 5½ inches

Materials
- Omega #2 nylon thread: 1 spool mint green
- Size 8 steel crochet hook or size needed to obtain gauge
- 2 yds 2¼-inch-wide polyester gathered lace
- Yarn needle

Gauge

10 sc = 1 inch

Check gauge to save time.

Pattern Notes

Weave in loose ends as work progresses.

Join rnds with a sl st unless otherwise stated.

Rose

With nylon thread, sc over gathered edge of entire length of lace, pushing hook gently through mesh of lace (see inset); do not fasten off.

Fold lace in half. Beg at cut end, sc through both top lps of both layers of lace for 4 sts, fold lace back onto itself (to start spiral of the lace) so there are 4 layers of lace. Hold so long piece of lace is toward you and short piece is to the back, sc through back lps of first layer, front lp of 2nd layer, and front lp of layer that has already been sc tog. Continue in spiral until all of lace is formed into a spiral, do not fasten off.

Handle

Row 1: Ch 35, sl st to outer round of spiral at opposite edge, sl st in next sc of spiral, turn, sc in each ch, sl st in next sc of spiral, turn.

Rows 2–4: Sc in each sc across handle, sl st in next sc of spiral, turn. At the end of Row 4, do not fasten off.

Leaf

Make 3

Row 1: Ch 8, sl next 8 sts of outer round of spiral, sl st into next st of spiral, turn.

Row 2: Ch 2, work 15 dc over ch, turn.

Row 3: Ch 2, sl st around vertical bars of sc below center of handle, 2 dc in each dc across, sk 4 sc of spiral, sl st around vertical bars of next sc, turn.

Row 4: [Ch 3, sk 2 dc, sc in next dc] rep across, ending with ch 1, dc in last dc, turn. (10 ch-3 sps)

Rows 5–12: [Ch 3, sc over next ch-3 sp] rep across, ending with ch 1, dc in last ch-3 sp, turn.

Row 13: Ch 1, dc in last ch-3 sp, fasten off.

Rep Rows 1–13 for each rem 2 leaves, attaching green mint as desired on rose back. ✄

Pretty Checks Pot Holders

Design by Maggie Petsch

The effective use of long stitches creates dimensional textures and a delightful check design in these durable and pretty pot holders. The pattern works up quickly in size 3 thread, so it's easy to make them in colors for all seasons!

Skill Level: Beginner

Size: 7 inches square

Materials
- J. & P. Coats Speed-Cro-Sheen crochet cotton size 3 (100 yds per ball): 3 balls white, 1 ball each forest green #449, Spanish red #126, navy #486 and delft blue #480
- Size 0 steel crochet hook or size needed to obtain gauge
- 3 (1⅛-inch) plastic rings
- Tapestry needle

Gauge
5 sts = 1 inch; 6 rows = 1 inch
Check gauge to save time.

Pattern Notes
Weave in loose ends as work progresses.

Join rnds with a sl st unless otherwise stated.

To change color in sc, insert hook in last st before color change, yo with working color, draw up a lp, drop working color to WS, yo with next color and draw through rem 2 lps on hook. Do not fasten off color not in use, carry up side of work until needed again.

Pattern Stitch
Long sc: Insert hook into sc in 3rd row below, yo, draw up a lp to height of working row so that work does not pucker, yo, draw through 2 lps on hook.

Green Pot Holder
Back
Row 1 (WS): With forest green, ch 30, sc in 2nd ch from hook, sc in each rem ch across, changing to white in last sc, turn. (29 sc)

Row 2: Ch 1, sc in each st across, turn.

Row 3: Rep Row 2, changing to forest green in last sc, turn.

Row 4: Ch 1, sc in first sc, [long sc in next sc, sc in next sc] rep across, turn.

Row 5: Ch 1, sc in each st across, changing to white in last sc, turn.

Rows 6–37: Rep Rows 2–5.

Rnd 38: Ch 1, 2 sc in same st as beg ch-1, sc in each of next 27 sc, 3 sc in corner st, working over side edge of rows, work 27 sc evenly sp to next corner, 3 sc in first ch of opposite side of foundation ch, sc in each of next 27 chs, 3 sc in last ch, working over side edge of rows, work 27 sc evenly sp, sc in same st as beg sc, join in beg sc, fasten off.

Front
Rows 1–37: Rep Rows 1–37 of back.

Rnd 38: Rep Rnd 38 of back, changing to forest green in last sc, fasten off white.

Joining
Rnd 1: Holding WS of front and back tog and working through both thicknesses, ch 1, sc in each sc around, working 3 sc in each center corner sc, join in beg sc.

Rnd 2: Ch 1, sc in each sc around, working 3 sc in center corner sc, join in beg sc, fasten off.

Hanging ring
Rnd 1: Attach forest green to plastic ring, ch 1, fill ring with sc sts so that no portion of the ring shows, join in beg sc, leaving a length of yarn, fasten off.

With rem length of yarn, sew hanging ring to top left corner of pot holder.

The beauty of a house is harmony,
The security of a house is loyalty,
The blessing of a house is children,
The comfort of a house is contentment,
The glory of a house is hospitality,
The joy of a house is love.

—Unknown

Red Pot Holder

Rep the same as for green pot holder, using Spanish red in place of forest green cotton.

Blue Plaid Pot Holder
Back
Row 1 (WS): With navy, ch 30, sc in 2nd ch from hook, sc in each rem ch across, changing to delft blue in last sc, turn. (29 sc)

Row 2: Ch 1, sc in each st across, turn.

Row 3: Rep Row 2, changing to navy in last sc, turn.

Row 4: Ch 1, sc in first sc, [long sc in next sc, sc in next sc] rep across, turn.

Row 5: Rep Row 2, changing to white in last sc, turn.

Row 6: Rep Row 2.

Row 7: Rep Row 2, changing to navy in last sc, turn.

Row 8: Rep Row 4.

Row 9: Rep Row 2, changing to delft blue in last sc, turn.

Rows 10–37: Rep Rows 2–9, ending last rep with Row 5.

Rnd 38: With white, rep Rnd 38 of green pot holder.

Front
Rows 1–37: Rep Rows 1–37 of back.

Rnd 38: Rep Rnd 38 of back.

Joining
Rnds 1 & 2: With navy, rep Rnds 1 and 2 of green pot holder.

Hanging ring
Rnd 1: With navy, rep Rnd 1

of hanging ring as for green pot holder. ✂

The Friendship Basket

On a shelf in the closet
Sits a basket that I've made
To hold the colorful pot holders
And dishcloths I've crocheted.
Now for special occasions
I don't run from store to store.
I take my gifts from my basket—
Handmade means so much more.
To thank a hostess or welcome
New neighbors to my town,
I just open up the closet
And take the Friendship Basket down!

Basket-Weave Pot Holder & Hot Pad

Designs by Dot Drake

Simple strips of single crochet interlaced in traditional basket-weave style create the old-fashioned appeal of these colorful pot holders and hot pads. They're fun to do and make great last-minute shower or hostess gifts!

Skill Level: Beginner

Size: 7 inches square

Materials
- Worsted weight 4-ply cotton yarn (50 grams per ball): 1 ball each pink, yellow and pale green
- Size G/6 crochet hook or size needed to obtain gauge
- Straight pins
- Yarn needle

Gauge
4 sc = 1 inch
Check gauge to save time.

Pattern Notes
Weave in loose ends as work progresses.

Join rnds with a sl st unless otherwise stated.

Pot Holder
Strips
Note: *Make 8 each yellow and pink.*

Row 1: Ch 25, sc in 2nd ch from hook, sc in each rem ch across, turn. (24 sc)

Row 2: Ch 1, sc in each sc across, fasten off.

Assembly
Working on a flat surface, working outward from center, weave strips in basket weave style positioning strips so that no sps show between strips, pin strip tog.

Border
Rnd 1 (RS): Attach pale green in any strip on outer edge, removing straight pins as work progresses, ch 1, sc evenly sp around, working 3 sc in each corner st, join in beg sc, turn.

Rnd 2 (WS): Ch 1, sc in same sc as beg ch, tr in next sc, [sc in next sc, tr in next sc] rep around, at any corner in pattern work [sc, ch 8, sc] for hanging lp, join in beg sc, fasten off.

Hot Pad
Strips
Note: *Make 8 each yellow and green.*

Rows 1 & 2: Rep Rows 1 and 2 of pot holder.

Assembly
Rep assembly the same as for pot holder.

Border
Rnd 1: With pink, rep Rnd 1 of pot holder border.

Rnd 2 (WS): Ch 1, sc in same sc as beg ch, tr in next sc, [sc in next sc, tr in next sc] rep around, join in beg sc, fasten off. ✄

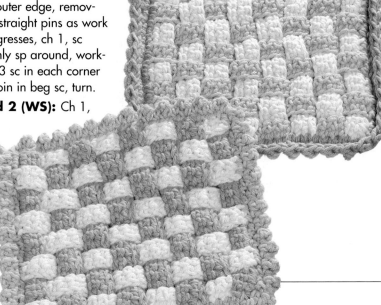

Tunisian Mosaic Pillow

Design by Margret Willson

Alternating colors and three variations of Tunisian crochet create the distinctive houndstooth pattern in this pillow with panache. Decorative tassels add the finishing touch!

Skill Level: Intermediate

Size: 14 inches square

Materials
- Worsted weight yarn: 5 oz each linen and white
- Size K/10½ afghan crochet hook or size needed to obtain gauge
- Size H/8 crochet hook
- 14-inch square pillow form
- Yarn needle

Gauge

7 sts = 2 inches; 8 rows = 2 inches

Check gauge to save time.

Pattern Notes

Weave in loose ends as work progresses.

Join rnds with a sl st unless otherwise stated.

To change color, on return row, with 2 lps rem on hook, bring new color under and to the left of current color, yo and draw through both lps.

Pattern Stitches

Tunisian simple (ts): Insert hook under next vertical bar, yo, draw up a lp and retain on hook.

Tunisian knit (tk): Insert hook from front to back through work and below chs formed by previous return row, to right of front vertical thread but to left of corresponding back thread, yo, draw up a lp and retain on hook.

Tunisian sl st (tsl st): Insert hook into st as if to work Tunisian simple, but do not draw yarn through, continue working leaving sl st on hook.

Pillow

Make 2

Row 1: With linen, ch 49, [insert hook in next ch, yo, draw up a lp and retain on hook] rep across. (49 lps on hook)

Row 2: Yo, draw through first lp on hook, [yo, draw through 2 lps on hook] rep across, change color in last yo.

Row 3: With white, [tk, ts, tsl st] rep across.

Row 4: Rep Row 2.

Row 5: With linen, [tsl st, ts, tk, ts] rep across.

Row 6: Rep Row 2.

Rep Rows 3–6 until there is a total of 27 white strips.

Last row: With linen, work as for Row 5, but complete each st as a sl st (as each st is completed, draw through st on hook), fasten off.

Joining

Holding WS of pillow tog and working through both thicknesses, attach linen in any corner, ch 1, [3 sc in corner st, sc evenly sp across edge] rep around, inserting pillow form before working 4th side, join in beg sc, fasten off.

Tassel

Make 4

Cut 23 strands of white, each 10 inches long. Holding all strands tog even, tie a separate length of yarn tightly around center of bundle. Holding by separate length tied at center, tie another 10-inch length around bundle 1¼ inches below top, blend these ends into tassel. With rem ends tied at center of bundle, attach tassel to corner of pillow. ✄

Lupines in the Snow Doily

Design by Dot Drake

The distinctive bonnet shape of the lovely lupine wildflower is reflected in the delicate beauty of this exquisite doily, stitched in luscious shades of lilac and lavender against a snow-white background.

Skill Level: Advanced

Size: Approximately 18 x 27 inches

Materials

- Crochet cotton size 10: 300 yds white (A) and 150 yds each lilac (B) and lavender (C)

- Size 7 steel crochet hook or size needed to obtain gauge

Gauge

Lupine = 1¼ inches

Check gauge to save time.

Pattern Notes

Weave in loose ends as work progresses.

Join rnds with a sl st unless otherwise stated.

Pattern Stitches

Ch-4 p: Ch 4, sl st in 3rd ch from hook.

Joining p (jp): Ch 1, sc in indicated p, ch 1.

Lupine

Note: Make 10 each with B and C.

Rnd 1 (RS): Ch 5, join to form a ring, ch 1, *sc in ring, ch 10, remove hook from lp, insert hook from RS to WS in top of last sc made, pick up dropped lp, draw through st on hook, [5 sc, ch 3, {3 sc, ch 3} twice, 5 sc (3 p made)] in ch-10 lp, rep from * 3 times, join in beg sc, fasten off. (4 petals)

First Motif

Rnd 1 (RS): With A, ch 8, remove hook from lp, insert hook into first ch made, pick up dropped lp, draw through st on hook, ch 1, 5 sc in ring, jp to first p on any petal of any lupine, **[{3 sc, ch 3} twice, 5 sc] in working ch-8 ring, *ch 16, remove hook from lp, insert hook in 8th ch from last, pick up dropped lp, draw through ch, ch 1, 5 sc in ch-8 ring just made, jp in last p made on previous ch-8 ring *, 3 sc in working ch-8 ring, jp in next p on same petal of lupine, [3 sc, ch 3, 5 sc] on working ch-8 ring, rep from * to * once, [3 sc, ch 3, 3 sc] in working ch-8 ring, jp in next p on same petal, 5 sc in working ch-8 ring †, ch 8, join to form a ring, ch 1, 5 sc in ring, jp in first p on next petal of lupine, rep from ** around, ending last rep at †, join in beg sc on first ch-8 ring. (12 ch-8 rings)

Rnd 2: With RS facing, **ch-4 p, ch 1, *[5 sc, ch 3, {2 sc, ch 3} twice, 5 sc] in next ch-8 sp *, ch 8, remove hook from lp, insert hook in first ch of ch-8 just made, pick up dropped lp, draw through st on hook, ch 1, [5 sc, ch 3, {3 sc, ch 3} twice, 5 sc] in ch-8 ring just made (corner lp made), rep from * to * once, rep from ** around, join at base of beg ch-4 p, fasten off.

STITCH KEY	
B	Lupine made with B
C	Lupine made with C
F-B	Fill-in motif made with B
F-C	Fill-in motif made with C
—	JP

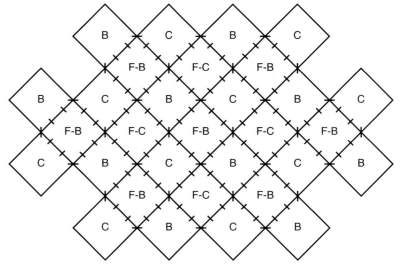

**Lupines in the Snow
Joining Diagram**

Second Motif

Rnd 1: Referring to joining diagram for color selection of lupine, rep Rnd 1 of first motif.

Rnd 2: With RS facing, **ch-4 p, ch 1, *[5 sc, ch 3, {2 sc, ch 3} twice, 5 sc] in next ch-8 sp *, ch 8, remove hook from lp, insert hook in first ch of ch-8 just made, pick up dropped lp, draw through st on hook, ch 1, [5 sc, ch 3, 3 sc, jp to center p on any corner lp on previous motif, 3 sc, ch 3, 5 sc] in ch-8 ring just made (one corner lp joined), complete as for Rnd 2 of first motif.

Rem 18 Motifs

Rnds 1 & 2: Rep Rnds 1 and 2 of 2nd motif, joining each motif on as many corners as are indicated on joining diagram.

Fill-in Motif

Note: *Make 7 with B and 4 with C.*

First lupine

Rnd 1 (RS): Referring to joining diagram for color selection, ch 5, join to form a ring, ch 1, *sc in ring, ch 8, remove hook from lp, insert hook from RS to WS in top of last sc made, pick up dropped lp, draw through st on hook, [5 sc, ch 3, 3 sc, jp to center p on 2nd ch-8 sp on Rnd 2 of any motif, 3 sc, ch 3, 5 sc] in ch-8 lp, rep from * once, working jp to center p on first ch-8 sp of next motif, **sc in ring, ch 8, remove hook from lp, insert hook from RS to WS in top of last sc made, pick up dropped lp, draw through st on hook, [5 sc, ch 3, {3 sc, ch 3} twice, 5 sc (3 p made) in ch-8 lp, rep from ** once, join in beg sc, fasten off. (4 petals)

Second–fourth lupines

Rep instructions for first lupine, working jps to motifs and to previous lupines as indicated on joining diagram.

Fill-in Motif Center

Make 11

Rnd 1 (RS): With A, ch 6, join to form a ring, ch 1, 16 sc in ring, join in beg sc.

Rnd 2: Ch 1, sc in same st as joining, ch 3, sc in first p on any lupine on fill-in motif, ch 3, sk next sc on Rnd 1, sc in next sc, *ch 3, sc in next free p on next petal of lupine, ch 3, sk next sc on Rnd 1, sc in next sc, rep from * around, ending with ch 3, sl st in beg sc, fasten off. ✄

We need not power or splendor, wide hall or lofty dome; the good, the true, the tender, these form the wealth of home.

—Sarah J. Hale

Morning Sunlight Table Runner

Design by Carol Alexander

Bring a bit of sunshine indoors to brighten your decor with this light and airy table accent that works up beautifully in lustrous sport weight yarn. Easy, join-as-you-go motifs make it simple, with no sewing required!

Skill Level: Intermediate

Size: 17½ x 42 inches

Materials
- J. & P. Coats Luster Sheen Sport weight yarn (150

yds per ball): 780 yds buttercup #227

- Size D/3 crochet hook or size needed to obtain gauge
- Tapestry needle

Gauge

Rnd 1 of motif = 1 inch in diameter; motif = 4¾ inches

Check gauge to save time.

Pattern Notes

Weave in loose ends as work progresses.

Join rnds with a sl st unless otherwise stated.

Pattern Stitches

Shell: 7 tr in indicated st.

Triple picot (trp): [Ch 3, sl st in 3rd ch from hook] 3 times.

Picot (p): Ch 3, sl st in 3rd ch from hook.

Joining picot (jp): Ch 1, sl st in corresponding picot on previous motif, ch 1, sl st in 3rd ch from hook.

Joining triple picot (jtp): Work center picot of tr picot as a joining picot.

First Motif

Rnd 1 (RS): Ch 8, join to form a ring, ch 1, 24 sc in ring, join in beg sc. (24 sc)

Rnd 2: Ch 1, sc in same sc, sc in each of next 2 sc, *ch 8, drop lp from hook, insert hook in 2nd sc of last 3-sc made and draw dropped lp through, work 13 sc over ch-8 sp **, sc in each of next 3 sc of Rnd 1, rep from * around, ending last rep at **, join in beg sc. (8 lps; 24 sc)

Rnd 3: Sl st in each of next 6 sc of first lp, ch 1, sc in same sc as beg ch, *sc in each of next 3 sc of same lp, ch 2, sc in 6th sc of next lp, sc in each of next 3 sc of same lp, ch 7 **, sc in 6th sc of next lp, rep from * around, ending last rep at **, join in beg sc. (32 sc; 4 ch-2 sps; 4 ch-7 sps)

Rnd 4: Ch 1, sc in same sc as beg ch, sc in each of next 3 sc, *3 sc in next ch-2 sp, sc in each of next 4 sc, 9 sc in next ch-7 sp (corner) **, sc in each of next 4 sc, rep from * around, ending last rep at **, join in beg sc. (80 sc)

Rnd 5: Ch 1, sc in same sc as beg ch, sc in each of next 10 sc, *ch 5, sk next 4 sc, shell in next sc (5th sc of 9-sc corner group), ch 5, sk next 4 sc **, sc in each of next 11 sc, rep from * around, ending last rep at **, join in beg sc.

Rnd 6: *Ch 3, sk next 4 sc, [2 dc, trp, 2 dc] in next sc, ch 3, sk next 4 sc, sl st in next sc, sl st in each of next 5 chs, sc in next tr, hdc in next tr, dc in next tr, [tr, p, tr] in next tr, dc in next tr, hdc in next tr, sc in next tr, sl st in each of next 5 chs, sl st in next sc, rep from * around, fasten off.

Second Motif

Rnds 1–5: Rep Rnds 1–5 of first motif.

Continued on page 171

My Blue Heaven Throw

Design by Melissa Leapman

Stitched in cloud-soft cotton worsted weight yarn, this snuggly throw is a heavenly delight! A combination of pretty shells and dimensional post stitches creates a sophisticated look with sumptuous textures!

Skill Level: Beginner

Size: 45 x 55 inches

Materials

- Peaches 'n Cream worsted weight cotton (2½ oz per skein): 24 skeins light blue #28
- Size H/8 crochet hook or size needed to obtain gauge
- Yarn needle

Gauge

Large shell = 1½ inches wide; 8 dc rows = 3½ inches

Check gauge to save time.

Pattern Notes

Weave in loose ends as work progresses.

Join rnds with a sl st unless otherwise stated.

Ch-3 counts as first dc throughout.

Pattern Stitches

Small shell: [Dc, ch 1, dc] in indicated st.

Large shell: [3 dc, ch 1, 3 dc] in indicated st.

Throw

Foundation row (WS): Ch 203, 2 dc in 5th ch from hook, [sk next ch, 2 dc in next ch] twice, sk next ch, dc in next ch, *ch 2, sk next 3 chs, small shell in next ch, ch 2, sk next 3 chs, dc in next ch, [sk next ch, 2 dc in next ch] 3 times, sk next ch, dc in next ch, rep from * across, turn.

Row 1 (RS): Ch 3, sk first dc, *[2 dc between next 2 dc] 3 times **, fpdc around next st, large shell in next ch-1 sp, sk next dc, fpdc around next st, rep from * across, ending last rep at **, dc in top of ch-3, turn.

Row 2 (WS): Ch 3, sk first dc, *[2 dc between next 2 dc] 3 times **, bpdc around next fpdc, ch 2, small shell in next ch-1 sp, ch 2, sk dc sts of large shell below, bpdc around next fpdc, rep from * across, ending last rep at **, dc in top of ch-3, turn.

Row 3 (RS): Ch 3, sk first dc, *[2 dc between next 2 dc] 3 times **, fpdc around next bpdc, large shell in next ch-1 sp, fpdc around next bpdc, rep from * across, ending last rep at **, dc in top of ch-3, turn.

Rep Rows 2 and 3 until throw measures approximately 54 inches, ending with Row 3.

Last row: Ch 3, sk first dc, *[2 dc between next 2 dc] 3 times **, bpdc around fpdc, ch 3, sc in ch-1 sp, ch 3, bpdc around next fpdc, rep from * across, ending last rep at **, dc in top of ch-3, fasten off.

Border

Rnd 1 (RS): Attach yarn in top right corner, ch 1, work 171 sc across top of throw, 3 sc in corner st, 205 sc across left side edge of rows, 3 sc in corner, 171 sc across opposite side of foundation ch, 3 sc in corner, 205 sc across right side edge of rows, 3 sc in next corner, join in beg sc.

Rnd 2: Ch 4, sk next sc, [dc in next sc, ch 1, sk next sc] rep around outer edge, working [{dc, ch 1} 3 times and dc] in each center corner st, join in 3rd ch of beg ch-4.

Rnd 3: Ch 1, [sl st, ch 2, dc] in next ch-1 sp, [sl st, ch 2, dc] in each rem ch-1 sp around, join, fasten off. ✂

Fringed Squares Rug

Design by Ruthie Marks

The lushly fringed squares on this delightfully different rug make you want to wiggle your toes in the fluffy yarn! Kids will love this fun design for their room, and it also makes an extra-absorbent rug for the bathroom.

Skill Level: Beginner

Size: 27 x 35 inches

Materials

- Coats & Clark Red Heart Super Saver worsted weight yarn: 14 oz light sage #631 (A), 7 oz Aran #313 (B), 1 oz each cornmeal #320 (C) and pale plum #579 (D)
- Size G/6 crochet hook or size needed to obtain gauge
- Size I/9 crochet hook
- 2¼-inch square cardboard
- Yarn needle

Gauge

With hook size G, 6 sc = 2 inches; 7 rows = 2 inches

Check gauge to save time.

Pattern Notes

Weave in loose ends as work progresses.

Join rnds with a sl st unless otherwise stated.

Rug Strip No. 1

Make 4

Row 1: With hook size G and A, ch 12, sc in 2nd ch from hook, sc in each rem ch across, turn. (11 sc)

Row 2: Ch 1, sc in each st across, turn.

Rows 3–12: Rep Row 2, at the end of Row 12, change to size I hook.

Row 13: Ch 1, sc in first st, [ch 1, sk next st, sc in next st] rep across, turn. (6 sc; 5 ch-1 sps)

Rows 14–24: Rep Row 13, at the end of Row 24, change to size G hook.

Rows 25–36: Ch 1, sc in each st across, turn. (11 sc)

At the end of last rep, change to size I hook.

Rows 37–48: Ch 1, sc in first st, [ch 1, sk next st, sc in next st] rep across, turn. (6 sc; 5 ch-1 sps)

At the end of last rep, change to size G hook.

Rows 49–96: Rep Rows 25–48.

Rows 97–108: Ch 1, sc in each st across, turn. At the end of last rep, fasten off.

Rug Strip No. 2

Make 3

Row 1: With hook size I and A, ch 12, sc in 2nd ch from hook, [ch 1, sk 1 ch, sc in next ch] rep across, turn. (6 sc; 5 ch-1 sps)

Rows 2–12: Ch 1, sc in first st, [ch 1, sk next st, sc in next st] rep across, turn.

This door will open at a touch to welcome every friend.

—Henry Jackson van Dyke

At the end of last rep, change to size G hook.

Rows 13–24: Ch 1, sc in each st across, turn. (11 sc)

At the end of last rep, change to size I hook.

Rows 25–36: Ch 1, sc in first st, [ch 1, sk next st, sc in next st] rep across, turn. (6 sc; 5 ch-1 sps)

At the end of last rep, change to size G hook.

Rows 37–108: Rep Rows 13–36. At the end of last rep, fasten off.

With RS facing, and alternating rug strips, sew strips tog.

Edging

Rnd 1 (RS): With hook size G, attach A in any st on outer edge, ch 1, sc evenly sp around, working 3 sc in each corner, join in beg sc.

Rnds 2–4 (RS): Ch 1, sc in each sc around, working 3 sc in each center corner sc, join in beg sc.

Rnd 5 (RS): Ch 1, reverse sc in each sc around, join in beg reverse sc, fasten off.

	P		A		C
V		P		A		C
	V		P		A
C		V		P		A
	C		V		P
A		C		V		P
	A		C		V
P		A		C		V
	P		A		C

Fringed Square Placement

X	X	X	X	X
X	X	X	X	X
X	X	X	X	X
X	O	O	O	X
X	O	O	O	X
X	O	O	O	X
X	O	O	O	X
X	O	O	O	X
X	X	X	X	X
X	X	X	X	X
X	X	X	X	X

Fringed Square

Fringe

Wrap yarn around 2¼-inch cardboard, cut at one edge (fringe pieces will measure 4½ inches in length). With hook size G, follow charts and attach 2 strands of yarn in each ch-1 sp. Fold 2 strands in half, insert hook under ch-1 sp, draw strands through at fold to form a lp on hook, draw cut ends through lp on hook, pull gently to secure. ✄

Morning Sunlight Table Runner

Continued from page 168

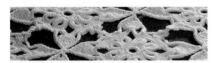

Rnd 6 (joining rnd): Work same as Rnd 6 of first motif to first corner of joining side, on joining side, work each corner p as a jp and the trp at center of side as a jtp, complete rem of rnd same as for first motif.

Make and join 22 more motifs the same as 2nd motif, joining motifs 3 x 8.

Note: *When joining a corner to previously joined corners, work joining sl st into center of previous joining.*

Border

Rnd 1 (RS): Attach buttercup in p at right corner of short side of runner, ch 1, *[sc, ch 4, sc] in corner p, [ch 7, sk next tr, dc and hdc of corner group, sc in next sc, ch 9, sl st in center p of next trp, ch 9, sc in first sc of next corner group, ch 7, sc in corner p joining] twice, †ch 7, sk next tr, dc and hdc of corner group, sc in next sc, ch 9, sl st in center p of next trp, ch 9, sc in first sc of next corner group, ch 7 †, [sc, ch 4, sc] in corner p, rep between [ ] 7 times, rep from † to † once, rep from * once, join in beg sc.

Rnd 2: Sl st into corner ch-4 sp, ch 3 (counts as first dc), [dc, ch 2, 2 dc] in same ch-4 sp, *7 dc in each ch-7 sp and 9 dc in each ch-9 sp across to next corner **, [2 dc, ch 2, 2 dc] in corner ch-4 sp, rep from * around, ending last rep at **, join in 3rd ch of beg ch-3.

Note: *On the following rnd, adjust spacing of sts as needed when working on each side in order to accommodate st sequence between opposite sides.*

Rnd 3: Sl st into corner ch-2 sp, ch 4 (counts as first tr), [tr, trp, {2 tr, trp} twice and 2 tr] in same sp as beg ch-4, *ch 2, sk next 4 sts, [sc, p, sc] in next st, [ch 2, sk next 4 sts, {2 tr, trp, 2 tr} in next st, ch 2, sk next 4 sts, {sc, p, sc} in next st] rep across, ending in 5th st from next corner sp (adjusting sts to accommodate st sequence), ch 2, sk next 4 sts **, [{2 tr, trp} 3 times and 2 tr] in corner sp, rep from * around, ending last rep at **, join in 4th ch of beg ch-4, fasten off.

Block runner to finished size. ✄

Gifts Well Given

We would like to recognize the following dedicated organizations for their tireless and compassionate efforts to make the lives of people and animals in need brighter, more comfortable and secure. We hope you will consider them, as well as charitable organizations in your own community, when donating your crochet time and talents for charity.

HATS FOR THE HOMELESS

Hats for the Homeless was created in memory of John Carroll, a young man who would annually gather his friends during the holiday season and, together with them, roam the streets of New York giving warm hats, scarves and gloves to the homeless. After John's sudden death in 1998, it became the mission of Hats for the Homeless to continue his tradition of bringing warmth and comfort to the less fortunate.

Through Hats for the Homeless, hats, scarves and gloves are collected throughout the year, gift-wrapped and distributed to a large population of urban homeless. The organization welcomes donations from anyone who would like to crochet, knit or purchase a new hat, scarf or pair of gloves to send them.

Wrapping donated gifts would be very helpful. For more information on Hats for the Homeless, visit their Web site at www.hats4thehomeless.org, e-mail them at info@hats4thehomeless.org, or write to Hats for the Homeless, 905 Main St., Hackensack, NJ 07601.

HUGS FOR HOMELESS ANIMALS

Hugs for Homeless Animals (H4HA) is a multiservice, nonprofit organization dedicated to helping homeless and displaced animals worldwide. Their popular Snuggles Project was established by H4HA president and founder Rae French in 1996 to provide security blankets, called "Snuggles," to shelter animals as a comforting reprieve from their hard, cold surroundings and to help them feel less alone.

The Snuggles Project asks for donations of handmade blankets to local humane societies and animal shelters. The blankets can be crocheted, knitted or sewn in the following guideline sizes: 14 x 14 inches (small), 24 x 24 inches (medium) and 36 x 36 inches (large). They may be cotton or acrylic in any color and should not have fringe that animals can chew off and swallow. Yarn or thread ends should be double-knotted and securely woven into the fabric. Snuggles are great projects for kids or people learning how to crochet, knit or sew because the blankets don't have to be perfect. The animals love them any way they can get them!

For more information about the Hugs for Homeless Animals organization, plus free crochet, knitting and sewing patterns to make Snuggles blankets, visit their Web site at www.h4ha.org.

NEWBORNS IN NEED

Newborns in Need is a charity devoted to providing essentials for sick and needy premature and newborn infants whose mothers literally have nothing. Babies are going home from the hospital in nothing more than a disposable diaper, and sometimes "home" is a shelter for battered women or the homeless.

Founded in 1992 by Carol and Richard Green of Houston, Mo., Newborns in Need provides over 21,000 much-needed preemie and newborn items each month to individuals, medical centers, hospitals, homeless shelters, adoption agencies, sheriff's offices and food pantries throughout the United States.

NIN gratefully accepts crocheted, knitted and sewn blankets, clothing, accessories, toys and other needs such as burial layettes, as well as donations of yarn, crochet cotton, fabric, flannelette, stuffing, batting, ribbon and sewing notions for NIN's 11,000 volunteers to use in making these items.

To find out how to help or get information on starting a local NIN group, visit their Web site at www.newbornsinneed.org, e-mail them at info@newbornsinneed.com, or contact Newborns in Need, P.O. Box 385, 403 W. State Route 17 N, Houston, MO 65483-1932, (417) 967-9441.

PROJECT LINUS

Project Linus is a 100 percent volunteer, nonprofit organization dedicated to providing love, warmth and comfort to children who are seriously ill, traumatized or otherwise in need through the gifts of new, handmade, washable blankets and afghans lovingly created by volunteer "blanketeers."

Founded in 1995 by Karen Loucks-Baker of Parker, Colo., and named after the blanket-carrying character in the *Peanuts* comic strip, Project Linus now has over 300 chapters in the United States and has delivered over half a million security blankets to children around the world. The project has been featured in leading magazines and on the Rosie O'Donnell and Oprah Winfrey shows.

For more information and a listing of national chapters, visit their Web site at www.projectlinus.org, which also has links to numerous free patterns to make crocheted, knitted or quilted blankets. You may also contact them at Project Linus National Headquarters, P.O. Box 5621, Bloomington, IL 61702-5621, (309) 664-7814.

RAIN (RESCUING ANIMALS IN NEED)

RAIN is an organization dedicated to the no-kill rescue of companion animals that face no alternative but euthanasia in animal shelters, and to providing adoption services, veterinary care and fostering for them.

RAIN also offers public education on responsible pet guardianship and holds regular adoption events. Potential adopters are screened and counseled to ensure that pets are adopted into safe and loving homes.

Rescued animals fostered by RAIN are lovingly cared for in a home environment and socialized for adoption. Prior to adoption, they are spayed or neutered, vaccinated, tested for infectious diseases, treated for fleas and worms, micro-chipped and given a clean bill of health.

Included on RAIN's wish list of donations are pet blankets and accessories such as collars, leashes and toys that are either purchased or handmade by crocheting, knitting or sewing. For more information, visit their Web site at www.rainanimals.org, e-mail them at donate@rainanimals.org, or contact Rescuing Animals in Need Inc., P.O. Box 189394, Sacramento, CA 95818, (916) 492-7977.

Give plenty of what is given to you, listen to compassion's call; don't think the little you give is great, or the much you get is small.

—Phoebe Cary

WARMING FAMILIES

As a project of the One Heart Foundation, Warming Families is an all-volunteer service that delivers blankets, clothing and other warm items to the homeless, domestic violence shelters and nursing homes.

Warming Families receives no financial funding, and all donations of time and materials are given directly to helping needy recipients. Donated items may be purchased or handmade. The Warming Families Web site offers many free crochet, knitting and craft patterns to make afghans, blankets, toys, dolls and all types of warm clothing and accessories for all ages from infants to seniors.

For more information, visit their Web site at www.warmingfamilies.org, e-mail project leader Kaye Rogers at crochetfever@cs.com, or write One Heart Foundation, P.O. Box 757, Provo, UT 84603.

WARM UP AMERICA!

Warm Up America! is a project sponsored by the Craft Yarn Council of America that is dedicated to keeping people in need warm with handmade afghans and blankets. They ask for volunteers, working together with family, friends or groups, to crochet or knit 7 x 9-inch sections, assemble them into afghans and distribute them to needy recipients in their own communities.

When this is not possible, the Council will gladly accept donations of individual sections or strips needing assembly, or completed afghans. They also welcome entire afghans that are crocheted or knitted in any colors from any patterns. The Council distributes completed blankets to social service agencies who have contacted their office.

For more information on the Warm Up America! project, plus free crochet and knitting patterns for making afghan sections, afghan assembly tips, and basic crochet and knitting instructions, visit their Web site at www.craftyarncouncil.com/warmup.html. Donated items should be sent to Warm Up America!, 1500 Lowell Road, Gastonia, NC 28054.

Remember Our Veterans

Please contact your state and local Veterans Administration offices for information on how you can help veterans in your community. Volunteers are always needed who can donate time to drive veterans to medical appointments or give clerical support for busy clinics. There is also a continual need for donations of food, clothing, blankets, personal items and other materials to help homeless and disabled veterans, and those in hospitals, rehab centers and nursing homes. If many give just a little, it adds up to a lot for those who gave so much.

General Instructions

Please review the following information before working the projects in this book. Important details about the abbreviations and symbols used are included.

Hooks

Crochet hooks are sized for different weights of yarn and thread. For thread crochet, you will usually use a steel crochet hook. Steel crochet-hook sizes range from size 00 to 14. The higher the number of the hook, the smaller your stitches will be. For example, a size 1 steel crochet hook will give you much larger stitches than a size 9 steel crochet hook. Keep in mind that the sizes given with the pattern instructions were obtained by working with the size thread or yarn and hook given in the materials list. If you work with a smaller hook, depending on your gauge, your project size will be smaller; if you work with a larger hook, your finished project's size will be larger.

Gauge

Gauge is determined by the tightness or looseness of your stitches, and affects the finished size of your project. If you are concerned about the finished size of the project matching the size given, take time to crochet a small section of the pattern and then check your gauge. For example, if the gauge called for is 10 dc = 1 inch, and your gauge is 12 dc to the inch, you should switch to a larger hook. On the other hand, if your gauge is only 8 dc to the inch, you should switch to a smaller hook.

If the gauge given in the pattern is for an entire motif, work one motif and then check your gauge.

Understanding Symbols

As you work through a pattern, you'll quickly notice several symbols in the instructions. These symbols are used to clarify the pattern for you: brackets [], curlicue brackets {}, asterisks *.

Brackets [] are used to set off a group of instructions worked a number of times. For example, "[ch 3, sc in ch-3 sp] 7 times" means to work the instructions inside the [] seven times. Brackets [] also set off a group of stitches to be worked in one stitch, space or loop. For example, the brackets [] in this set of instructions, "Sk 3 sc, [3 dc, ch 1, 3 dc] in next st" indicate that after skipping 3 sc, you will work 3 dc, ch 1 and 3 more dc all in the next stitch.

Occasionally, a set of instructions inside a set of brackets needs to be repeated, too. In this case, the text within the brackets to be repeated will be set off with curlicue brackets {}. For example, "[Ch 9, yo twice, insert hook in 7th ch from hook and pull up a loop, sk next dc, yo, insert hook in next dc and pull up a loop, {yo and draw through 2 lps on hook} 5 times, ch 3] 8 times." In this case, in each of the eight times you work the instructions included in brackets, you will work the section included in curlicue brackets five times.

Asterisks * are also used when a group of instructions is repeated. They may either be used alone or with brackets. For example, "*Sc in each of the next 5 sc, 2 sc in next sc, rep from * around, join with a sl st in beg sc" simply means you will work the instructions from the first * around the entire round.

"*Sk 3 sc, [3 dc, ch 1, 3 dc] in next st, rep from * around" is an example of asterisks working with brackets. In this set of instructions, you will repeat the instructions from the asterisk around, working the instructions inside the brackets together.

Buyer's Guide

When looking for a special material, first check your local craft stores and yarn shops. If you are unable to locate a product, contact the manufacturers listed below for the closest retail source in your area.

Bernat
P.O. Box 40
Listowel, ON N4W 3H3 Canada
www.bernat.com

Caron International
Customer Service
P.O. Box 222
Washington, NC 27889
(800) 868-9194
www.caron.com

Coats & Clark
Consumer Service
P.O. Box 12229
Greenville, SC 26912-0229
(800) 648-1479
www.coatsandclark.com

Elmore-Pisgah
204 Oak St.
Spindale, NC 28160
(800) 633-7829

Lion Brand Yarn Co.
34 W. 15th St.
New York, NY 10011
(800) 258-9276
www.lionbrand.com

SolarActive International
18740 Oxnard St. #315
Tarzana, CA 91356
www.solaractiveintl.com

The Thread Exchange Inc.
P.O. Box 1409
Weaverville, NC 28787-1409
(800) 915-2320
www.sewtruce.com

TMA Yarns
206 W.140th St.
Los Angeles, CA 90061

STITCH GUIDE

Front Loop (a)
Back Loop (b)

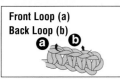

Chain (ch)
Yo, draw lp through hook.

Slip Stitch Joining
Insert hook in beg ch, yo, draw lp through.

Front Post/Back Post Dc
Fpdc (a): Yo, insert hook from front to back and to front again around the vertical post (upright part) of next st, yo and draw yarn through, yo and complete dc.
Bpdc (b): Yo, reaching over top of piece and working on opposite side (back) of work, insert hook from back to front to back again around vertical post of next st, yo and draw yarn through, yo and complete dc.

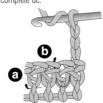

Single Crochet (sc)
Insert hook in st (a), yo, draw lp through (b), yo, draw through both lps on hook (c).

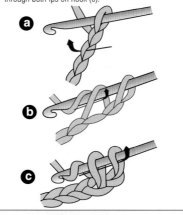

Half-Double Crochet (hdc)
Yo, insert hook in st (a), yo, draw lp through (b), yo, draw through all 3 lps on hook (c).

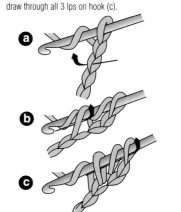

DECREASING

Single Crochet Decrease
Dec 1 sc over next 2 sts as follows: Draw up a lp in each of next 2 sts, yo, draw through all 3 lps on hook.

Double Crochet Decrease
Dec 1 dc over next 2 sts as follows: [Yo, insert hook in next st, yo, draw up lp on hook, yo, draw through 2 lps] twice, yo, draw through all 3 lps on hook.

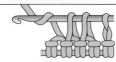

Double Crochet (dc)
Yo, insert hook in st (a), yo, draw lp through (b), [yo, draw through 2 lps] twice (c, d).

Treble Crochet (tr)
Yo hook twice, insert hook in st (a), yo, draw lp through (b), [yo, draw through 2 lps on hook] 3 times (c, d, e).

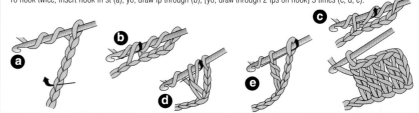

SPECIAL STITCHES

Chain Color Change (ch color change)
Yo with new color, draw through last lp on hook.

Double Crochet Color Change (dc color change)
Drop first color, yo with new color, draw through last 2 lps of st.

Reverse Single Crochet (reverse sc)
Working from left to right, insert hook in next st to the right (a), yo, draw up lp on hook, complete as for sc (b).

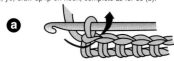

Stitch Abbreviations
The following stitch abbreviations are used throughout this publication.

beg	begin(ning)
bl(s)	block(s)
bpdc	back post dc
ch(s)	chain(s)
cl(s)	cluster(s)
CC	contrasting color
dc	double crochet
dec	decrease
dtr	double treble crochet
fpdc	front post dc
hdc	half-double crochet
inc	increase
lp(s)	loop(s)
MC	main color
p	picot
rem	remain(ing)
rep	repeat
rnd(s)	round(s)
RS	right side facing you
sc	single crochet
sk	skip
sl st	slip stitch
sp(s)	space(s)
st(s)	stitch(es)
tog	together
tr	treble crochet
trtr	triple treble crochet
WS	wrong side facing you
yo	yarn over

Crochet Hooks

METRIC	US
.60mm	14 steel
.75mm	12 steel
1.00mm	10 steel
1.25mm	8 steel
1.50mm	7 steel
1.75mm	5 steel
2.00mm	B/1
2.50mm	C/2
3.00mm	D/3
3.50mm	E/4
4.00mm	F/5
4.50mm	G/6
5.00mm	H/8
5.50mm	I/9
6.00mm	J/10

Yarn Conversion
OUNCES TO GRAMS

1	28.4
2	56.7
3	85.0
4	113.4

GRAMS TO OUNCES

25	⅞
40	1⅜
50	1¾
100	3½

Crochet Abbreviations

US	INTL
sc—single crochet	dc—double crochet
dc—double crochet	tr—treble crochet
hdc—half-double crochet	htr—half treble crochet
tr—treble crochet	dtr—double treble crochet
dtr—double treble crochet	trip—triple treble crochet
sk—skip	miss

YARNS
Bedspread weight .... No. 10 cotton or Virtuoso
Sport weight .... 3-ply or thin DK
Worsted weight .... thick DK or Aran

Check tension or gauge to save time.

Special Thanks

Designs
To the very creative and diversely talented crochet designers whose work appears in this book.

Eleanor Albano-Miles
Mini Purselette, page 78

Articles
To Rose Pirrone for sharing some interesting and noteworthy information about crochet in bygone days.

How Old Sweaters Became New, page 11; Before There Was Fiberfill, page 65

Poetry
To Amy Ballard for her insightful and touching rhymes that stir our emotions and inspire our charitable aspirations.

My Favorite Sweater, page 13; Warm Hands, Warm Heart, page 25; Forgotten Heroes, page 36; The Afghan Givers, page 46; Sharing Cuddles, page 56; The Blanket, page 70; The Handy Tote, page 81; My Helpers, page 90; Adopting Spot, page 99; Cat & Mouse, page 109; Someone Else's Grandma, page 119; The Pattern Library, page 129; The Littlest Needs, page 136; Lullaby, page 152; The Friendship Basket, page 163

Quotations
To the wonderfully wise and witty individuals, past and present, named or unknown, whose meaningful and inspiring words appear throughout this book.

Accessories
To Pier 1 of Longview, Texas, for providing accessories for several of our projects.

Charities
To the charitable organizations—those featured in this book and all others worldwide whose efforts make life better for people and animals—for their invaluable contributions to making the world a brighter place for those living in the shadows of need.

Carol Alexander
Morning Sunlight Table Runner, page 168

Kazimiera Budak
Pretty in Plum Scarf & Ski Band, page 8

Carol Carlile
Sunshine Dots Blanket, page 139

Cindy Carlson
Many Textures Tote, page 88

Bendy Carter
Broomstick Lace Cradle Blanket, page 137; Doggie Barbells, page 104; Feline Monitor Perch, page 102; His & Her Dog Sweaters, page 106; Love My Pet Mat & Toys, page 108; Play Tunnel, page 96; Preemie Wardrobe, page 140; Puzzle Sweater, page 21; Terry Pet Mat, page 101; Toss & Twist Game, page 52; Woven Jewel Blankie, page 100

Carol Decker
Water Bottle Holders, page 85

Rosalie DeVries
Aurora, page 42; Dream Catcher, page 48

Margaret Dick
Chevron Strips, page 128

Dot Drake
Basket-Weave Pot Holder & Hot Pad, page 164; Fireside Chat, page 44; Lupines in the Snow Doily, page 166; Colorful Windmills, page 38

Katherine Eng
Southwest Baskets, page 92

Darla Fanton
Magic Purple Passion Purse, page 82

Anne Halliday
Vineyard in the Valley, page 46

Karen Isak
Fun-Time Play Books, page 66

Rosanne Kropp
Strawberry Parfait Ensemble, page 134

Melissa Leapman
Hunter's Lodge, page 35; Neutral Tones Pullover, page 12; Shawl-Collar Cardigan, page 114; My Blue Heaven Throw, page 169

Sheila Leslie
Mother-Daughter Hat & Mittens, page 26

Ruthie Marks
Cozy Pet Bed & Blanket, page 98; Fringed Squares Rug, page 170; Warm & Soothing Heat Pack, page 123

Maria Merlino
Young Miss Winter Warmer Set, page 18

Joyce Messenger
Chill Chasers Hat & Scarf Set, page 28

Beverly Mewhorter
Harry the Horned Lizard, page 64

Nancy Nehring
Dainty Scallops Lingerie Bag, page 84; Rose Bath Pouf, page 161

Shirley Patterson
Baby Mittens, page 138

Maggie Petsch
Pretty Checks Pot Holders, page 162

Carolyn Pfeifer
Let Freedom Ring, page 36

Sharon Phillips
Accessory Pockets, page 79; Beddy-Bye Booties, page 117

Darlene Polachic
Braided-Look Pet Rug, page 110

Cora Rattle
Anniversary Sachets, page 125;

Janet Rehfeldt
Crayon Box Afghan & Pillows, page 69; Family Foot Warmers, page 14

Sandy Rideout
Carnival Colors Layette, page 144

Karen Rigsby
Pocket Shawl, page 130

Rena V. Stevens
Summer Roses Lap Robe, page 118

Brenda Stratton
County Fair Sleeping Bag, page 58; Hearts & Gingham Afghan, page 158

Kathleen Stuart
Convertible Mittens, page 24; Sweetie Pie Baby, page 146

Aline Suplinskas
Mint Twinkle Blanket, page 147

Debbie Tabor
Butterfly Buddy Pillow, page 72

Amy Venditti
Chair Pouch, page 90

Kathy Weese
Li'l Friends Sleeping Bags, page 61

Michele Wilcox
Kitty & Puppy Neck Nuzzlers, page 62; North Country Caps, page 9; Play With Me Bear, page 56

Margret Willson
Tunisian Mosaic Pillow, page 165; Weekender Pullover, page 10

Glenda Winkleman
Aspen Twist, page 40; Sweet Dreams Poncho & Blanket, page 149

Shirley Zebrowski
Cozy Shrug, page 122; Plentiful Pockets Tote, page 80

Lori Zeller
Baby Garden Headbands, page 148